"Troy and Dawn never disappoint in offering thoughtful insights and practical advice for students' use of digital tools in inquiry-based research, writing, collaboration, and media production. Theirs are voices from a real classroom as they demonstrate sensitivity to the realities of meeting standards, assessing (and grading) student work, and teaching students to cultivate responsible digital identities. Along the way, we hear not only their voices, but also the voices of students in text examples and through QR codes in each chapter that lead to classroom videos. Teachers, whether digital veterans or those who are just beginning to experiment with these tools, will appreciate the practical advice and concrete and easily adaptable lesson plans for authentic, collaborative inquiry in any middle school or high school classroom. This book is not about learning to use digital tools; it's about using digital tools to inquire, to collaborate, to reflect, to create, and to share ideas with global audiences and with us."

—SANDY HAYES
Past President, National Council of Teachers of English

"While we live in an age of connectedness, the challenge of cogently connecting students with language and learning in order to help them intelligently interpret what they read, see, and hear—as well as with the language they utilize when composing their own ideas, questions, and reflections—constitutes a formidable hurdle. Mix in the fact that the sands are shifting beneath all of our feet year-to-year as new tools are created at a rate that feels impossible to keep up with and the need for thoughtful guidance on how to amplify students' literacy skills in the modern-day classroom becomes self-evident. Kudos to Troy and Dawn for stepping so smartly into the shoes of thoughtful literacy leadership and publishing a tool kit on how to bring inquiry-driven digital research projects into the classroom. This book is a real win-win: rife with practical lesson plans, chock full of meaningful reflections that use theory as a foundation to materialize strong academic practice. In other words, BIG HOME RUN!"

—ALAN SITOMER
California Teacher of the Year Award Winner

"Teaching writing is hard, and when we see writing as inquiry, teaching writing is really messy. Adding digital technologies and the vast network of the Internet to the mix can be overwhelming as we try to help students navigate how they consume and how they might create. Reed and Hicks acknowledge these difficulties of teaching research while providing a road map that makes the teaching of inquiry feasible. They detail concrete lesson ideas that could be adapted to any age level, any discipline. Their unit, focused on culture and identity, is designed using essential questions; it involves multiple opportunities for low-stakes writing; it integrates various media; it develops necessary skills of digital and media literacy alongside more traditional research skills. They expertly marry the principles of Connected Learning with a long tradition of scholarship into best practices in teaching writing. In short, this book is good teaching. *Research Writing Rewired* inspires me to redesign my own assignments and to make inquiry, not just a written research paper, the heart of research in my classroom."

—**KRISTEN HAWLEY TURNER, PhD**
Associate Professor, Fordham University Graduate School of Education

"In this very practical and powerful book, Dawn Reed and Troy Hicks present a rich case example of what classrooms can be when we marry the tradition of inquiry-driven learning with the powerful digital tools of the Internet age. This is what college- and career-ready standards look like when students' authentic questions are at the center."

—**ELYSE EIDMAN-AADAHL**
Executive Director, National Writing Project

RESEARCH
WRITING
REWIRED

Lessons That Ground
Students' Digital Learning

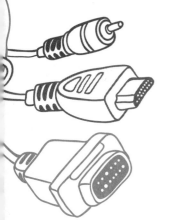

Dawn Reed / Troy Hicks

Foreword by Peter Smagorinsky

http://resources.corwin.com/writingrewired

CL CORWIN
LITERACY

FOR INFORMATION:

Corwin

A SAGE Company

2455 Teller Road

Thousand Oaks, California 91320

(800) 233-9936

www.corwin.com

SAGE Publications Ltd.

1 Oliver's Yard

55 City Road

London EC1Y 1SP

United Kingdom

SAGE Publications India Pvt. Ltd.

B 1/I 1 Mohan Cooperative Industrial Area

Mathura Road, New Delhi 110 044

India

SAGE Publications Asia-Pacific Pte. Ltd.

3 Church Street

#10-04 Samsung Hub

Singapore 049483

Publisher: Lisa Luedeke

Editorial Development Manager: Julie Nemer

Development Editor: Renee Nicholls

Assistant Editor: Emeli Warren

Production Editor: Melanie Birdsall

Copy Editor: Melinda Masson

Typesetter: C&M Digitals (P) Ltd.

Proofreader: Wendy Jo Dymond

Indexer: Amy Murphy

Cover Designer: Rose Storey

Interior Designer: Scott Van Atta

Marketing Managers: Maura Sullivan and
Rebecca Eaton

Photographs by Dawn Reed and Troy Hicks.

Printed in the United States of America

ISBN 978-1-4833-5898-7

This book is printed on acid-free paper.

SUSTAINABLE FORESTRY INITIATIVE

Certified Chain of Custody
Promoting Sustainable Forestry
www.sfiprogram.org
SFI-01268

SFI label applies to text stock

15 16 17 18 19 10 9 8 7 6 5 4 3 2 1

Contents

At-a-Glance Lesson Summaries   ix

Foreword   xiv

   Peter Smagorinsky

Acknowledgments   xvi

Preface: Reading, Writing,
and Inquiry With Adolescents   xviii

   Why "Rewire" Research Writing?   xix

   The Contents of This Book   xx

   Our Guiding Principles   xxii

Introduction: Framing Student Inquiry   1

   Considering Our Goals   1

      The Five *T*s: Teens, Timing, Topics, Texts, and Technology   2

      MAPS: A Heuristic for Writing and Thinking   6

   The Big Picture: Broad Curricular Considerations   7

      Essential Questions   8

      Selecting Online Tools   12

   Additional Curricular Components   13

      KQED Do Now and Critical Media Literacy   15

      Youth Voices   16

      Technology Decisions   18

      Disciplinary Literacy   20

      Differentiation   20

   Final Considerations   21

Chapter 1. Introducing Research, Inquiry, and Connected Learning 23

Preview Lesson: Thinking Through a Cultural Lens 25

Lessons for Week 1

Lesson 1. Exploring Digital Identities 30

Lesson 2. Cultural Conversations Online: Joining Youth Voices and Reading Collaboratively 35

Lesson 3. Beginning the Cultural Conversation 39

Lesson 4. Exploring Visual Culture Through Food Wrappers and Analyzing Visual Culture 44

Lesson 5. Introducing Ethnography and the Culture Collage Assignment 50

Reflections on Embracing Inquiry in the Connected Classroom 54

Chapter 2. Getting Started With Inquiry Work: Visual Literacy and Literature Circles 57

Lessons for Week 2

Lesson 6. Visual Literacy and Design 59

Lesson 7. Culture Collage Sharing 62

Lesson 8. Literature Circles 72

Lesson 9. Fashion and Image in American Culture 81

Lesson 10. Reading Images: Fact or Fiction? 83

Lesson 11. Personal Inquiry Reflections 86

Reflections on Mentor Texts for Analysis and Developing Inquiry Questions 90

Chapter 3. Laying the Groundwork for Research Writing: Developing Close Reading Skills and Organizing Digital Spaces 91

Lessons for Week 3

Lesson 12. Literature Circle Meeting 1: Engaging in Active Discussions 95

Lesson 13. Self-Assessment and Reflection   98

Lesson 14. Language in American Culture   105

Lesson 15. Literature Circle Meeting 2:
Close Reading of Passages   110

Lesson 16. Questioning and Speculating   113

Reflections on Developing Close Reading
Skills and Organizing Digital Spaces   117

Chapter 4. Embarking on the Inquiry-Based Research Essay: Collaboration, Citation, and Credibility   119

Key Features of the Inquiry-Based
Research Essay Assignment   120

Mode   120

Media   121

Audience   121

Purpose   122

Situation   122

Assessment   122

Lessons for Week 4

Lesson 17. Literature Circle Meeting 3:
Intertextual Connections   123

Lesson 18. Researching Skills and Tips:
Exploring Sources   128

Lesson 19. Researching (Online and
in the Library Media Center)   143

Lesson 20. Writing and Researching Workshop   145

Reflections on the Research Process   148

Chapter 5. Writing Workshop and Media Projects: Responding, Revising, and Reflecting   149

Lessons for Week 5

Lesson 21. Literature Circle Meeting 4:
Final Thoughts and Reflection   151

Lesson 22. Writing Workshop and Peer Response   154

Lesson 23. Media Work   160

Lesson 24. Cultural Questions and Media Literacy   166

Lesson 25. Workshop: Inquiry-Based Research
Essay and Media Projects   173

Lesson 26. Reflection and Publication of the
Inquiry-Based Research Essay   177

Lesson 27. Exploring Basic Copyright Issues:
Copyright, Fair Use, Creative Commons, and
the Public Domain   181

Lesson 28. Reflecting, Sharing, and
Celebrating the Final Media Project   186

Reflections on the Writing Process   198

Chapter 6. Final Reflections and Conclusions   199

Assessment: A Flexible, Rhetorical Approach   201

Purposeful Technology Integration   203

Conclusions   204

References and Further Reading   208

Index   215

About the Authors   227

Visit the companion website at
http://resources.corwin.com/writingrewired
for videos, handouts, and slide show presentations.

At-a-Glance Lesson Summaries

Chapter 1. Introducing Research, Inquiry, and Connected Learning

Preview Lesson: Thinking Through a Cultural Lens

Reading through a culture lens is a focus for the inquiry work described in the example unit in this book. By viewing a TED Talk by Sheikha Al Mayassa, students begin thinking about artifacts and characteristics of culture. To think about their own beliefs, students collect images that represent their culture.

Lesson 1. Exploring Digital Identities

As students develop their digital footprint, they explore what it means to create a digital identity and represent themselves online.

Lesson 2. Cultural Conversations Online: Joining Youth Voices and Reading Collaboratively

Students create their profile for the Youth Voices network. They review models of existing profiles and develop questions for inquiry.

Lesson 3. Beginning the Cultural Conversation

While reading a brief article by a millennial author, students discover how one writer understands her own identity. They also use digital tools to annotate the text.

Lesson 4. Exploring Visual Culture Through Food Wrappers and Analyzing Visual Culture

By analyzing one particular artifact of culture—food wrappers—students uncover biases and assumptions related to American culture (Part 1). As students view three different videos, they apply what they have discovered about culture and begin thinking about visual literacy and design (Part 2).

Lesson 5. Introducing Ethnography and the Culture Collage Assignment

Using photography as one tool for exploring culture, students begin to think like ethnographers and, quite literally, explore different perspectives of their classroom through a cell phone camera's lens.

Chapter 2. Getting Started With Inquiry Work: Visual Literacy and Literature Circles

Lesson 6. Visual Literacy and Design

While we are surrounded by images, ads, and icons, it is rare that we take time to understand how these visuals are constructed. In this lesson, we provide students with a "crash course" in visual literacy and design.

Lesson 7. Culture Collage Sharing

As a formative assessment, the opportunity to share their cultural collages gives students a chance to articulate inquiry questions and gain perspective on what their peers are exploring as they are questioning for the purpose of developing curiosities and specific inquiry topics for further research.

Lesson 8. Literature Circles

Diving into discussion of their shared reading, students work together to identify reading goals and to think about what artifacts and characteristics of culture may become evident in their novels.

Lesson 9. Fashion and Image in American Culture

Exploring the cultural artifacts of fashion, students again become ethnographers and discover how trends in clothing shape our individual and cultural identity.

Lesson 10. Reading Images: Fact or Fiction?

In a digital era where image manipulation is part of everyday media and advertising, helping students identify strategies for critically consuming visuals becomes the focus for this lesson.

Lesson 11. Personal Inquiry Reflections

As students engage in reading and critical questioning, we guide them through a process of reflection to help clarify their inquiry questions and prepare them for deeper research in the weeks ahead.

Chapter 3. Laying the Groundwork for Research Writing: Developing Close Reading Skills and Organizing Digital Spaces

Lesson 12. Literature Circle Meeting 1: Engaging in Active Discussions

Students purposefully discuss how to have an intentional discussion. Then, students engage in their literature circle meeting discussion and take notes in a digital space to share their ideas with others.

Lesson 13. Self-Assessment and Reflection

As students continue to work on close reading for literature circles, taking time to self-assess their reading and writing work is important for their reflection and continual development in reading, writing, and discussing.

Lesson 14. Language in American Culture

Students explore the role of language in American culture through an all-class review of a contemporary commercial and trending conversations surrounding this text as a means to begin exploration of socially mediated research. Then, students engage in reading various articles with close reading strategies.

Lesson 15. Literature Circle Meeting 2: Close Reading of Passages

Students build their ideas and knowledge through literature circle discussion and close reading of text passages. Students mark reading excerpts for a careful critical read of the text.

Lesson 16. Questioning and Speculating

Now that students have been critically reading and forming inquiry questions, time to pull ideas together is important. In this lesson, students write reflective blog posts that question, speculate, and build connections between inquiry questions and their literature circle books. Additionally, students respond to classmates on their blog posts.

Chapter 4. Embarking on the Inquiry-Based Research Essay: Collaboration, Citation, and Credibility

Lesson 17. Literature Circle Meeting 3: Intertextual Connections

In addition to the discussion focused on questions, reading passages, and culture elements, students add another layer to their literature circles by bringing in additional outside texts that relate to their books and inquiry questions.

Lesson 18. Researching Skills and Tips: Exploring Sources

Students share prior knowledge about research (Part 1) and build onto their repertoire of approaches to research by exploring primary and secondary sources (Part 2). Together teachers and students tackle the Wikipedia conversation by exploring the role of Wikipedia in research (Part 3).

Lesson 19. Researching
(Online and in the Library Media Center)

Students engage with research from multiple sources, including print texts in the library. Additionally, students are able to work with adult researchers to share their research process.

Lesson 20. Writing and Researching Workshop

During the writing process, students need to review their work and the learning they have done with writing all year. Through review of various approaches to writing that students have already encountered and time to work and collaborate with peers and the teacher, students progress in their writing process.

Chapter 5. Writing Workshop and Media Projects: Responding, Revising, and Reflecting

Lesson 21. Literature Circle Meeting 4:
Final Thoughts and Reflection

As students wrap up their work with the reading of their literature circle books, they continue to have rich conversations about their questions, dialectic journals, and culture logs. They also write a final reflection post and respond to their peers on Youth Voices.

Lesson 22. Writing Workshop
and Peer Response

When students complete a final self-assessment reflection on their work with literature circles, they move into a focused peer response of their inquiry-based research essays. Students identify specific areas of focus for feedback they would like to receive from their peers.

Lesson 23. Media Work

When students are well on their way with their inquiry-based research essay, another layer is added to their thinking by assigning a media assignment. In this lesson, students brainstorm ideas and explore audiences and purposes for their work.

Lesson 24. Cultural Questions and Media Literacy

Through exploration of the topic of celebrity obsession, students engage in media literacy arguments of adjusting or remixing an image from a website using Mozilla X-Ray Goggles. This media literacy assignment provides an idea for the media project and reiterates the role of checking sources and reliability for critical reading and research.

Lesson 25. Workshop: Inquiry-Based Research Essay and Media Projects

As part of the writing process, students review how to provide citations for their research and integrate researched work into their writing. Additionally, students work on media projects as they begin the brainstorming and drafting phase of this work.

Lesson 26. Reflection and Publication of the Inquiry-Based Research Essay

In this lesson, students reflect in writing on their process and product of the inquiry-based research essay. Then students meet in literature circles to share their work and celebrate their learning. Students then have the opportunity to publish their work online to share with their personal learning networks.

Lesson 27. Exploring Basic Copyright Issues: Copyright, Fair Use, Creative Commons, and the Public Domain

Students explore the basics of copyright and fair use through music, discussion, and websites as reference material. Additionally, students apply a fair-use reasoning guide to their media drafts.

Lesson 28. Reflecting, Sharing, and Celebrating the Final Media Project

To reinforce the importance of intentionality in composing, as well as for the audience to fully understand the media project, students write a reflection to share with the teacher, share their work with others, and celebrate their work through publication and informal sharing of work with the class.

Foreword

> Now that the overhead projector has been tried out with reported success in a number of large lecture situations, it seems time for a new experiment in size of class, using lay readers and the overhead projector as aids to composition instruction.
>
> —Richard Braddock, Richard Lloyd-Jones, and Lowell Schoer, *Research in Written Composition*

Braddock, Lloyd-Jones, and Schoer (1963, p. 46) made the above observation on the promising new technology of the overhead projector following their review of writing research covering the 20th century through the early 1960s.[1] Each introduction of new technologies brings new waves of excitement, advocacy, and possibility to educational settings, from (chronologically speaking) televisions to personal computers to the continually emerging devices that are introduced each week. The idealistic rhetoric that accompanies new technologies, however, is rarely realized in practice.

One teacher I know teaches at a school that provided spanking-new tablets for all students to modernize their learning. But when she passed them out to her class, instead of recognizing the tablets as electronic learning devices, they began using them as props in a provocative dance.

At another school I recently visited, the bandwidth available for Internet access was so weak that every time students took a new standardized test,

---

1. Braddock et al. (1963) also stated that, with regard to "lay readers" who relieve teachers' grading loads, "a conclusion valid for a high school in, for example, a university community where *there are many competent faculty wives who would like to be lay readers* has little meaning for a less fortunate community where there is no abundant supply, if any, of people competent to mark compositions" (p. 46, emphasis added). The times, they are a-changin'.

which was often, nobody else in the school could get online lest the test takers lose their connections and test scores decline.

It turns out that just investing in technology only provides potential. How that potential is realized is a function of other changes that need to take place, in terms of both supporting resources and technological conceptions, so that the tools of technology are put to good use.

I recently read an article that helps explain the problem. Mi Song Kim (2012) found that just being given the tools of technology *without simultaneously learning corresponding psychological tools for using it appropriately* is insufficient for sound educational practice. So, passing out tablets to students who have developed no appropriate technological psychological tools—ways of thinking that are in tune with the technology's functions and intended purposes— can result in students using them as props for a lascivious dance, an activity for which their cultural knowledge is considerable.

In *Research Writing Rewired: Lessons That Ground Students' Digital Learning*, Dawn Reed and Troy Hicks once again show that they grasp this important principle. They are not simply passing out the devices and expecting learning to happen, which seems to happen far too often. Old-timers might remember all the excitement over WordStar, the cutting-edge word processing program that was so fabulous that nobody could figure out how to use it, leaving staffroom closets full of what, at the time, was one of the most expensive pieces of software on the market.

Rather, the collaboration of the authors—a current classroom teacher and a former one with expertise in how technology works in school—is grounded in educational realities and how technology works to promote learning. This is not a textbook handed down by authorities whose knowledge comes from ivory towers that are remote from real students and classrooms. Theoretically strong and practically oriented, the ideas in this book should greatly benefit those teachers who are eager to join the technological revolution but whose muskets keep jamming as they struggle with not only the new and ever-changing features of each new device but a schooling context that has yet to keep pace with their affordances.

Troy and Dawn's goal is to do more than provide a catalog of devices. More important, they detail the psychological tools that are involved in infusing classroom life with digital possibilities. That typically takes a reordering of how to conceive of writing (and other forms of composing— art, music, and so on) as an expression of thinking mediated by technologies and what they afford. The field has, I think, enough idealistic conceptions of technology to last another century or two. This book answers the far more urgent need to provide ways of thinking that make technology a useful tool and not just another high-priced device destined for the dustbin.

—Peter Smagorinsky
Distinguished Research Professor, The University of Georgia

Acknowledgments

> *Education is what remains after one has forgotten what one has learned in school.*
>
> —Albert Einstein

This book is about questioning and investigating through thoughtful reflection and exploration. To the teachers and learners who inspire curiosity, thank you. To our mentors, colleagues, publishers, students, friends, and family for your support of this book, we are grateful. We especially thank Dawn's students who learned with us through this inquiry unit. You were open to collaborative learning in class and sharing your work with other learners throughout our book project. Thank you for taking a risk and trusting the research process and us, as your teachers, as a part of the learning experience. To the parents and guardians of Dawn's students, thank you for supporting learning for not only your students but also other teachers and learners as we share our experiences with others.

Thank you to Okemos Public Schools for support of this project. Thanks to Matt Ottinger and Cailey Dingman-Sanchez; the video work was possible with your help. Okemos Public Schools Librarian Sandy Fields, thank you for being a thinking partner related to research, technology, libraries, and learning, and for sharing your insights with us in your writing. Thank you to Okemos High School English department for your support and for engaging students in rich learning opportunities. To Central Michigan University, Troy appreciates the sabbatical opportunity that allowed him time to spend six weeks in Dawn's classroom. Thank you to our colleagues who have inspired many of these curriculum ideas and shared resources with us over the years. For our friends in the National Writing Project, Red Cedar Writing Project, and Chippewa River Writing Project, thank you for your support and inspiration.

To the Corwin Literacy team, especially Lisa Luedeke, Julie Nemer, Emeli Warren, Melanie Birdsall, Melinda Masson, Rose Storey, Maura Sullivan, and Rebecca Eaton, and to development editor Renee Nicholls, your feedback was invaluable, and we appreciate your support of rewiring of the research process.

Thank you to Paul Allison, Chris Sloan, and Karen Fasimpaur, the gurus of Youth Voices. Matt Williams of KQED and Paul Oh from Teaching Channel, formerly of the NWP, thank you for collaborating through work with KQED's Do Now.

Thank you to Dànielle DeVoss from Michigan State University (MSU) for graciously sharing materials for our curriculum in this book and for inspiring us to dig into media and visual work.

Thank you to Peter Smagorinsky for writing the foreword and reminding our profession just how far we've come (and how far we still have to go) in order to achieve the goal of purposeful technology integration.

To Janet Swenson, from MSU and Red Cedar Writing Project (RCWP), you are mentor to both of us; thank you for constantly challenging us to embrace rich, thoughtful learning moments with our students.

To our families for being patient with us in the time it takes to work on a book and for cheering us on. To Sara, Troy's spouse, who supports the work of teachers and time for Troy to collaborate with others. To Michael, Dawn's spouse, for bringing laughter to writing times and for recognizing this was an important work to create.

Preface

Reading, Writing, and Inquiry With Adolescents

> *I am not a teacher, but an awakener.*
> —Robert Frost

Over the past twenty years, English teachers have been confronted with a variety of challenges and opportunities related to the changing nature of texts and language. In particular, two major transformations have occurred:

- Educational standards like the Common Core have become more prominent both in the United States and around the world, raising serious questions about student learning, teacher effectiveness, and the fundamental goals of education.

- The Internet has changed our lives, affecting the way that we produce, publish, and encounter texts, and expanding our content area of English language arts expertise to include film, media, and digital literacies.

The key principle that remains the foundation of our work is the task of teaching English, which involves connecting students with language and helping them interpret what they read, see, and hear, as well as the language they employ when sending their own ideas, questions, and reflections out to the world. We agree with Randy Bomer's (2011) description of the type of English class we must create for our students:

> The agenda of supporting each student in developing the habits and projects in literacy allows an English class to be designed as a unified and simple curriculum that can contain much diversity and complexity, as we all learn what a literate life is made of, while diverse individuals pursue projects that are meaningful to them. (p. 6)

Indeed, it is specifically because of the two transformations outlined earlier—the increasingly myopic view of standards and assessments that dominate the current discourse about schools, as well as the changing nature of communication and commerce in our global world—that we as teachers must support individual students even more thoughtfully now than we have done in the past. Diverse classrooms require us to acknowledge individuality while, at the same time, helping students develop effective literacy skills for both college and the workplace, as well as for their civic and personal lives.

In this unique moment, where we feel substantive changes could happen for teaching and learning, we are committed to connect students through language and help them learn how to read and write their worlds. Specifically, our goal for *Research Writing Rewired: Lessons That Ground Students' Digital Learning* is to explore how teachers can help students integrate inquiry-based research approaches with digital reading and writing in the classroom—and assess those approaches effectively.

WHY "REWIRE" RESEARCH WRITING?

Let's face it. The "research paper" has a bad reputation. Tedious note taking. Copying and pasting from sources. No critical thinking. Shallow arguments. And so on.

This book challenges the negative stereotypes in several ways:

- It exhibits the role that inquiry plays in sparking creativity and producing authentic writing.

- It demonstrates how students and teachers can work collaboratively to explore research processes *and* create engaging products, employing a variety of modes and media.

- It describes methods for integrating and employing technology, including a number of free resources that are available on the web and apps on smartphones and tablets.

- It shows why we—as teachers, researchers, and writers ourselves— enjoy the research process, a stance that can empower our students as they become researchers, too.

Throughout this book, as well as in our classrooms, we work to help students develop the skills they need to act as genuine researchers, not to merely finish a research paper. These skills are transferable to other projects they will do in school and in other contexts and are critical to college, career, and civic readiness.

Throughout this book, as well as in our classrooms, we work to help students develop the skills they need to act as genuine researchers, not to merely finish a research paper.

THE CONTENTS OF THIS BOOK

The chapters in this book describe an inquiry-based unit we created for Dawn's high school English classroom.[1] The unit integrates digital writing and research, as many projects today do in some way or another. However, we aimed to make this integration a seamless process. We didn't just integrate technology when it seemed convenient; instead, a variety of technologies were integral to the research process. Additionally, we share our reflections on student learning, as well as the reflections of Dawn's students on what they've learned. While some readers may be able to take our unit and use it in its entirety, we recognize that this is rarely possible with any professional text, nor is that our goal here. Rather, we wanted to share research practices and technology tools that could be modified and used in a variety of classroom situations and circumstances. Our sincere hope is that the book will inspire you to engage in thoughtful inquiry with your own students, using digital tools that will rewire their research and writing experience.

Through our students' inquiry and research, we highlight digital writing tools, in the form of both web services and apps for mobile devices. The purpose of sharing these tools is not to define a single, preset suite of tools that students must go through in order to complete a research project. Nor is it our intention to propose a certain linear order. Rather, books need to be a bit more orderly than our teaching sometimes is; so, while we have organized the digital writing tools roughly in the order in which they might be used, we want to acknowledge the recursive and messy nature of the writing process during research. Students could use any or all of these tools at any time. You may choose to focus in on one tool at a time in order to help students develop their skills and, more importantly, learn how to create an effective and accurate research project. Moreover, we recognize that every teaching context is different. While this book is based on our work within Dawn's high school classroom, throughout the text we offer what Swenson and Mitchell (2006) have called "extensions and adaptations" to help readers identify what "would be necessary for the lesson to work as well with diverse groups of students in other contexts and/or that might enrich the demonstration in its current context" (p. 6).

Dawn often captures her vision of purposeful technology integration in the classroom with the common aphorism "Dream big, start small." While we

---

1. Throughout the book, we (Dawn and Troy) employ we, us, and our to describe the work that we did over six weeks in Dawn's classroom. Troy, as a teacher educator and researcher, was able to collaborate with Dawn throughout the process and interacted with students as a co-teacher. This close working relationship allowed us to craft the book in this first-person plural voice.

acknowledge that it can be a challenge to integrate everything at once, the ideas in this book will inspire you to start so you can get to the dream of creating your own inquiry-based, technology-rich unit and, in turn, rewire the research and writing process for your students.

Chapter Descriptions

In the **introduction**, we explore the development of our technology-infused inquiry-based curriculum. This chapter describes the pedagogical and practical moves we made to promote sophisticated thinking and rich writing experiences. These decisions extend beyond the unit we are describing here to teaching decisions that we make each day. These moves include our considerations of the five *T*s: teens, timing, topics, texts, and technology. We also explain how we teach students to use the MAPS heuristic for writing and thinking. Traditionally, this heuristic includes mode, audience, purpose, and situation. As you will see, we've added another essential *M* to this heuristic: media.

The introduction also examines broad curricular considerations, including essential ideas, unit objectives, and assessment. We look at curricular components such as technology decisions and differentiation. Our goal is to provide readers with a clear overview of the unit we created for Dawn's students, including the thinking process behind that creation.

In **Chapters 1 through 5,** we go into the classroom as we guide students through the inquiry process week by week, including lessons and handouts. Additionally, we offer technology tips, as well as extensions and adaptations for lessons, suggesting other topics, resources, or tools that you may find useful as your students consider different content, time frames, or inquiry questions.

While we have neatly broken these chapters into weeklong segments of instruction, please understand that the actual unit was not quite this tidy. The lessons presented in the book are based on a fifty-five-minute class period, but in our case, some class periods were shorter. Also, while all the lessons are presented as sequential, we recognize that some could be interchanged and taught in a different order, developed further, broken into several classroom periods, and/or used as a frame for an entire unit.

In **Chapter 6,** we return to the principles that we lay out in the introduction, reflecting on what Dawn's students learned throughout the inquiry. We also briefly explore the issue of assessment, discussing how and why we evaluated and responded to the various pieces of writing—from initial blog posts through the dual summative assessments: an inquiry-based research essay and media project.

Finally, we invite you to go online at http://resources.corwin.com/writingrewired to experience the short videos we have created to complement and extend the content of this book. In each chapter, you will find QR codes that will lead you to classroom videos that illustrate how Dawn taught these lessons. These videos are designed to be examples for teachers as you create your digital reading and writing workshop.

OUR GUIDING PRINCIPLES

Both of us can trace many of the pedagogical principles that guide our instruction back to our experience as writing consultants at the Michigan State University (MSU) Writing Center. This is where we each discovered the central tenet captured in Stephen North's foundational article "The Idea of a Writing Center" (1984):

> [I]n a writing center the object is to make sure that writers, and not necessarily their texts, are what get changed by instruction. In axiom form it goes like this: Our job is to produce better writers, not better writing. (p. 438)

This goal, simple as it sounds, suggests that teaching writing no longer is about fixing errors; instead, it requires making a shift in our thinking about what it means to work with students to help them develop and improve their skills as writers. Our goal is to teach skills that students will carry with them throughout their education and into their career. The aim of completing a single project is not enough.

> Our goal is to teach skills that students will carry with them throughout their education and into their career. The aim of completing a single project is not enough.

We have also learned a great deal from our experiences with MSU's Red Cedar Writing Project, a site of the National Writing Project (NWP)—a network of nearly two hundred sites where K–12 teachers and university faculty work together to develop meaningful professional development opportunities centered on writing. Among the stated principles of the NWP, one in particular stands out for us as we consider our relationship as collaborators over the past decade, and specifically related to this project:

> Teachers who are well informed and effective in their practice can be successful teachers of other teachers as well as partners in educational research, development, and implementation. Collectively, teacher-leaders are our greatest resource for educational reform. (NWP, n.d.)

We take this stance as educators and researchers, and it has guided many of our collaborations (e.g., Hicks & Reed, 2007; Reed & Hicks, 2009) as well as our work with other teachers (e.g., Autrey et al., 2005; Borsheim, Merritt,

& Reed, 2008; Hicks, Busch-Grabmeyer, Hyler, & Smoker, 2013; Hicks et al., 2007; Homan & Reed, 2014; Hyler & Hicks, 2014; Olinghouse, Zheng, & Reed, 2010).

As teachers of writing—and, since both of us are active as leaders in professional development settings, as teachers of other teachers—we follow three guiding principles in our approach to English instruction:

1. We create a focus on inquiry-driven research.

2. We give students a variety of writing experiences.

3. We support connected learning in the English classroom.

In the following sections, we discuss each of these elements in more detail to help you make effective choices for your own classroom and curriculum.

Guiding Principle 1: Create a Focus on Inquiry-Driven Research

In Ken Macrorie's classic book on rethinking what it means for students to be researchers, *The I-search Paper* (1988), in the unpaginated preface, he makes the case for individual agency in the research process:

> I search. That's the truth of any inquiry. Re-search doesn't say it, rather implies complete detachment, absolute objectivity. Time to clear the miasma and admit that the best searchers act both subjectively and objectively. . . . (n.p.)

Macrorie warns that too often—and particularly in school assignments—the act of research has become mired in a quest for what others have to say. Thus, the types of writing that tend to happen in school quite often become what Anne Whitney (2011) describes as "schoolish." Instead, we should help students approach research as a personal quest, an individual inquiry.

More recently, Jim Burke, the author of *What's the Big Idea? Question-Driven Units to Motivate Reading, Writing, and Thinking* (2010), outlines the use of questions as a teaching strategy, beginning with Socrates and tracing the idea of inquiry all the way up to Wiggins and McTighe (2005). While Burke is clearly an advocate for helping students ask questions, he also makes the case that questions alone are not enough to drive curriculum or teaching. Specifically, he notes that

> students who are guided by questions need help learning how to steer their way through such uncharted waters. Without guidance and

accountability, students can wander from the topic they are investigating, arriving at the final with little more than a summary or an
extended digression. (Burke, 2010, p. 40)

In other words, unless teachers provide proper scaffolding and support,
inquiry-based instruction can quickly turn into mass chaos. We have found
that an inquiry-based approach to learning and writing requires that students be taught explicitly, through

- Models of quality writing

- Feedback on their own writing

- Opportunities to explore various genres, audiences, and purposes
  for writing

Research, from this perspective, is generated from authentic questions and
individual needs; teachers and students, working together, generate big
questions that can inspire sustained writing over the course of the entire
unit and across multiple writing opportunities.

Though teachers encourage students to make choices throughout an inquiry-driven unit, we do not leave them to go it alone; this approach also requires a great deal of teacher guidance, scaffolding, and support.

Again, it is worth reiterating that, even though teachers encourage students
to make choices throughout an inquiry-driven unit, we do not leave them to
go it alone; this approach also requires a great deal of teacher guidance, scaffolding, and support. Teachers use their personal experiences as readers and
writers to make their own questioning and thinking process visible for students. At the same time, they encourage students to select topics that are in
some way tied to the students' own interests, experiences, and/or passions.
Teachers also collaborate with students as they ask questions, and they help
students explore their findings through rich and thoughtful discussions that
encourage critical thinking.

Guiding Principle 2: Give Students a Variety of Writing Experiences

Just as Ken Macrorie inspired a shift in our approach to personal inquiry,
research in writing instruction over the past thirty years has demonstrated
that we must provide students with a variety of writing experiences,
support them through the process, and invite them to think about various genres, audiences, and purposes (Applebee & Langer, 2013; Graham
& Perin, 2007; Hillocks, 1986). For instance, in their book *Beyond the
Five-Paragraph Essay* (2012), Campbell and Latimer note that it is essential
to move students into more detailed and enhanced writing:

We need to change how we structure our classrooms and how we support students as writers. . . . This process will not be easy, and we have discovered [it] can be messy, and even frustrating, for teachers and students. When we move from asking students to follow a formula to developing an essay based on what they think about literature they have read, we put the emphasis on thinking—deep thinking. We want students to articulate this thinking and support it with evidence from the text. (p. 10)

While the Common Core has placed new emphasis on creating lessons that encourage deep thinking—supported with evidence—the concept has in fact been around for quite some time. In fact, standards documents such as the *Standards for the English Language Arts* (1996), from the National Council of Teachers of English (NCTE) and International Reading Association (recently renamed the International Literacy Association), have long advocated for the types of deeper reading, substantive writing, and engaging content now being suggested by the Common Core. This, in turn, leads us to articulate our own principles about teaching writing, as well as teaching digital writing.

Best Practices in Writing

Key writing skills should be part of any English language arts classroom—no matter what standards your state has in place, or what curriculum guide your school follows. These writing skills promote an ultimate goal of supporting students as critical thinkers, thoughtful readers, multimodal composers, and active citizens.

1. Students will become better writers through holistic, authentic, and varied writing experiences. Providing students with opportunities to write in various genres, for specific purposes and audiences, and with a variety of media will give them the best chance to succeed as writers. Specifically, we agree with the *Writing Now* research brief created by NCTE (2008a), which notes that

[r]esearch cannot identify one single approach to writing instruction that will be effective with every learner because of the diverse backgrounds and learning styles of students who respond differently to various approaches. (p. 1)

2. Process *and* product goals are an important part of inquiry. In *Writing Next* (2007), Graham and Perin highlight a number of specific factors that contribute to student growth as writers:

- The use of writing strategies
- Specific product goals

- Inquiry activities
- A process writing approach

3. Students need authentic purposes and audiences for their writing. Student ownership increases when students have real reasons to write. We agree with others, such as Zemelman, Daniels, and Hyde (2012), who also share this belief and support decreasing teacher control of decision making over topics and genres, in favor of student decision making.

4. Writing across the disciplines is important to student learning. To that end, many writing researchers now advocate techniques and approaches that encourage writing across the disciplines and that support English language learners (Applebee & Langer, 2013; Graham, MacArthur, & Fitzgerald, 2013; Jetton & Shanahan, 2012; Shanahan & Shanahan, 2008).

Best Practices in Digital Writing

Scholars in recent years have documented an increased use of digital writing as a means for students to express their ideas across genres and media. In *Because Digital Writing Matters* (2010), the National Writing Project (NWP), DeVoss, Eidman-Aadahl, and Hicks contend that "[d]igital writing matters because we live in a networked world and there's no going back. Because, quite simply, *digital is*" (p. ix, emphasis in original). Similarly, in *Teaching the New Writing: Technology, Change, and Assessment in the 21st-Century Classroom* (2009), Herrington, Hodgson, and Moran suggest that writing and assessment are changing as teachers "develop curricula that teach students to use new media to compose, [to] communicate with others for a range of purposes, and to understand and act in the world around them" (p. 14).

We concur. Digital writing skills are essential to the classroom as students engage in our global society.

1. Through work with digital writing, learners embrace a wide variety of audiences and purposes for their writing. Additionally, they work on skills and "practices that attend to the wide range of functional, critical, and rhetorical skills" (NWP et al., 2010, p. 13).

2. Digital writing work demands collaboration in a class that is

committed to purposeful, audience-oriented writing . . . digital tools [allow] such writing to happen more efficiently and more powerfully than ever before and in a variety of new media. (NWP et al., 2010, p. 45)

3. Teachers must foster work with digital writing. Integrating digital tools does not simply happen incidentally as students have opportunities to be on the computer or use their smartphones; teachers must include these tools in purposeful instruction. For instance, as later chapters will show, it is possible to incorporate digital writing conversations in the context of writing workshop with the following results:

> [B]y building on the writing workshop principles of inquiry and choice, conferring and response, examining author's craft, publishing beyond the classroom, and broadening our visions of assessment, digital writing tools can sometimes supplement, sometimes enhance, and sometimes completely change the ways in which we work with writers. (Hicks, 2009, p. 125)

Throughout this book, you will see us help students integrate digital tools into their research and writing as a natural part of inquiry, thinking, questioning, reading, and writing.

Of course, all of this work must be done with careful critical reflection, so that we're not just engaging in technology for technology's sake. Specifically, "teachers need to understand how and why to employ technology in specific ways" (Hicks & Turner, 2013, p. 126). Table P.1 contrasts the qualities of poorly designed research writing lessons with well-designed inquiry-based learning and notes how teachers can now include digital writing tools to elevate them even further. Knowing that, as a profession, our writing instruction has not always been the strongest, we outline our own set of principles in Table P.1, principles that shift from older paradigms of "good writing" to newer ideas about integrating inquiry and digital writing tools.

Guiding Principle 3: Support Connected Learning

Based on our involvement with the NWP and the fact that we both enjoy using technology to support student writers, we have become more interested in the principles of connected learning as articulated by the Connected Learning Research Network (CLRN). This group of scholars—including Mimi Ito, Kris Gutiérrez, Sonia Livingstone, Bill Penuel, Jean Rhodes, Katie Salen, Juliet Schor, Julian Sefton-Green, and S. Craig Watkins—has been exploring the ways in which people, especially teens, learn in out-of-school contexts and through the use of social media.

> Integrating digital tools does not simply happen incidentally as students have opportunities to be on the computer or use their smartphones; teachers must include these tools in purposeful instruction.

Table P.1 Putting Our Writing Principles in Practice

	Poorly designed research paper assignments have been . . .	Well-designed inquiry-based research, thinking, and writing assignments have been . . .	Now we should also think about how to incorporate digital writing tools so these lessons can become . . .
Inquiry	Teacher- or subject-driven, with little to no input by students. Teachers provide a general list, and students select their topic off the list.	Inquiry-driven, with genuine questions developed by students and their interests.	Inquiry-driven, with students exploring various forms of media and creating their own personal learning network throughout the research process.
Process	Formulaic, with step-by-step organization and deadlines to support the goal of a "final" draft.	Recursive, with students reading, writing, thinking critically, and reflecting over time with journaling and working with peers.	Recursive, often beginning with journaling or blogging (and replying to others), becoming a more formal document later on.
Format of the Writing	Full of requirements, such as having a certain number of note cards and paying close attention to citation styles, often at expense to the actual content of the writing itself.	Full of options for how to find and cite different information, with thoughtful explanations from the teacher about why and how to build them into the students' own writing.	Opportunities to examine and critique other sources (both highly credible and less credible), integrating them into the students' writing with the correct context and supporting evidence from primary and secondary research.
Audience and Purpose	Written for the teacher, not meant for a broader audience.	Written for a broader audience, including peers, the community, and experts.	Written for a global audience, open to commentary, collaboration, and critique.
Assessment	Evaluated on the ability to adhere to the conventions of MLA, APA, or Chicago style, with clear thesis and organization (product focus).	Evaluated on conventions and citations, thesis, and organization, with some attention on the process of research, writing, and reflection (process focus).	Evaluated on critical conversations addressed in the paper, as well as thesis, organization, and conventions and citations, plus reflection on the process. Also, evaluated over time on the publicly shared research process using digital writing tools.

In an infographic created by the CLRN and Digital Media & Learning Research Hub, *connected learning* is defined as

> a model of learning that holds out the possibility of reimagining the experience of education in the information age. It draws on the power of today's technology to fuse young people's interests, friendships, and academic achievement through experiences laced with hands-on production, shared purpose, and open networks.

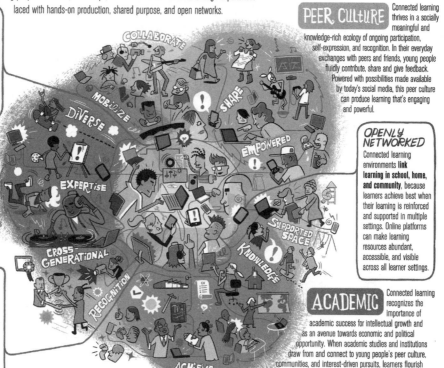

Principles of Connected Learning

Source: Connected Learning Research Network and Digital Media & Learning Research Hub.

These scholars go on to argue that connected learning, as a pedagogical approach, makes learning relevant to all students through real-life work and the need to constantly adapt to new learning contexts. They advocate for

> broadened access to learning that is *socially embedded, interest-driven, and oriented toward educational, economic, or political opportunity.* Connected learning is realized when a young person is able to pursue a personal interest or passion with the support of friends and caring adults, and is in turn able to link this learning and interest to academic achievement, career success or civic engagement. This model is based on evidence that the most resilient, adaptive, and effective learning involves individual interest as well as social support to overcome adversity and provide recognition. (Ito et al., 2013, p. 4, emphasis in original)

We see connected learning as a model for thinking about who our students are as readers and writers, and about what they are capable of creating with new media and social networks and for a variety of audiences and purposes, including civic engagement. Teachers who support connected learning in the classroom help students create relationships between the various literacy contexts of their lives through careful, critical thinking.

Teachers who support connected learning in the classroom help students create relationships between the various literacy contexts of their lives through careful, critical thinking.

This approach to teaching is discussed in a variety of presentations and publications (e.g., Garcia, 2014; Jenkins & Kelley, 2013; see also digitalis .nwp.org). We see the core tenets of connected learning as critical to the manner in which students experience their work, both inside and outside the classroom. The students you will meet in this book explored various technologies (e.g., Wikispaces, Google Docs, and the Youth Voices social network); we also asked them to create their own media composition. While we asked students to research their topics using reliable web databases and published books, we also encouraged them to conduct their own research. By positioning students as active agents in the research process, much as Macrorie began to argue for decades ago, we allowed them to be connected learners as well as readers and writers who participated in broader conversations across their own classroom, community, and the Youth Voices network.

We selected culture awareness and analysis as the focus of our inquiry project because it involves the deep exploration of fiction and nonfiction texts, and calls for visual and media literacy. In the pages that follow, we show teachers how to consider multiple and overlapping needs related to writing instruction and create an opportunity for students to

- Engage fully in the inquiry process
- Explore a topic of importance to them

- Use a variety of digital tools to support their research and writing
- Receive support and opportunities to write for a variety of purposes and audiences

Most important, as English teachers create lessons that focus on inquiry-based learning, offer a variety of genuine writing experiences, and guide students through rich explorations of connected learning, they provide learners with instruction that is progressive, student-centered, technology-rich, and critically literate. They give students the tools they need to successfully navigate new media, express themselves in thoughtful ways, and fully participate in our connected culture.

*Thank you, Troy, for your friendship and for
helping me share my teaching stories.*

*For my students, teachers and mentors.
You inspire me to reflect upon, engage in, and
embrace my craft of teaching, and I am grateful.*

*Thanks to my parents, Joseph and Lorretta Budzyn,
who taught me to view myself as a writer.*

*For Michael, you teach me to enjoy the wonders of every day;
thank you for bringing joy and love to my story.*

—Dawn

*Thanks to you, Dawn, for your many years of friendship and
collegiality beginning in our time at the writing center and stretching up to
the present. Time spent with you and your students working on this unit was
invaluable for me as a teacher, as a teacher educator, and as a parent.*

*And, thanks to my dad, Ron Hicks, who forced me to write my first research
paper on a computer way back in tenth grade. A CD-ROM encyclopedia and
WordPerfect rewired my passion for writing, and I've never been far from a
keyboard since.*

—Troy

Introduction

Framing Student Inquiry

> Truths are as much a matter of questions as answers.
>
> —Ozzie Zehner, *Green Illusions*

"Reading Our World and Exploring Perspectives: Identity and Culture" was created in the spirit of Peter Smagorinsky's "conceptual units," which devote four to six weeks to *"sustained attention to a related set of ideas"* (Smagorinsky, 2007, p. 111, emphasis in original). Learning in this unit will help students develop approaches to critical thinking and refine literacy skills that they can transfer to other contexts. Our inquiry-based approach to research asks students to work collaboratively, with the teacher as facilitator and guide. Also, it requires active engagement, self-directed learning, and shared responsibility among individual students, small groups of students, and the teacher.

We offer our unit as one example of how you might employ the kind of teaching outlined in the preface and shown in Table P.1: an inquiry-driven approach to research that is rich with opportunities for connected learning and includes a variety of writing experiences. This chapter provides the context for our research project, considerations of what we have come to call the "five *Ts*," MAPS (a thinking tool for writers), and a variety of other curricular components that we considered.

CONSIDERING OUR GOALS

We built this unit with research and connected learning as primary focuses. Yet we also considered end goals for students that address the following:

- What skills will they carry with them—as readers, writers, researchers, and thinkers—into other contexts and situations, in school and beyond?

- How can we help students to critically read various texts—including literature, images, videos, websites, and cultural artifacts (such as fashion or food wrappers)—through an exploration of their own inquiry questions?

We also considered what information and guidance students would need to be able to create a vision for their writing as well as their final media product. At the same time, we wanted to be flexible enough to allow students some creative freedom and keep their learning differentiated. Ultimately, we wanted to provide an inquiry-based approach where students had investment in rich learning opportunities.

Another goal was to ensure that students learned how to engage in conversations, essentially beginning the process of developing their own personal learning network, in digital spaces such as blogs, wikis, and social networks (Beach, Anson, Breuch, & Swiss, 2008; Hicks, 2009; Hicks & Reed, 2007; Kajder, 2010; Reed & Hicks, 2009; Richardson, 2010; Richardson & Mancabelli, 2011). However, there is more to teaching the process of digital writing than simply employing a tech tool. We knew that for students to refine their thinking and research processes, they would need to participate in critical conversations, including collaborative work inside of class, and digital conversations that extended beyond our four walls. Moreover, we wanted students to be able to synthesize their work into a pair of final pieces—an inquiry-based research essay and a media project—that demonstrated their learning throughout the course of their inquiry.

Both of these final projects, which are explained in more detail in Chapters 4 (inquiry-based research essay) and 5 (media project), are recursive research projects that build on work over the entire unit. Major features of these projects are explained in Table I.1, as we begin with the end goal in mind.

> There is more to teaching the process of digital writing than simply employing a tech tool.

To accomplish these final compositions, we knew that it would be essential to set up Dawn's classroom as a community focused on critical thinking and questioning, a move that Stock (1995) has described as creating a "dialogic curriculum." Students sometimes expect teachers to provide answers, but when we do so, we do not support the inquiry process. Instead, Dawn supports and guides students so they can figure out how to answer questions on their own. To rewire the research process, putting the responsibility on students as researchers, there are many elements that we must keep in mind. We turn our attention to these elements now.

The Five *T*s: Teens, Timing, Topics, Texts, and Technology

For students to engage in inquiry, teachers must establish and foster a culture of curiosity, taking into consideration the students in the room, their

Table I.1   Final Research Project Features

Inquiry-Based Research Essay	Media Project
• Inquiry focus determined by student researcher through work with reading various texts (literature circle book, common class articles and media texts, personal learning network blog posts) and writing (reflective journals and blog posts) related to big ideas and unit questions. • Recursive research process with students reading and writing related to their inquiry question. Students' active research with integration of personal surveys or interviews. • Writing focused on an overall purpose to construct a critical conversation around the topic and to convey an argument about their topic; writing audience to include their class, personal learning network, and a global audience. • Assessment based on developing an academic conversation and argument about their inquiry question.	• Explores inquiry focus from inquiry-based research essay using media. • Develops an argument about inquiry topic and conveys message using media in intentional ways. • Recursive process to develop project and unique modality based on an appropriate audience and purpose for the work as determined by the topic. • Assessment based on explanation of the intentional decisions in the media work.

experiences, and the relationships among members of the class. As Johnston (2004) explains, words that we speak in front of the class—as well as the language that we use in our lesson plans, assignment sheets, and feedback provided to students—affect "the subtle ways in which [teachers] build emotionally and relationally healthy learning communities—intellectual environments that produce not mere technical competence, but caring, secure, actively literate human beings" (p. 2). As you create units, draft essential questions, and foster curiosity in your own classroom, we encourage you to think carefully about the five *T*s—teens, timing, topics, texts, and technology—and how you position each as you describe them.

Teens

We are conscious of the numerous reports and research studies documenting the state of adolescent literacy. For instance, the opening pages of a report to the Carnegie Corporation, *Time to Act: An Agenda for Advancing Adolescent Literacy for College and Career Success* (2009), implore us:

> Every adolescent must have the opportunity to develop the necessary tools and skill-sets for ongoing active engagement with different kinds of text, critical thinking, and lifelong exploration and development. Improving literacy in grades 4–12 is the key to realizing this essential goal.
>
> We already know enough to raise the overall level of adolescent literacy in our schools. The time to act is now. (p. 2)

Our inquiry unit, which we used with ninth graders coming to the end of their freshman year, works to address the unique needs of adolescent learners. The unit's themes—culture and identity—are universal, and could be modified and used in middle school and upper secondary grades as well. Adolescents of any age can benefit from help navigating their emerging identity, articulating this identity, and considering how their identity is situated within the context of culture.

We designed specific activities to scaffold students' learning around the topic of culture. While we taught the unit at the end of the year, Dawn established a foundation for digital learning and inquiry throughout the year. Specifically, during the unit, we

- Explored the topic of culture through various readings

- Asked students to write and reflect on digital citizenship

- Selected high-interest texts and materials in a variety of media that were challenging but accessible

- Explored texts that students interact with on a daily basis, such as TED Talks, news articles, and Twitter chat responses to current events and contemporary narratives

- Strategically encouraged discussions to scaffold student learning in this area

Timing

This particular unit took place in the late winter and early spring, but in addition to setting the foundation, Dawn had taken care to prepare students to explore the theme of culture. Earlier in the year, when studying texts such as *To Kill a Mockingbird* (Lee, 1960) and *Romeo and Juliet* (Shakespeare, n.d.), students reflected and discussed the way in which the societal context, time period, and culture impacted the characters. In this way, students were rehearsing reading through a cultural lens. Additionally, they had previously engaged in conversations about digital citizenship; they understood that digital spaces were an extension of the classroom, and that they needed to adhere to an academic approach in the context of school. Students worked in online spaces, such as Google Drive and Gmail, and they had learned how to take screenshots and how to respond to one another through online peer review.

Careful coaching ensured that as students learned the technology they also learned that they needed to be resources to one another. They often worked collaboratively throughout the year on writing, and they supported one another to address technology needs. This eliminated the need for repeated step-by-step instruction; rather, Dawn was able to give one quick review on how to use a new online tool and then move on because students could figure it out by learning together. We agreed that it was essential for students to learn to problem-solve and overcome challenges together to create a classroom culture that ultimately supported the unit's goals of collaboration, transfer, and eventual independence. To ensure that students had adequate time to learn and to develop confidence with collaborative learning, we introduced the inquiry project toward the end of the school year.

> Careful coaching ensured that as students learned the technology they also learned that they needed to be resources to one another.

Throughout the year, when students had questions about how to do research or experienced technical difficulties (which are bound to occur at some point), Dawn modeled the habits of mind for writers from the *Framework for Success in Postsecondary Writing* (Council of Writing Program Administrators, National Council of Teachers of English, & National Writing Project, 2011), emphasizing flexibility and persistence. These tenets reinforced Dawn's problem-solving approach, taught students to recognize that stumbling blocks are a natural part of the learning process, and emphasized that it is OK to fail and take risks.

Topics

As we considered various topics for the unit, we asked ourselves the following questions:

- How can we help students analyze and synthesize texts that are challenging in both reading level and content?

- How can we help students wrestle with real questions, providing guidance without scripting them or moving in a lockstep manner?

- How can we give students flexibility within the broad theme of culture to pursue their own topics for research?

We selected cultural inquiry as our theme because it provided a wide range of individual subtopics that would be relevant to our students' lives. We also wanted to give students the opportunity to discover that while culture is something that impacts us all—including our learning, reading, and writing—we don't often recognize its power in our own lives.

Culture lacks a tangibility that students often crave; you can't touch it or capture it in a single image. But we were devoted to challenging our students to stretch themselves. We wanted to give them an opportunity to embrace the uncertainty that comes with inquiry and what ultimately accompanies it—discovery.

Texts

We selected relevant and interesting texts in a variety of media, which included print, visual, and multimedia, with the understanding that multiple texts in multiple modes could create a richer conversation as students would be able to read contemporary texts and modalities. These readings also served as mentor texts. We encouraged students to see our inquiry as an opportunity to become ethnographers and study the spaces in which they interact with others, embracing community and their own unique culture. Additionally, we chose a variety of classic and contemporary books that students could select for literature circles. As students prepared to "read" their world, we discussed the important role of perspective in observation, and ways they might carefully read what they see every day.

Technology

Prior to our inquiry unit, students had engaged in academic conversations with their classmates via class discussion and online in Google Drive, and had participated in conversations across class sections using Google Groups. As we moved more deeply into connected learning, we decided to also connect students with other students across the country through Youth Voices at youthvoices.net. We felt this connection would help students as they worked to develop inquiry questions related to the world and to hone their questions related to culture. We wanted technology to be a critical part of their composing processes for all aspects of the unit, from blog posts and essay drafts to their final inquiry-based research essay and media project. And, as we note throughout these pages, we also took steps to ensure that the use of technology was always combined with analysis of why and when to explore digital writing, as well as components of digital writing.

MAPS: A Heuristic for Writing and Thinking

The blend of the *T*s discussed in the previous section, as well as the stance we wanted to take in regard to critical pedagogy, made the unit both robust and complex. This wide array of technology, tools, and texts was exactly what we wanted to set up for students to establish a culture of inquiry, questioning, and exploration. To help guide us through the process, we used a heuristic, a tool for thinking called MAPS.

Described by Swenson and Mitchell (2006), MAPS helps writers consider the rhetorical situation in which they are writing. It includes the following four components:

- **Mode:** What the writer understands about the type, or genre, of writing, including the conventions of writing that make up the modality

- **Audience:** What previous experiences and knowledge of the intended reader the writer can assume, as well as recognition of what the audience may want to hear

- **Purpose:** The action that this writing will take, such as to inform or argue; the reasons the writer is composing this text

- **Situation:** The personal context for the writer (e.g., experience in the genre, comfort with the topic, preferences for writing) and the writing task (e.g., deadline, length, formatting requirements)

MAPS gives students and teachers a guide to formulate thinking about writing. Because of our focus on digital and multimodal texts, we also added another *M* (Hicks, 2009):

- **Media:** The publishing opportunities the writer has, such as blogs, podcasts, digital stories, and other forms of media; the tools writers use to compose, such as a collaborative word processor, a video editing program, or a wiki

Throughout the inquiry unit, we encouraged students to use the MAPS heuristic to make connections between *rhetoric* and successful *choice of media*. Dawn teaches rhetoric from an Aristotelian perspective as the art of communication, including strategies writers use to communicate to an audience. We extended discussions of MAPS to prompt students to consider the variety of media (e.g., text, audio, and video) that they could use most effectively for specific audiences and purposes.

> This wide array of technology, tools, and texts was exactly what we wanted to set up for students to establish a culture of inquiry, questioning, and exploration.

THE BIG PICTURE: BROAD CURRICULAR CONSIDERATIONS

Our inquiry unit would allow students to pursue individual interests within the broader topic of culture. As we planned for reading, writing, and connected learning, we also considered the following:

- Essential questions for students to explore
- Overarching literacy goals

- Unit objectives

- Common Core State Standards (CCSS)

- Assessment

- Effective ways to organize information for sharing and collaboration

Essential Questions

We designed this unit knowing that students need to be critical readers and writers in various places and spaces, and for various audiences and purposes. We wanted students to engage in critical reading of both fiction and nonfiction and real inquiry about their own lives as based on their identity and culture. To introduce the unit, we shared the handout on page 9 with students.

These overarching essential questions and tasks helped us establish a central frame for the way students would explore their research topics. We also planned to help students work on skill development as they addressed these questions and examined big ideas related to culture.

Extensions and Adaptations: Inquiry Unit Ideas

We chose to focus on culture and identity because it fit within the curriculum focus for ninth-grade students at our school and offered a focal point that worked with our curriculum goals. We aimed to explore a broad topic that would appeal to the interests of students and that was of personal and professional interest for us as well. This decision depended on more than the fact that we "liked" a particular book or genre of writing; instead, we aimed to ask engaging questions and guide students in their personal inquiry. Based on your students' grade level and anchor texts, as well as your teaching interests and context, you might wish to consider thematic approaches such as these:

- Conflict and resolution

- Relationships

- Freedom and liberty

- Coming of age and identity

- Courage and fear

- Transformation

- Growth and change

"Reading Our World and Exploring Perspectives: Identity and Culture" Essential Questions

HAND OUT

For all of human history, individuals and groups of people have worked to form their identities. Some elements of our identity are unique and specific to each of us. Other elements are shared and help us feel like part of a group. These elements are all part of our culture. Yet, we don't often pause to ask, *What is culture? How does our culture influence the way we view our world?* In our inquiry unit, we will explore the following essential questions:

- What is culture? How do various individuals, communities, and groups describe the characteristics of "culture"?

  ○ What are characteristics of culture? How do these characteristics influence and contribute to culture?

  ○ When are cultural characteristics seen as positive, and when are they seen as negative?

- What is cultural identity? How does my culture influence identity?

  ○ What is my own cultural identity in relation to my family and community?

  ○ How is American culture described through various forms of media, in my school, and in my community?

- How do these visions and elements of culture influence my life?

  ○ What are the artifacts of my culture (imagery, music, food, clothing, ceremonies, pop culture icons, etc.)?

  ○ How do I imagine these artifacts and characteristics of culture will continue to influence my life in the future?

In pursuit of answers to these questions and others, we will

- Identify and explain characteristics (e.g., freedom, individualism, the common good) that shape culture in families, in communities, and in the United States

- Select and analyze various cultural artifacts (e.g., food, music, clothing) that represent these characteristics of culture

- Recognize and elaborate upon various perspectives related to culture, broadly, and related to individual cultural identity specifically

For more ideas, note that Peter Smagorinsky and teachers enrolled in his courses at the University of Georgia continue to create and share a variety of instructional units: http://smago.coe.uga.edu/VirtualLibrary.

"Reading Our World and Exploring Perspectives: Identity and Culture" Objectives

As students conducted their research, we placed a focus on learning through careful reflection and analysis of texts. Within the unit, we organized learning experiences to help students meet the following objectives.

Students will be able to

- Examine different cultures to which they belong by analyzing cultural elements. In doing so, students will examine markers of identity, as well as specific aspects of culture as recognized in their reading, and how culture influences a text (written, visual, film, etc.)

- Explore cultural production through nonfiction and fictional texts by reading and responding to those texts

- Closely read various texts after modeled think-alouds, group reading, and individual practice

- Analyze a range of texts (e.g., traditional books, video, visuals, social media, and other cultural artifacts)

- Research elements related to cultural identity

- Identify and think critically about various artifacts of culture and cultural characteristics

- Utilize research through sharing of ideas related to the process of thinking when reading, writing, synthesizing, and composing research writing and media composition

- Compose an inquiry-based research essay by developing inquiry questions, refining inquiry questions into research topics, exploring research databases and various other sources related to the research topic, determining credibility related to research information, and synthesizing information related to research questions

- Revise the inquiry-based research essay into a media project to adjust for different purposes for compositions

Assessment

All the practices and products that comprise this inquiry lead us to assessment, a significant topic to consider and one that is much discussed in the field of education today. We'll provide a quick overview here of how we assessed students' work along the way (formative assessment) as well as their final products (summative assessment). In the final chapter, we include some additional thinking about assessment.

In sum, our assessment process was multilayered. While we did assign students a final grade, it included specific values or weights for each part of the project. We recognized that to move assessment beyond mere points in a grade book (a major—and fair—concern for Dawn's students as well as their parents/guardians), we needed to create a score that was designed to monitor learning and help students embrace learning. We recognized that to support future learning, assessment practices need to provide feedback for growth (Fisher & Frey, 2007; Hattie, 2008; Heritage, 2010; Popham, 2011), and they must articulate to students and parents/guardians strengths in student work as well as areas for students to continue to develop their skills. These formative assessments throughout the unit guided our teaching to monitor and support student learning.

Our final assessment also took into consideration the rhetorical moves (or, using the term we defined earlier, MAPS) of student writing, and we worked on utilizing self-assessment to help students monitor their learning and identify the moves they made in their own compositions. These steps helped students move beyond merely memorizing characters or plot points in a text to transferring their learning about reading and analysis to other texts.

The process of assessment can be tricky. Even though Dawn worked hard to help students see beyond the grade, well, grades still mattered, and moving beyond a focus on a grade can be hard for some students, especially given college entrance pressures. Moreover, the kind of critical thinking, reading, writing, and questioning established in this unit was not something that could be evaluated in a multiple-choice fashion. Instead, we ensured that both the process and the product were factored into our assessment and, importantly, student learners received ongoing feedback both in conversations and in written comments regarding their work, oral and written, individual and collaborative.

As you consider your own assessment practices, there are dozens, probably hundreds, of resources out there. As teachers of English, we would like to point out two recently published documents worthy of attention:

- *Formative Assessment That* Truly *Informs Instruction* (National Council of Teachers of English [NCTE] Assessment Task Force, 2013)

- *Framework for Success in Post-Secondary Writing* (Council of Writing Program Administrators, National Council of Teachers of English, & National Writing Project, 2011)

As statements from our professional organizations, these documents offer insights into current research and best practices related to curriculum planning, instructional design, and formative and summative assessment. The NCTE Assessment Task Force (2013) statement defines formative assessment as

> the lived, daily embodiment of a teacher's desire to refine practice based on a keener understanding of current levels of student performance, undergirded by the teacher's knowledge of possible paths of student development within the discipline and of pedagogies that support such development. (p. 2)

Both of these valuable professional documents informed our thinking for the inquiry unit, and we recommend reading and discussing them with your colleagues.

Selecting Online Tools

While choosing a particular educational technology is sometimes dictated by convenience, cost to the school, and district filtering policies, it should ideally be a process in which teachers

1. Engage in thoughtful consideration about the many options available (for a unit or course website, some options include blogs, wikis, social media, and course sites)
2. Choose something appropriate for the task and for their students

While both of us have experience in many platforms, for this unit we were committed to using an online tool that would provide openness, flexibility, and opportunities for student collaboration. We knew that the students were quite comfortable with using Google Docs for collaboration, and with checking Dawn's class blog for assignments, but neither of these venues provided all the features we wanted:

- Space for us to include daily lesson plans, links to assignments, and outside resources

- Space for students to create individual profile pages to pull together materials and notes in one location

- Space for students to create group pages for their literature circle team

- Opportunities for students to work together and co-construct a place for their notes, just like they were co-constructing analysis of a text through discussion

To that end, we chose to create the unit using Wikispaces.

A quick tour of the home page will allow us to explain some of those features (http://culture-study.wikispaces.com). As you view the annotated image on page 14, we also invite you to visit the wiki and explore for yourself via the link on our companion website (**http://resources.corwin.com /writingrewired**).

Wikispaces proved to be an effective choice for this project both in a technical and in a pedagogical sense. It served as a hub for daily activity in class, as well as for students outside of class.

Extensions and Adaptations: Course Management Technologies

The decision to use various tools is based on personal preference, literacy goals, district policy, and student interest. Here are a few other technology options to consider when creating a web-based unit that will allow for collaborative work:

- Course websites (e.g., Blackboard, Moodle, My Big Campus)

- School-based social networks (e.g., Edmodo, Schoology, Spruz, GroupSpaces, Wiggio)

- Blogs and wikis (e.g., Kidblog, Edublogs, Blogger, PBworks)

- Websites (e.g., Weebly, Google Sites, Google Classroom)

ADDITIONAL CURRICULAR COMPONENTS

While creating goals and objectives is an important step in designing a curriculum, we must also recognize that curriculum exists in context. In this inquiry unit on identity and culture, we worked to integrate various components that embraced connected learning, blending the students' interests with hands-on experiences that supported their inquiry through the use of collaboration and technology. Depending on the topic of your own inquiry-based unit, you may find that additional components similar to the ones described here can enhance your curriculum. Our connections with the National Writing Project led to the decision that we would connect with KQED Do Now and Youth Voices, and these are available for any teacher. Additionally, we outline decision making related to technology decisions, disciplinary literacy, and differentiation.

> While both of us have experience in many platforms, for this unit we were committed to using an online tool that would provide openness, flexibility, and opportunities for student collaboration.

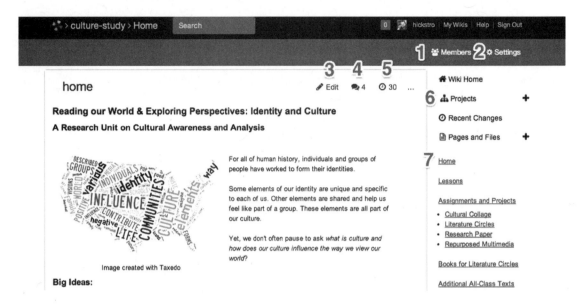

Home Page of the Class Wiki for "Reading Our World
and Exploring Perspectives: Identity and Culture" Unit

Source: http://culture-study.wikispaces.com.

Key:

1. **Members.** Teachers can add student members without requiring an e-mail address, or students can join the wiki using a course code. This can be a helpful way to invite students all at once and eliminate extra steps that a school may not yet be ready for.

2. **Settings.** This includes public/private settings and editing privileges. There are benefits to publishing work in a very public space such as opportunities to share work with others, opportunities to engage in digital citizenship activities, and the ease of access to material for various audiences. However, having a Wikispace that is only accessible to members offers less concern over publishing online or the potential for inappropriate work to be posted. When making a decision for your wiki settings, consider your objectives for learning and your comfort with the level of privacy for your students' work. You can always go back and change your settings to make material appear as public or private for others; just be sure to discuss any such changes with all student contributors.

3. **Edit.** It's important to note that each page can be edited by others unless you lock it. While it's possible to make pages revert back to previous revisions, you will want to actively manage your classroom's online space. Locking pages, such as lesson plans, makes it so that no one else can alter them. This is especially important because the material on your pages may impact your students' expectations and, if public, be viewed by parents, guardians, and administrators. You don't want students adding comments like "Class will be held at the sub shop!" or "Free pizza today!" That's where the locked feature comes in handy.

4. **Discussions.** Each page has a discussion forum. These forums can be a handy place to keep notes from class discussion. They can also give students a place to conduct critical conversations.

5. **Revisions.** Each page tracks revisions, and users can revert to previous versions if necessary. While wiki members cannot easily see line edits, as they can with Google Docs, they can see revisions on a wiki page, and this can be especially helpful if students accidentally write over one another's work.

6. **Projects.** During our unit, each literature circle group had its own wiki page within the main Wikispaces site. Sharing projects publicly allows students to see the work of other teams. Some teachers prefer not to do this in case it results in copying, but, of course, that could also happen without an online space. We contend that sharing projects publicly offers opportunities for collaboration and co-created thinking if teachers manage it with students for that clear purpose.

7. **Navigation Bar.** The contents of this bar can easily be edited and changed to suit students' projects. Establishing a navigation bar that can be modified and adjusted throughout the course of the unit offers a way for teachers to model lifelong organizational skills for students, along with the chance to show them how we rethink and reorganize ideas.

KQED Do Now and Critical Media Literacy

Prior to the unit on identity and culture, Dawn's students had already used social media to engage in conversations about civics and popular culture through their experiences with KQED, a radio, television, and Internet news source out of Northern California that works in connection with National Public Radio (NPR) and the Public Broadcasting Service (PBS). As its website explains, KQED Education offers a program called Do Now, which it describes as

> a weekly activity for students to engage and respond to current issues using social media tools like Twitter. Do Now aims to build civic engagement and digital literacy for young folks. (KQED, n.d.)

Dawn's students' previous KQED Do Now work had prompted discussions about the importance of

- Entering thoughtful conversations by reading carefully around a topic
- Exploring some of the conversations that are already happening
- Acknowledging those conversations
- Adding on to the conversation

Through this process, reading and researching become a natural part of participating in a thoughtful online, ongoing conversation.

KQED Education Do Now Website

Source: KQED Do Now.

To use Kenneth Burke's (1973) metaphor, participants who join a conversation first listen to retrace the path of the conversation and then eventually "decide that [they] have caught the tenor of the argument [and] put in [their] oar" (pp. 110–111). When we provide students with opportunities to write within social media or blogs engaged in conversation with others, we give them a chance to "put in their oar" by sharing the rich ideas that they have developed by careful reading. They engage in this work in socially mediated ways through their involvement in conversations that take place in digital spaces.

As part of our unit, students responded to weekly questions related to current news events through adding comments on a blog or tweeting a response. Additionally, they participated in creating media including remixed images to engage in rich analysis of text and visuals. Through their work with KQED Do Now, Dawn's students were able to act as genuine researchers who engage in collaborative conversations and build and adjust their ideas accordingly.

This work was influenced by the principles of connected learning, which suggest that learning happens beyond the walls of the classroom through engagement in smart, thoughtful critical conversations and compositions, and with informed citizens. Moreover, students practiced critical media literacy skills in this unit to analyze their world, including popular perceptions of teens and their own experiences related to identity and culture.

Youth Voices

We also asked students to engage in blogging to initiate digital conversations. To set up a space for this process, we turned to Youth Voices, which is

> a school-based social network that was started in 2003 by a group of National Writing Project teachers [who] merged several earlier blogging projects [and] have found that there are many advantages to bringing students together in one site that lives beyond any particular class. (Youth Voices, n.d.)

As the creators note on the Youth Voices website, blogging through a network makes it "easier for individual students to read and write about their own passions, to connect with other students, comment on each other's work, and create multimedia posts for each other." It also offers teachers and students an opportunity to "pool [their] knowledge about curriculum and digital literacies" (Youth Voices, n.d.).

While many educators are doing rich and thoughtful work with various blogging platforms, we turned to Youth Voices knowing the rich work here

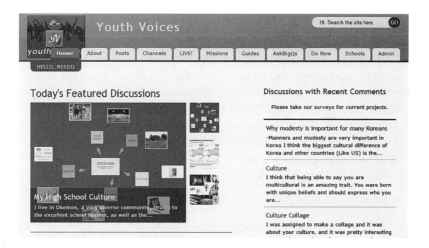

Youth Voices Website

Source: Courtesy of Youth Voices.

is specifically designed to support conversations among students. The site includes many valuable research tools and guides for writing moves that bloggers might make in their discussions, and allowed us to introduce Dawn's students to an established community that could quickly respond to the individual blogs they created.

We wanted students to be able to share their thinking along the way not only with their classroom peers but also through conversations in digital spaces with real authentic audiences beyond the classroom, school, and state. We also wanted students to journal both publicly and privately to have opportunities to make good decisions about when to move into public spaces and when to keep ideas private.

When teachers ask students to create blogs and to partake in digital conversations about their work, we help them

- Move research to another level beyond just stating what they found

- Put texts in conversation with one another for a rich synthesis of ideas

- Enter conversations where their ideas are more than just a lone, final project that is turned in for a grade and then disregarded

In this way, the entire process for creating the inquiry-based research essay becomes conversational, collaborative, and authentically situated in discussions that move thinking forward.

Technology Decisions

As we considered the best way to set up the unit to provide structure and guidance for students to engage in inquiry and research, to allow them the freedom to be creative, and to provide them with genuine opportunities to ensure that inquiry and writing are authentic, we knew that we also had to integrate technology in a purposeful and authentic way. While both of us are advocates for digital literacy and the integration of technology, we do so to meet academic goals and not simply to show that we can "use technology." Specifically, as we make technology decisions, we are constantly considering elements such as these:

- The *purpose* behind the technology

- How the technology might spark creativity or motivation

- What the tool is able to do and how that would impact the learning experience for the positive or the negative

- Ease of use and ease of access

- The benefit and the cost

- The ability for students to learn the technology fairly easily, so the focus stays on the learning of content and usage versus the details of the technology

We also need to establish times when it is best for students *not* to use technology. For example, when fostering questioning and inquiry, we need to offer students time before they simply search for answers on Google. We need to provide time for wonder, because without wonder there is no room for genuine creation. With technology, it is possible to quickly find an answer and move on; time away from technology, rather, can create space for small questions that may turn into big questions. Time to linger and think can produce even bigger answers as well.

> While both of us are advocates for digital literacy and the integration of technology, we do so to meet academic goals and not simply to show that we can "use technology."

Not all tools and technologies are the right match for all students at all times. We must remember that the collaboration tools and creation tools we use with students are not intended to make them experts with technology or to replace other valuable kinds of learning experiences. Students who struggle with certain tools and technology can still learn from their peers, the teacher, and many other resources. While students should learn how to use the tools, no student needs to be a perfect expert, and students should not become completely dependent on the technology.

In fact, during this inquiry, while all of our material and instructions were available to students online, students who missed class still struggled to catch up without also asking teachers or classmates what to do. One student remarked after the first week that it would be hard to use only the online material to follow what we were doing in class because the real-time conversation that surrounded the learning was so important. We live in a time that is embracing online education—and both of us are excited by this work—but we still recognize that in some contexts the social interaction and conversation in a shared space is pivotal to the students' learning experiences, as is the case with this particular experience.

In terms of the actual technology we used in class, Dawn's students were already using some of the collaboration tools we included in this unit, such as Google Drive and other Google education tools. Students had their own Gmail accounts associated with the district, and within the e-mail system it was easy to find students' and faculty members' e-mail addresses. Since all students were using Gmail, Dawn also used Google Drive in the classroom for various purposes. Students used it to turn in work to Dawn for feedback, to collaborate among peers with shared writing and feedback, and to share resources and other collaborative work in class-shared folders. While some students struggled with organizing folders and placing work in the correct folder, Dawn recognized the importance of encouraging students to be resourceful and persistent and engage in 21st century literacy learning. Google Drive also provided a way for students to engage in peer response in a place that was not public but could be shared in small groups.

Throughout the research process, we encouraged students to engage with various digital spaces. The following chapters provide full details, but here is a brief outline to show some of the ways students used technology throughout the unit:

- Students used Citelighter, a research tool, to take notes on what they were researching and to work with citations.

- Students used cell phones and cameras to be ethnographers and record images and video clips for further study.

- We modeled several tools students could use to create a collage, including Smore, ThingLink, VoiceThread, Padlet, and Capzles. Students also jumped in and shared programs that they enjoyed, such as Animoto, Mural.ly, and Loupe.

- Some students used audio and video to present their work.

As noted earlier, students don't have to be experts on each tool (in fact, neither do we). Rather, by exploring just a few of the elements of a variety of tools, students were able to determine if they wanted to learn more about the tool and further consider its possibilities.

Disciplinary Literacy

Throughout the unit on culture and identity, disciplinary literacy became part of the research process as students engaged in questions that they developed and explored because of individual interest. Working as true scholars, students often moved beyond the discipline of English as they were required to analyze data and explore writing in different fields to answer their questions, using academic vocabulary, specific genres, and rhetorical strategies unique to other disciplines.

We believe that if students are truly researching and acting as scholars, then they need to think big. While this book is written from an English language arts (ELA) perspective, there are lots of connections to other content areas. For instance, at the start of our cultural study, students selected various inquiry topics. Some included the role of analyzing history and how people have been treated in society throughout history or in war times. For this example, students referenced their history textbooks and shared insights from social studies courses with one another. Similarly, some students explored fashion and found themselves exploring the advertising industry for their research. Social sciences were another big area of exploration as students looked at the psychology of what it means to have certain standards for beauty or how colors are used in our society.

The practice of disciplinary literacy is sometimes even richer as seniors in high school prepare for college-level writing and start to explicitly explore writing in the disciplines. However, this scaffolding is important even in earlier grades, as students understand and engage in writing as thinking across all content areas. Introducing students to the many ways in which research can be designed, and how data can be collected and analyzed, and then written about, is a process that will serve them well throughout high school, college, and career.

Differentiation

While planning a unit, we must also consider the students' various learning needs. Within our classes, we have visual, auditory, and kinesthetic learners; we also have students with special needs and learning disabilities. A co-created curriculum, in which teachers give students the chance to participate in decisions and choose their own paths for inquiry, can be challenging for some students, particularly those who need more guidance. At times, teachers may find they need to make some modifications and adaptations to meet particular students' needs.

We believe in challenging all students to a high level that will expand their current skills and knowledge. With that in mind, we designed this unit to allow room for differentiation and individualized instruction—from choice, to technology assistance, to collaboration opportunities. In Dawn's classes, we were able to limit or modify different parts of the material as needed for individual students. As the following chapters show, we also scaffolded learning with one-on-one instruction.

FINAL CONSIDERATIONS

While we have tried to make our creation of this inquiry project as transparent as possible both in this book and through the companion online resources at **http://resources.corwin.com/writingrewired**, the moves you make as a teacher will still be based on your individual context as the students' teacher. As you continue to take this journey with us, we hope that you will also think about how you might extend our ideas to consider new pedagogical approaches for incorporating inquiry-based research, writing, and technology into your own classroom.

We believe that all teachers need to be knowledgeable and constantly learning to make educated professional choices. Sometimes that also includes the need to push back against confines, particularly the comment that "it's always been done this way." It's important to ask ourselves: "Have I thought about doing my work in a different way? What are the benefits, and what are the limitations, of various approaches?" Above all, we need to make it real. Students do not necessarily need to learn amazing organizational strategies and to create beautiful note card systems to succeed as researchers; after all, do professional researchers use them? Rather, they need opportunities to engage in genuine experiences that teach them that research and the synthesis of that research is a messy but highly rewarding process.

Throughout the process of developing or revising curriculum and scaffolding learning experiences for our students, there is a lot to figure out. We are teaching our classes, assessing student work, and much, much more. For instance, as we planned this work, we were doing our own research related to culture, exploring potential inquiry questions for ourselves, but also considering what students might appreciate, finding models and examples, considering various technology tools and weighing the benefits and costs of using each technology, reviewing the ties to our standards (CCSS), integrating disciplinary reading, scaffolding reading and writing strategies and skill building, exploring various texts for study, and considering what we as teachers had to learn about this topic. While all of this can be quite overwhelming, it's also exciting. This is indeed the teacher brain at work. And it is what rewiring the traditional, linear research process into one that is multifaceted, recursive, and ongoing is all about.

As we extend our work with students, our pedagogical focus on encouraging inquiry, providing students with many writing experiences, and giving students opportunities to engage in connected learning continues to guide our curriculum choices. In summary, we make the case that our class inquiry, "Reading Our World and Exploring Perspectives: Identity and Culture,"

- Addresses multiple ELA standards, incorporating fiction and nonfiction texts and inviting students to write in a variety of genres/purposes

- Acknowledges unique needs of adolescent learners, helping them articulate a sense of identity

- Questions popular perceptions of teens and culture presented in the media, sharing instead what students discovered about their own identities and communities

- Provides adequate structure and, at the same time, enough freedom for students to make good choices as readers, writers, and digital citizens

- Uses technology in an integrative fashion, not just as an add-on for its own sake

To that end, we encourage you to read this text not as a how-to guide but instead as a heuristic—a thinking guide—as one way to think about designing such a unit. The approach we describe is what worked for us, and you should feel free to adapt and modify the tools we have provided both here in the book and on the companion website as necessary. As you begin to co-construct an inquiry-based unit with your own students, giving them options, allowing them to choose their own paths, making adjustments (sometimes in the middle of a lesson), opening yourself up to student feedback during the process, and responding to your learners' needs, you will probably recognize, as we did, that there is no single "right" way that research like this can be taught. In this book and through the videos and examples you will find on our companion website, we hope to do for you exactly what we aim to do for our students: share, model, coach, and guide—and, in the process, rewire research writing.

1 Introducing Research, Inquiry, and Connected Learning

> *Research is formalized curiosity. It is poking and prying with a purpose.*
>
> —Zora Neale Hurston

No matter who we ask to think about the concept of culture, no matter what point they are at in their lives, it is a big issue to grapple with, to puzzle through. Asking ninth graders to think about it, especially at 7:45 in the morning, initially results in general bewilderment. This chapter shows how we effectively introduced students to the research, inquiry, and technology tools we used in the unit "Reading Our World and Exploring Perspectives: Identity and Culture."

As we considered how best to frame this broad idea and help students break the work into manageable chunks, we identified a number of overlapping goals:

- Integrate technology in a robust and appropriate manner

- Invite students to begin their own inquiry process

- Teach students how to participate in a variety of digital spaces as productive digital citizens

We aimed to develop a shared sense of *artifacts of culture*, which we referred to as representations of a cultural characteristic (art, music, fashion, food, traditions, language, etc.), and *characteristics of culture*, which we referred to as abstract and metaphorical or "thinking about culture" (e.g., the trait of being individualistic).

In terms of technology, we introduced or reminded students of the following technologies:

- Wikispaces, our class site for this work, including daily agendas with links and handouts

- The Youth Voices social network, where students would post their blogs and respond to the posts of others

- Google Apps for Education, including Drive, Docs, and Slides, for collaborative work to share ideas, comment on one another's work, and compose together

We also explored digital citizenship, asking students to think about how they represented themselves in existing online spaces, such as social networks outside of school, and how they could create academically appropriate—yet still personal—digital identities related to topics inspired through work in school. As we consider the ways in which this approach rewires the research and writing process, we encourage you to pay particular attention to the ways that students develop their own interest-driven questions, how they join a personal learning network of other engaged students, and how they use technology to explore and annotate texts.

For their inquiry, we asked students to think about big questions focused on identity and culture, knowing that some would "wobble" with the ideas being presented. As Fecho (2013) notes,

> as teachers and students venture into dialogically primed spaces, they often do so with questions and doubt. It is in such spaces where . . . wobble (Fecho, 2011) happens, an indication that change is occurring and attention should be paid. (p. 117)

These moments where students—and teachers—"wobble" are important for learning, as we grapple with big questions and consider, explicitly, what we are learning and why we are learning it.

Charles Fort in *Wild Talents* (1998) wrote, "One can't learn much and also be comfortable." Challenges that initially feel uncomfortable can be a key part of learning. This is the "wobble," or the moment when students are grappling with a big idea and not always getting it. Serious writers and professionals in other contexts often wrestle with such moments of uncertainty. It reflects critical thinking and real-life learning. But to establish a classroom for teachable moments that are uncomfortable, we need to be ready for mess and ready for challenges.

This chapter spans the first section of the unit, from the Preview Lesson through Lesson 5. We want to remind our readers that, in addition to the lesson outlines, links to all handouts and resources referenced in this book are available on the companion website, **http://resources.corwin.com /writingrewired.**

Beginning in this chapter and continuing through Chapter 5, we will share each lesson, including its purpose, its context within the inquiry unit, a handout for the lesson, and extensions and adaptations for consideration.

> Challenges that initially feel uncomfortable can be a key part of learning. This is the "wobble," or the moment when students are grappling with a big idea and not always getting it.

PREVIEW LESSON: THINKING THROUGH A CULTURAL LENS

The purpose of this lesson is to help students

- Define and begin to establish a shared thinking space

- Explore artifacts that represent a culture and offer a tangible connection to the culture's characteristics

- Determine characteristics of culture and analyze abstract and metaphorical characteristics of a culture

- Engage in initial brainstorming of cultural images based on student perception

- Preread key ideas for the unit of study

Reading and Responding to a Common Text

To introduce the inquiry unit, we asked students to read the transcript while viewing Sheikha Al Mayassa's (2010) TED Talk *Globalizing the Local, Localizing the Global*. (The transcript for many TED Talks can be accessed by clicking on a visible link on each video page: "View interactive transcript.") In this TED Talk, Al Mayassa explores the cultural identity of Qatar through examples of fashion, food, and technology. In this conversation, she additionally breaks down the importance of gender roles in understanding and disseminating cultural identity. When we selected this video, we recognized that Al Mayassa's talk is quite hefty in terms of both the type and number of ideas, especially for ninth graders, but we wanted to present students with a text that addressed our cultural focus, as well as challenged them so that they knew we would be working at a high level of sophistication in our conversation.

As we introduced this TED Talk, we invited the students to read and listen for the general messages and concepts presented about culture, not to understand every detail of Al Mayassa's presentation. After they viewed the video, we asked them to write and reflect on the speech and then discuss it. Through class discussion, we captured ideas from Al Mayassa's transcript and posted them in the discussion tab of our unit culture study wiki, as this website served as a class hub across all the sections of Dawn's courses; when students posted on this site, students in all class sections could observe ideas expressed by students from Dawn's other classes who were also studying this talk. For instance, some students identified cultural artifacts in Al Mayassa's speech—fashion, religion, tradition, food, mobile phones, and social media—and others found smart ideas as points to share, such as how sometimes cultures are misunderstood. In some cases, students latched on to key phrases, and in other instances, they were able to identify characteristics and artifacts of culture such as Al Mayassa's *abaya* (traditional dress), the role of women in a traditionally patriarchal culture, and new representations and interpretations of art. Al Mayassa also poses important questions that the students pointed out, including "What should culture in the 21st century look like?"

Reflective Writing and Thinking: Generating Initial Ideas

After exploring this initial text for our cultural study, we prompted students to engage in a quick activity of collecting images for their own TED Talk.

By asking students to identify five images that represent a culture, we intentionally created a task that was both quick and thought-provoking. We also set up the exercise to provoke cognitive dissonance as students "wobbled" with questions related to culture, such as *"What is culture?"* and *"How do we participate in it?"* We explained that their goal for the assignment was to capture quick first impressions of a culture so they could, by the end of the inquiry unit, have an artifact to return to as a reminder of their initial thinking related to culture.

During this activity, a student turned to Dawn and asked, "What are we doing? What will we do with this work?" He understood that this first assignment involved selecting images and participating in a conversation related to culture, but he wanted Dawn to identify the final destination. What would the end product be? Dawn replied, "We're going to be exploring culture and our questions related to culture. We'll be on a journey of inquiry together." To succeed as researchers, students must learn to be comfortable embarking on journeys for the purpose of exploration without a prescribed final destination as the main goal. Of course, we had the end goal in mind, but we also intentionally were building in flexibility and intentional time to question and explore without a scripted response or format. After all, research should impact our thinking, and a predetermined idea is not being informed by research, just proven.

Still others didn't jump ahead to try to determine the major end product but rather grappled with what culture to represent and whether or not to include an image related to a culture that they belonged to but did not participate in. For instance, one student recognized that while fast food plays an important role in American culture, she did not eat it. In that sense, the conversation among students was even better than we had expected. Students started asking questions: "Should I just represent American culture?" "Should it be my ethnic culture?" "Can it just be teenage culture?"

Initially, the students wanted us to answer these questions for them. Instead, we explained that they had to develop answers to these questions in the inquiry process and learn to be comfortable with the wobble and the challenge of exploring ideas through reading, writing, and researching as a means to refine their thinking and make purposeful decisions for a composition.

Collaborative Writing and Thinking: Sharing Initial Ideas

Students began the quick collection of cultural images on Friday, developed them over the weekend, and shared them on Monday. During that class period, students observed that they found pictures to be powerful messages of culture, citing the cliché that "a picture is worth a thousand words."

We then asked students to share their TED Talk images and writing in a Google folder. Using the commenting and highlighting tools in Google Drive, students could respond to one another through a digital adaptation of "ink shedding." In this peer response practice, students share original writing with one another and, as they read, "shed ink" on (or, more literally, underline) spots that they find interesting, that they appreciate, or that otherwise resonate for them in each other's work (Ashbaugh, 2007). Students may also praise a text or pose thoughtful questions by inserting margin comments.

One student, Allison,[1] shared her work with the class. She had highlighted the social media aspects of culture. With an image of the Facebook logo, Allison wrote,

> Facebook represents our culture because it allows us to express ourselves and tell others our thoughts. It is a huge social media outlet, which can affect how people react to different events and how they react to each other. It is positive because it allows people to share their thoughts and feelings, but is negative because it can also open people up to ridicule.

This note received a few comments, including one from Beverly, who said,

> I hugely agree with this. I also think that although the Internet can connect people who are far away, it has taken control over people's lives. People can spend hours on end just staring at a lit-up screen.

Thaarini followed Beverly's comment:

> I agree with both of you guys. People can express themselves on social media, but it also takes up their lives because they can get absorbed into it.

Through this discussion with comments in a Google presentation, students were starting the inquiry process as they engaged in conversation surrounding

---

1. With their parents' permission, we identify all students by their real first names. We thank them for allowing us to bring their voices to this book.

Preview Lesson. Thinking Through a Cultural Lens

We see artifacts of culture all around us—clothes, buildings, signs, and more. Yet, we don't often slow down to understand what these artifacts say about our culture, or our identities as individuals. Today, we are going to view a TED Talk from Sheikha Al Mayassa from Qatar, who invites us to think about her culture and how it is changing in the 21st century.

Activity 1: Viewing a TED Talk

This presenter shares her thoughts about how the country of Qatar is changing in the modern era. As you watch, we encourage you to think about some of the artifacts that she presents as well as what those artifacts demonstrate about the characteristics of her culture.

Cultural Artifact	What does this demonstrate about Qatar?

Activity 2: Creating Your Own TED Talk

Now it's your turn. Imagine that you must deliver a TED Talk tomorrow, in which you describe your own culture like Al Mayassa did in her talk. Please do the following:

- Find at least five images that represent characteristics and/or artifacts of your culture. Import those images into separate slides in a Google presentation.

- Next to the image, explain how your image represents culture. Consider why you selected this image. Also, consider various perspectives. Think about it: Is this a positive or negative representation? Why or why not? What does it suggest about culture, cultural values, and cultural identity?

images. Inquiry was naturally developing and being co-created through collaborations with peers.

Interestingly, Allison made the move to feature cultural groups. She examined not only American society at large with social media but also her school culture with a focus on academics and grades, as well as her own ethnic culture. In this way, she started brainstorming about various cultures and their influence on our lives. Another student, Amjid, shared his work with the class. It was clear he appreciated and respected his religious culture, as he joyfully shared images that reflected his Islamic culture, such as making a pilgrimage to Mecca.

Across the classroom, diverse backgrounds and experiences were highlighted as students appreciated hearing one another's stories. Through our shared Google folder, students visited one another's work, viewing images and representations of culture and commenting on the choices other students made for this same task. Students began to recognize that the work was both personal (i.e., each student could relate to it personally as culture is important to self, family, and community) and public (because the content that was represented often informs many of the things that happen in our society, communities, and cultures).

> Inquiry was naturally developing and being co-created through collaborations with peers.

Extensions and Adaptations for the Preview Lesson

To introduce various thematic units, teachers can use different modes and media for engaging texts. When choosing a mentor text, it's important to think about whether or not students will find it accessible, as well as applicable and relevant. To adapt this lesson, consider using different introductory material or a different TED Talk or film. The text of focus could also be a song or image related to the topic. Several websites, including Edudemic, feature TED Talks for Classrooms.

LESSON 1. EXPLORING DIGITAL IDENTITIES

The purpose of this lesson is to help students

- Activate prior knowledge about digital citizenship

- Discuss factors impacting choices to post writing online

- Revisit and refine ideas about digital citizenship and responsibilities related to posting work online

- Introduce ideas related to questioning

- Explore the writing of a digital profile

Composing for Online Spaces

In Lesson 1, Dawn made a number of teaching moves related to prompting student reflection about publishing online and digital identity. To see the lesson, watch Video 1.1. Students in Dawn's class had already explored the concept of digital citizenship throughout the school year, and it was also clear that they had learned about Internet safety in middle school. Earlier in the year, students had talked about the scary (though sometimes overblown) news reports of Internet predators and the importance of digital safety. They had also shared stories of ways in which people make inappropriate moves in digital spaces—moves that can have real implications for school and job opportunities. Consequently, this portion of our initial teaching happened relatively quickly, but other teachers may need to spend more time on this broad subject with their own students.

watch it here

Video 1.1

http://resources.corwin .com/writingrewired

To read a QR code, you must have a smartphone or tablet with a camera. We recommend that you download a QR code reader app that is made specifically for your phone or tablet brand.

Some Considerations for Posting Work Online

When we teach from a rhetorical perspective, we focus on encouraging students to carefully consider their audience. This also means that students need to recognize that what they put online stays online and could follow them as writers, as content can stay associated with their name. This reality is an exciting one, but it also comes with certain responsibilities.

As teachers, we need to consider that if students post content online that contains errors or immature viewpoints, it could possibly jeopardize some aspects of their future college and career goals. There are times when people evaluate others without knowing the context, especially in a digital space.

To honor our students, we need to think about giving them choices—not just because the publishing medium is digital, but also to help them own their work. Specifically, we need to address the role of digital safety head on and allow students and their parents/guardians to make choices about when and what to post.

We contend that, at least in our digital class space, thoughtful learning around the role of digital citizenship can happen even if a student makes a mistake. Supporting students in these situations, as well as setting them up for success with their digital identity, is important. We also acknowledge that if we are teaching digital literacy skills, we need to do so in digital spaces and invite students to participate in real digital conversations.

In Lesson 1, we asked students to write about how they make choices in what they post online and their understanding of a digital identity. Students quickly came up with answers and jotted them on our wiki discussion forum. General responses noted the importance of keeping audience in mind and the need to think twice before posting. For instance, one student said, "Before you post—think about how you sound or how much information you post. Even if it is not a finished piece, you still need to think before posting." Students described digital identity, noting, "Who you are—everything you post online—helps show who you are. How you portray yourself across the Internet (what you post, pictures, what you say)—this characterizes you for those who don't know you." Students further mentioned that digital identity is important for college and jobs and can be very positive.

Additionally, students mentioned that they saw publishing work online as a valuable way to get feedback on their writing, but that this opportunity required them to be open to criticism too. In this way, students embraced writing online for the purpose of sharing process work and also final published work. They understood that they had to be careful in their thinking because an audience would be present in the digital space and that, when they post online, they are leaving behind their digital footprint.

Creating an Online Profile

This lesson intentionally placed the development of a profile with the conversation about digital citizenship, digital identity, and digital footprints. In some educational settings, students are positioned to avoid social networks for their own safety. However, we contend that they will need to operate within these spaces for their education and careers. Networking for many jobs includes using social media resources for the purpose of gaining a job (e.g., through LinkedIn), demonstrating credibility of skills, and sharing resources and learning collaboratively. When a student told Dawn that she does not like computers, Dawn replied, "If you want to operate in this world, whether or not you *like* computers is less important than *how and when you use them.*"

The Internet is full of people trying on different personas and identities in various spaces, and students need to recognize different purposes for online spaces. As such, the development of their academic profile is an important one. To create an effective profile, students must learn how to identify their audience and consider how they might be perceived in a digital space. For this lesson, students wrote about themselves for an academic audience, and to support their work with inquiry, part of this lesson was to develop five "self" and "world" questions; selected questions developed by various students are shown in Table 1.1.

Of course, looking at these initial questions, any middle or high school teacher (or parent of a teen) can understand why students are asking these types of questions. Taken out of context, they could seem trite, or cliché.

Table 1.1   Student "Self" and "World" Questions

Examples of "Self" Questions for Student Profiles	Examples of "World" Questions for Student Profiles
• What job am I going to get? • Are there some aspects of my culture that I don't know about? • Will I ever get married/have kids? • What would be a great new hobby for me? • How do others perceive me? • Where are my strengths? • Is my life already planned out for me? • Am I "normal"? • Am I capable of making a significant mark on the world? • What most surprises others about me? • What one sentence best describes me? • What will I do when I grow up?	• How was the universe created? • Will there ever be a way to get rid of pollution? • When will our world end? • Are humans inherently flawed? • How do I know "reality" isn't just some elaborate dream? • What happens when we die? • How large is the universe? Is there intelligent life out there? • How much about the universe do we really know? • Will all the nations on Earth ever get along? • What does the future hold? • Will humans ever leave Earth?

As we designed an inquiry-based unit, we wanted to honor and understand these pressing questions in our students' lives while, eventually, pushing them to ask more critical, specific questions about their own identity and the broader influences of culture.

Extensions and Adaptations for Lesson 1

There are a variety of existing curricular materials available to help teachers develop conversations about digital citizenship. Resources that we trust are from Common Sense Media (www.commonsensemedia.org), the Digital ID project (http://digital-id.wikispaces.com), and Digital Citizenship (www.digitalcitizenship.net). Each site offers activities that can be taught in one class period or as an entire unit. We encourage you to visit these sites and adapt the lessons as needed for your own students.

Lesson 1. Exploring Digital Identities

Digital identities include how we present ourselves and interact in digital spaces. Our digital footprints also speak to this identity as we leave tracks that give information about ourselves in online spaces. How will you craft your digital identity? How does what we leave behind in our footprints have implications for our futures? How will you make purposeful decisions as you craft your digital identity?

Activity 1: Writing, Reflecting, and Discussion

Writing time:

- As a critical thinker and writer, what do you need to consider when writing in an online space?
- What value is there in sharing ideas that are not "final draft" quality in an online space?
- What do you need to consider when posting ideas that are final polished pieces of writing?
- What does it mean to have a digital identity?
- What is your identity in a public online space? How will you participate in online academic communities?

Share responses: Pair share, class share

Class discussion: What do we believe about digital citizenship and safe digital identities?

Activity 2: Brainstorming Ideas for Your Profile

We will be joining a social network of students whose academic experience includes engaging in online discussion with students across the nation. Part of joining this community includes the opportunity to develop your own profile.

You may make an avatar for your profile picture. You can also add to your profile to share information about yourself. Your first task is to compose your profile information.

For your profile, you can be as simple as stating your grade in school, an interest or two, or recent books you have read. You can also develop this further if you like.

You do need to write five "self" and five "world" questions to think about inquiry questions, and you may also use them in your profile. See http://youthvoices.net/questions for a guide to writing your questions.

In our next lesson, we will review examples and work on revision.

Password Management

Managing digital spaces can be a challenging task for adults, let alone for students. While students need to make their own choices with parent/guardian input on how to manage these spaces, we do offer a few tips for students to manage passwords.

We have heard the idea that "the best password is the one that you can't remember," which sounds, of course, paradoxical. Really, it makes a good deal of sense in that we should remember a single master password, one of significant complexity that we can then use to access our other passwords. Online services like LastPass (https://lastpass.com) and downloadable programs like KeePass (http://keepass.info) allow users to generate secure passwords for websites, store those passwords, and access their entire collection with a single master password.

These password management tools are an essential component of how we teach our students to become smart digital readers and writers.

LESSON 2. CULTURAL CONVERSATIONS ONLINE: JOINING YOUTH VOICES AND READING COLLABORATIVELY

The purpose of this lesson is to help students

- Review and revise profile work through careful practices of providing feedback to others

- Develop profiles on the Youth Voices network to join an academic community conversation

- Explore voice and tone for writing in online spaces

- Refine "self" and "world" questions as a step toward developing clear inquiry questions

Identity and Tone for Online Spaces

Throughout the school year, Dawn's class discussed the importance of entering conversations in online spaces. She explained that just as they would choose an appropriate tone for talking to their friends, parents, or teachers in various settings, students needed to select the proper language and tone for Youth Voices, a space for academic discourse. She introduced students to Youth Voices as a space for serious, yet still personal, writing and thinking, and noted that given this digital setting, she expected them to refrain from using only "digitalk," or language acceptable for online communications outside of academic settings that may include abbreviations, emoticons, and other shortened textual forms (Turner, 2012, 2014), as well as from engaging in the types of social banter that are acceptable in other online spaces.

Thus, we asked students to generate a draft of their profile in Google Docs, including and building on their five "self" and five "world" questions. As they reviewed one another's work, we asked them to consider response questions:

- *What do you appreciate about this author's profile? How does he or she use his or her voice to accentuate positive aspects of his or her personality and interests?*

- *What might you suggest that he or she add or revise? What do you want to know more about?*

- *How might he or she incorporate his or her "self" and "world" questions into the profile? They don't need to be a list of the questions necessarily, but how could those ideas be sprinkled throughout the author's description of himself or herself?*

As students read one another's profiles, they answered these questions and, in turn, generated more ideas for their own writing. Building in purposeful peer response provided time for students to work on their writing and engage in revision. Additionally, emphasis on peer response for student profiles was an intentional decision. We wanted students to think about what they were writing and how to address the audience and purpose of Youth Voices. While students could quickly compose a profile and post it, spending more time on revision for this first publication on the website set the tone for careful thinking, writing, and revising of work students would post on Youth Voices. Through this work, students also reflected on the conversations about digital literacy and what they post online by the simple step of taking more time to review their work instead of the popular approach of write and post—without much reflection or revision—that students often experience on social media sites. In Video 1.2, Dawn helps students think about developing inquiry questions through their profile work, while keeping purpose and audience in mind.

watch it here

Video 1.2
http://resources.corwin
.com/writingrewired

Joining Youth Voices

To conclude the first part of this lesson, we asked students to join Youth Voices, an online academic community (http://youthvoices.net). We suggest that you set up your account and school page on the Youth Voices site before asking students to create profiles, as this step will allow you to make students members and link to individual student pages from a Youth Voices page specifically for your school and your students.

Lesson 2. Cultural Conversations Online: Joining Youth Voices and Reading Collaboratively

HAND OUT

Collaboration is important to our shared thinking. By brainstorming ideas with one another, we can generate more possibilities for writing. Also, we can make our own work better by offering feedback to one another.

Today's work focuses on reviewing our profiles to get another perspective and share ideas with collaborative reading.

Activity 1: Reading a Mentor Text

Read the example profile below. Highlight, underline, or put a star next to elements of the profile that stand out to you as important to know or that demonstrate voice as a writer.

- What do you appreciate about this profile?

- What might you suggest that the author add or revise?

- How might the author further incorporate "self" and "world" questions into his profile?

Youth Voices Logo

Source: Youth Voices Logo, http://youthvoices.net/ Used with permission.

My name is Bob. I attend Okemos High School, and I am a freshman. I enjoy reading science fiction books, and I enjoy playing soccer. Other interests of mine include hanging out with friends, listening to music, and learning how to play the guitar. I enjoy socializing with friends at sporting events and on social media. I have a cat and dog, and two sisters. I enjoy sharing ideas with others. I am interested in the universe, and I wonder if alien life-forms exist. Does the government cover up alien interactions? What would I find if I visited another planet? Are any aliens like those we watch on Star Wars? I am also interested in paleontology. My favorite dinosaurs are the Triceratops and Tyrannosaurus rex. I would love to go on a dinosaur dig. I wonder, How many fossils are yet to be found? How did the dinosaurs go extinct? In what ways can our society work to prevent such destruction from happening again? Are any alien life-forms similar to dinosaurs?

(Continued)

(Continued)

Activity 2: Review Profiles

In small groups, review your profile drafts. In Google Drive, share your profile draft with your writing group. Respond to one another using the following questions:

- What does each profile suggest about the author?
- In what ways is this profile appropriate for an academic social network?
- Review the writer's "self" and "world" questions. Do the questions make sense to other readers? If not, why not?
- What might be revised so that others understand the writer's questions?
- In what ways might the questions spark further research or discussion with others on Youth Voices?
- Offer any other constructive comments or questions for the writer.

Activity 3: Join Youth Voices (or Your Class's Online Community)

- Create an account at http://youthvoices.net/user/register.
- Copy and paste your revised profile from Google Drive into your bio on Youth Voices.
- Create your profile!

Extensions and Adaptations for Lesson 2

Extensions of the profile work are also important to consider. How students introduce themselves in online spaces can relate to personal narrative writing. Students might share a top-ten list about themselves, inquiry questions, or even a personal narrative, poem, or digital story to introduce themselves into the community.

Additionally, the technology that students use to create their social network could be Edmodo, Schoology, Nicenet, Chalkup, Google Classroom, or any number of other appropriate tools. Other social network options include Wiggio, Spruz, GroupSpaces, and Ning. While these services are generally "free," be mindful that some of them (Spruz and Ning) may have fees if you go over a certain amount of users on the site.

We recommend Youth Voices because it is maintained by teachers connected with the National Writing Project and because we know that students are encouraged (and taught how) to participate in ongoing conversations across classrooms and communities. Perhaps you want to start with something smaller or more self-contained with one of these other tools, yet know that you—and your students—would be welcomed in the Youth Voices community.

LESSON 3. BEGINNING THE CULTURAL CONVERSATION

The purpose of this lesson is to help students

- Review and use reading strategies for a careful close reading of a common text

- Collaborate and share thinking related to culture and identity

- Build ideas and thinking related to culture and identity

- Establish clear classroom community guidelines for discussing issues related to culture

Digital Reflections on Collaborative Reading

In this lesson, students engaged in a close reading of a common text. To continue the culture conversation, we used Katie Soe's "The Great Cultural Divide: Multiethnic Teens Struggle With Self-Identity, Others' Perceptions" (2006). This text was interesting to students because it is written by a teen and includes experiences that some students understood firsthand. So, what happened when we had students respond to the article digitally? Many students used the comment and highlighting feature in Google Docs not only to comment on the article but also to reply to one another's comments. In our diverse setting, some students discovered that they could relate to the article about being from a multiethnic background. Others recognized that they could not relate directly but that the points in the piece were very important and insightful. Students were also able to identify characteristics and artifacts in the article that reflect culture.

Some learners related very personally to the article, noting how they identify themselves on forms that require them to select an ethnicity. One student wrote,

I can totally relate to this. I hate having to mark "other." It feels like I'm different from everyone, like an alien.

Later in the unit, another student replied to this student's post, noting,

If you're an alien, you're a cool alien :)

And the first student replied at the beginning of her spring break:

aw thanks :3

In this way, students continued to interact with texts even after we'd studied them in class. They also engaged in conversations with their reading in interesting ways as commenting on the text and even interactive commenting with peers, and moved the learning from reading to writing.

We had originally selected Soe's article in part because it would raise the concept that there are various differences in our classroom related to culture. As such, it was a good setup for a review of the need to respect and appreciate our differences and different opinions. We established a few ground rules for discussion, such as "Comments should allow an opportunity for everyone to be heard" and "We learn a lot when we disagree; accept different opinions and be open to learning from others," and we offered students the opportunity to add to the discussion expectations. This conversation about the text and our discussion expectations allowed students to build on their thinking related to culture in a very manageable way. Additionally, they continued to practice their careful critical reading skills and marking of a text.

Using Google Drive and Google Docs as a Tool for Annotation

Google Drive—a cloud-based suite of software including a word processor, spreadsheet, and slide-style presentation tool—is available for free for anyone who creates a Google account. Dawn's school district already subscribed to Google Apps for Education, thus providing her students access to these tools when they logged in with their school network ID.

Often cited for its collaborative, real-time writing and editing capabilities, Google Docs can also be creatively repurposed for a variety of tasks. In this case, Dawn chose to use Google Docs as a space for the students to respond to writing. To do this, she

1. Navigated her web browser to a site with the article "The Great Cultural Divide" by Katie Soe

2. Copied the entire article and pasted it into a new Google Doc

3. Created a shared folder in Google Drive named "First Hour" for the class, and invited students to this folder, using their Gmail addresses

4. Shared the Google Doc with her entire class by placing it in the shared "First Hour" folder

5. Instructed students either to use the "make a copy" function to create their own version, or to place comments in the shared Google Doc

Of course, the copy-and-paste move here offered Dawn a good opportunity to talk about plagiarism as well as copyright and fair use. In this case, Dawn was asking students to use copyrighted material for an educational purpose, commenting upon it, and identifying elements of culture. During this lesson, Dawn modeled her thinking about this concept by taking on the role of a student and pondering aloud as a student might. Specifically, Dawn noted that she was not attempting to use any part of Soe's article for quoting in her own writing, nor would she ever try to pass Soe's writing off as her own, a clear act of plagiarism. Instead, in this case, she was repurposing the original work for an educational purpose, an allowable fair use of the copyrighted material.

Extensions and Adaptations for Lesson 3

There are a variety of ways to work with students and text annotation, such as arranging students in different groups based on lesson objectives or using different tools for annotation. From e-books to social bookmarking notes, technology opportunities abound.

Lesson 3. Beginning the Cultural Conversation

At this point, we return to our first set of essential questions: What is culture? How do various individuals, communities, and groups describe the characteristics of "culture"? Also, consider two related subquestions:

- What are characteristics of culture? How do these characteristics influence and contribute to culture?

- When are cultural characteristics considered positive, and when are they considered negative?

You are going to use your abilities as a critical reader to explore an article by Katie Soe, "The Great Cultural Divide: Multiethnic Teens Struggle With Self-Identity, Perceptions." As you read, we want you to consider Soe's perspective, and to make connections to your own cultural experience.

Archives of American Art,
Eitaro Ishigaki

Source: Wikimedia Commons.

Activity 1: Reading Strategy Review

Discussion Review: What reading strategies do we already know and use? In teams, write a list of at least six strategies you can use when wrestling with a challenging text.

Activity 2: Close Reading of "The Great Cultural Divide"

Group leader: Copy and paste the text from "The Great Cultural Divide" into a new Google Doc and share with your group.

Group reader: Read the article aloud as everyone else will use the commenting and highlighting tools to take notes on the reading. Every group member should highlight at least three important points from the article and include at least one comment.

Summarize: After your group discusses the article, capture notes and write a four- to five-sentence summary of what your team identifies as the key ideas of this article. Also, include at least one question that still remains for your group. Post the summary to our online class space for Lesson 3.

Activity 3: Reflection

Individually, please write a brief reflection on Soe's article. How do you relate to her argument that "because people have different ideas about how ethnicity should be expressed, this can be a source of frustration and disappointment"? Do you agree or disagree? Why?

Classroom Management in Virtual Spaces

It is inevitable that students will make mistakes. After all, isn't making mistakes part of learning? Still, when students take missteps online, the consequences may be permanent, so it's essential to discuss digital citizenship. Share examples with students too; stories from the news about people who have used digital spaces inappropriately can be discussed for the purpose of learning and making smart decisions in online spaces.

Particular issues to discuss and watch out for include using racist, sexist, classist, or other stereotypes or posting inappropriate or suggestive words.

During our inquiry unit on "The Great Cultural Divide," a student silently waved Dawn over to her screen to show her that another student (they couldn't tell who) had inserted a swear word in the title.

Dawn chose to tackle this behavior head on. She stopped the class and immediately had students write answers in response to the following questions:

- *What responsibility do I have to my class, my classmates, and my learning?*
- *How do I want to be treated? What do I need from others to be treated as a mature learner?*

All the students brought up the idea of "respect" in their writing while referring to their classmates and/or teacher, noting that this respect needed to extend to their digital conversations. It was clear that they valued and respected their learning community.

No one confessed to adding the swear word, but several students apologized on behalf of the group. Dawn realized it was less important to identify and discipline the writer than to have the entire class see the impact such behavior could have on their learning, reminding them of the responsibility they had for their classroom learning community.

Here are a few tips for classroom management in virtual spaces:

- Review student expectations for behavior in digital spaces just like you would in your physical classroom.
- Help students understand publishing decisions and variance between spaces.
- Discuss academic personas versus personal personas.
- Review implications for inappropriate posting both in and out of class.
- Manage your moves as a teacher. If you are worried about students writing in online spaces, start with a tool that offers monitoring.
- Extend your proximity to include not only moving near students, but also looking at their screens. This does not have to be onerous, but students need to see the teacher monitor and to have consequences if they get off task.
- Establish a classroom community and know your students on both your physical and digital classroom spaces. Students might behave differently in each space.

A few ways to work on annotating with students could include the following:

- Diigo (free, with premium services; web-based)

- Evernote (free, with premium services; web-based)

- Genius or Lit Genius (free, web-based tool for annotating)

- Hypothes.is (free, web-based service for annotating, collaborating, and organizing work)

- NowComment (free, web-based tool for collaborative commenting)

- OneNote (a component of Microsoft Office)

LESSON 4. EXPLORING VISUAL CULTURE THROUGH FOOD WRAPPERS AND ANALYZING VISUAL CULTURE

The purpose of this lesson is to help students

- Explore arguments about culture

- Review the role of visual texts in our construction of cultural ideas

- Question various texts in our everyday world, such as the food wrapper

- Analyze the rhetorical moves of a food wrapper

- Develop and build upon our definitions and understandings about culture

- Analyze various aspects of a culture as based on a food wrapper

- Explore the role of business, technology, legalities, and safety, presumptions all present in the text of a food wrapper

- Continue to support learning communities through the common practices of reading, discussing, and writing

Reading a Food Wrapper: Questioning Cultural Artifacts

At this point, students had viewed a TED Talk, explored images related to culture, and engaged in a shared reading of a brief nonfiction text. To further their thinking about culture and texts, we asked students to bring a food wrapper to class (a move we learned from Dànielle DeVoss). Even though this is a simple task, some students were surprised by the nature of this request. A food wrapper? We also gave students the challenge of being creative in their food wrapper selections so that we might have the chance to share a broad range of material. Some embraced this challenge, looking for a unique type of food, while others simply grabbed the nearest candy bar wrapper for the assignment.

When students prepared to analyze their food wrappers as text that offers messages that teachers often don't consider, we asked big questions to prompt students to consider the cultural artifacts involved:

- What does it mean that a lot of wrappers are shiny or the inside of a wrapper is made with silver paper? What marketing considerations might be part of packaging?

- Why is it that natural colors—such as green and blue—or pictures of nature are found on packages that promote sugary foods?

- What does color psychology have to do with understanding our food wrappers?

This food wrapper exercise helped students examine perspectives and carefully read the world around them. By answering questions, students were also prompted to form more questions.

For instance, one student brought in an energy bar with a banner proclaiming "High in Protein!" This raised a series of questions about our cultural assumptions related to the typical American diet, as well as dieting as a way to lose weight, which led to further questions about our perceptions on healthy weight levels and body image. These views were held in contrast to reading this wrapper as a product to help a culture that might not have access to meat for protein requirements in a diet.

Thus, a relatively simple claim on just one wrapper created its own inquiry process through a brief class discussion. As students worked in small groups, each person asked similar questions about everything from candy to ramen noodles, from potato chips to bottled water. During class, in the discussion tab of the wiki, students wrote about their ideas related to questioning the food wrapper.

Analyzing Visual Culture

In addition to prompting students to explore the questions about food wrappers, we asked them to view a slide show titled "Analyzing Visual Culture," which originated from one of our mentors, Professor Dànielle DeVoss at Michigan State University. Available on the companion website at http://resources.corwin.com/writingrewired, this slide show offers various definitions of culture, thus echoing the work that students engaged in before their analysis of food wrappers. It also establishes the argument that culture revolves around digital technologies, cultural ideas and artifacts are remixed and repurposed, meaning is created across various modalities, and meaning can be contested.

Through the arguments made in the slide show, we explored the impact of technology on culture and the role we play in society as not only consumers of texts but also producers of texts. DeVoss uses the term *prosumers*, originally coined by Alvin Toffler in his book *The Third Wave* (1980). Moreover, we explored the role of remixing to create new messages, a concept important to composing texts with digital media. Popular references in society constantly deal with textuality, and we examined the role of remixed material across modes and media as oral, visual, and textual elements are combined. As part of this activity, we wanted students to begin to recognize meaning that is made based on modality. This understanding is important for students as they engage with a variety of texts, and we continued to define texts as not only the printed word but also visual compositions and speeches, and even food wrappers.

Furthermore, we explored the role of parody in our society. For instance, there is a genre of video trailers that have become even more popular with the emergence of YouTube: parody horror trailers. Users will take existing footage and—under the provisions of fair use in the Copyright Act of 1976—create parody horror trailers. Many exist on YouTube, some of amateur quality and others that are quite exemplary ranging from *Willy Wonka* to *Frozen* to *Mrs. Doubtfire*. We examined the *Scary "Mary Poppins"* video as one way to remix texts and understand how it can change meaning (Rule, 2006).

> We explored the impact of technology on the role we play in society— not only as consumers of texts but as producers of them.

At the same time, we also explored the changing nature of texts with the role of technology by viewing cultural anthropologist Michael Wesch's brief film *Web 2.0: The Machine Is Us/ing Us* (2007), which explores the malleable nature of digital texts. In this film, Wesch blends a variety of screen captures and screencasting of activity on his computer to argue that digital text is different from print text. Along the same lines, we considered the manner in which text, communication, and education are changing by viewing the *Did You Know? Shift Happens* video, which demonstrates the changing nature of our society in the 21st century, especially as it is influenced by technology. This informational film, originally created by educators Karl Fisch and Scott McLeod in 2007, outlines dozens of facts about the changing nature of our digital world (and has, itself, been remixed numerous times). Just as we had students explore concepts about culture by examining the food wrappers, we used these films to help them consider the idea that meaning can be created by composing with various media and remixing content.

Lesson 4 (Part 1). Exploring Visual Culture Through Food Wrappers

As we look at the world around us, exploration of cultural artifacts and visual culture can help us read and understand our world. Consider the essential questions:

- How do artifacts and characteristics of culture influence your life?

  - What are artifacts of your culture, such as images, music, food, clothing, ceremonies, or pop culture icons?

  - What do artifacts of culture suggest about cultural characteristics? (For instance, if an artifact is a protein bar, what does this demonstrate about culture? Does it suggest that our culture needs protein or is obsessed with body image?)

  - How do you imagine these artifacts and characteristics of culture will continue to influence your life in the future?

Activity 1: Defining Culture

As a team, develop a response to the following questions and post it in our online class space:

- What is culture? What is American culture?

- What characteristics are important to culture?

- How might these questions be important to our reading of literature and our world?

Activity 2: Food Wrapper Analysis

Look at the wrapper and identify what it tells us about the culture the wrapper is from. In a group document, write down everything you might assume about this culture by looking at these wrappers.

- What kind of assumptions does this document make of its audience?

- What are you expected to know when you look at this?

- What sort of legal, safety, or other presumptions does this make?

- What does it tell us about business in that culture? Systems of measurement in that culture? Technology in that culture?

Activity 3: Arguments About Visual Culture

Based on our work with exploring ideas related to culture, we can make some general arguments about visual culture. We will look at a slide presentation, adapted from

(Continued)

(Continued)

Dànielle DeVoss at Michigan State University, as a way to think about how images and culture connect. Consider these questions as you view the slides:

- How do you define culture? Why do you define culture in this way? What value is there in defining culture?

- What are some of the factors that influence culture? Why are these significant?

- How does the changing nature of texts impact culture? How do digital spaces impact culture? What impact does that have on your understanding about culture?

- What texts do you consume? What texts do you produce? How would you define a "prosumer" culture? How are you a part of that culture?

- How is meaning made in a culture? How are visuals a part of culture?

- What role do remixing, remaking, and rehashing have in how we define culture?

Lesson 4 (Part 2). Analyzing Visual Culture

Based on our work with exploring ideas related to culture, we can make some general arguments about culture.

Think about your ideas inspired by the "Analyzing Visual Culture" presentation as you consider the following video arguments and their implications.

	Did You Know?	Scary "Mary Poppins"	Web 2.0: The Machine Is Us/ing Us
What do you notice about the design of the video? What do you notice about the color scheme? Camera angles? Text and captions?			
What does each video suggest about our culture? What message do you take away from the video? What role do remixing, remaking, and rehashing have in this video?			

watch it here

Video 1.3

http://resources.corwin
.com/writingrewired

After viewing their food wrappers from this new perspective, students expressed that they both enjoyed the process and learned how to analyze one form of text in a deep manner. This activity was a scaffold for deeper analysis that would come later in the inquiry process, helping them to question various assumptions about texts, as well as to recognize many types of texts that could be important in their study of culture and identity. As this lesson ended, students were primed to begin our exploration of the definition of ethnography the next day. Conversations from this lesson about visual literacy and arguments about culture are shared in Video 1.3.

Extensions and Adaptations for Lesson 4

Teachers might structure this lesson in different ways by varying the guided notes page or asking different questions of texts. Additionally, students could explore various texts for analysis. A few texts for consideration could be

- Advertisements
- Art
- Magazines
- Songs

While not all ads on this site are school appropriate, carefully selected images from Adbusters can be used effectively to demonstrate the power and pervasiveness of advertising (see www.adbusters.org). Additionally, Renee Hobbs and her colleagues at the Media Education Lab (see http://mediaedlab.com) have created a variety of interactive and useful lessons, including a set of resources including Powerful Voices for Kids (http://powerfulvoicesforkids .com) and My Pop Studio (www.mypopstudio.com).

LESSON 5. INTRODUCING ETHNOGRAPHY AND THE CULTURE COLLAGE ASSIGNMENT

The purpose of this lesson is to help students

- Consider various perspectives as a way to see the world from a different view and support the role of questioning

- Explore the concept of ethnography and apply it to understanding the need to read carefully and closely

- Review the need to be ethnographers to collect and create a culture collage

- Practice being both producers and consumers of texts

Becoming Digital Ethnographers: Embracing Culture Through Perspective

By the end of this first week, we wanted students to begin seeing themselves as both consumers and producers of culture, with the ability to understand and interpret various forms of text in their world. Greene (1981) explores the importance of "perceiving and noticing" as a part of aesthetic education, which we contend is an important part of the research process. She further notes that students

> ought to have opportunities, in every classroom, to pay heed to color and glimmer and sound, to attend to the appearances of things from an aesthetic point of view. If not, they are unlikely to be in a position to be challenged by what they see or hear; and one of the great powers associated with the arts is the power to challenge expectations, to break stereotypes, to change the ways in which persons apprehend the world. (Greene, 1981, pp. 136–137)

In this spirit, we invited students to be ethnographers in our classroom community. We asked them to think about the definition of ethnographers as people who study culture through careful consideration of perspectives from observation, interviews, and analysis of artifacts.

To begin the lesson, we asked students to team up and take pictures with one another of interesting angles and perspectives in our classroom. Within a matter of seconds, students were standing on tables and lying on the floor to get interesting pictures that we would not always see in a classroom. In Video 1.4, you can see Dawn explain the instructions to capture pictures with a different perspective.

Looking at the classroom through a new lens also led students to the conversation about being ethnographers within their own culture to explore its rich perspectives and artifacts. While this exercise was engaging for students because it was fun, it was also purposeful because few of them had thought about photography in this manner before. Most were accustomed to taking snapshots or, as was popular at the time, "selfies." However, most had not thought about composing an image by choosing a different perspective, framing the shot, or thinking purposefully about the message that they intended for the image to convey. The process of "re-seeing" the classroom, a space where students can often zero in on their own personal space and small group, reminded all of us that taking time to rethink our perspective is useful. And it's not lost on us that this teaching move would honor Mr. Keating from *Dead Poets Society* (Weir & Schulman, 1989), the teacher who invited his students to stand on a desk and look around the room to see from a different perspective. Students were also beginning a research process by experiencing the work of ethnography.

watch it here

Video 1.4
http://resources.corwin
.com/writingrewired

Extensions and Adaptations for Lesson 5

There are various ways for students to be ethnographers. Whether they take on the role of ethnographers in the classroom or around the school, the experience of "looking" is an important one. In addition to taking photos of the classroom, students could engage in a mini-lesson to analyze photographs related to perspective. Teachers might also prepare a more focused lesson on being an ethnographer in students' homes and neighborhoods. Finally, students could also explore existing photo sets on Flickr, Picasa, or other photo-sharing services.

The Culture Collage Assignment

The final piece of this week included an introduction to the Culture Collage Assignment, which asked students to consider perspectives and collect images of their culture (see the handout on page 55). The timing of this assignment, on the day before spring break, was intentional; rather than starting a novel for the literature circles (as we describe in Chapter 2), we agreed that a flexible creative assignment would work well to keep students engaged in questions of culture during the break. Obviously, this assignment could also fit during a week or over a weekend too. One of the goals for this assignment was to have students synthesize the ideas that they had been exploring through the first week's lessons. The assignment was designed to be interesting for teens, as well as to offer students an opportunity to explore various media and modalities. Additionally, the writing that students would eventually do related to their collage and would demonstrate the need for purposeful moves crafted in various compositions. We knew this skill was

Zoya, with Anna, capturing a panoramic image.

Lesson 5. Introducing Ethnography

> *As an ethnographer, you are, of course, interested not only in the facts but also in what those facts mean and how they might help you to explain the culture you are studying. Therefore, you will need to create the kinds of research questions which would answer not only what is happening in front of your eyes but also why it is happening and what its significance is for the culture you are investigating. You also need to ask the kinds of questions that would help you discern patterns in the events or behaviors you observe, you make connections between people, incidents, and events.*
>
> —Pavel Zemliansky

How do people study culture? Ethnographers engage in research by conducting

- Primary research, which includes observing, interviewing, surveying, photographing, and collecting cultural artifacts. Researchers then analyze these resources through a critical interpretive lens to make meaning from what they have seen, heard, and experienced.

- Secondary research, which includes searching for existing articles, books, websites, photos, videos, and other materials related to the researcher's topic, created by others.

Activity 1: Being Ethnographers

Ethnographers consider things from various perspectives, much like we might see in different photos. In teams, take pictures in our classroom that offer a perspective that you might not always see. For instance, you might lie under a table or stand on a desk. You can't stay in your seat for this . . . or can you? For example, here is a panoramic image from Zoya:

Zoya's Panoramic Photograph of Our Classroom

Activity 2: Sharing Your Findings

Post your images in our online class space. Compose a brief response about perspectives in our shared classroom space. See if you can be the most creative here!

essential for their learning, and it would also be important for the decisions they would make in their media project later on. In this way, we continued to scaffold student experiences to prepare them for later work.

While students were not too excited about the prospect of having real "home-work" over the break, they were interested in gathering photos and images related to their culture. This project also prompted conversation about what was going on in their world. Students who were traveling to different places for their break were expected to think about how the places and spaces they visited impacted their culture. Students who were staying home were asked to think about the role of their culture in their everyday places.

REFLECTIONS ON EMBRACING INQUIRY IN THE CONNECTED CLASSROOM

At the end of the first week of instruction, we could tell that the students were overwhelmed yet enjoying the variety of lessons and ideas that had been presented to them. Given that this first week of lessons was intended to help spark their thinking and spur their inquiry process, we felt as though we had accomplished that goal. They had created their initial TED Talk quick draft presentation, which was, as we noted, meant to encourage the wobble as students were thinking carefully about their own culture and what they valued. A few other specific reflections related to our overall teaching and learning goals follow.

As we consider the five *T*s—teens, timing, topics, texts, and technology—we feel that a number of strategic moves helped create the groundwork to consider cultural influences and elements related to culture. Our conversations in the classroom and work in digital spaces were intentionally focused on fostering questioning and inquiry. As mentioned, we had students develop "self" and "world" questions while considering the cultural focus. We also had students get set up with various digital spaces.

Teaching in an inquiry-based, student-centered context creates an interesting paradox both for us as teachers and for students. On one hand, we recognize schools and classrooms as spaces that require a certain degree of order and coherence (e.g., daily and weekly routines, marking periods and semesters, lesson objectives and unit goals). Still, as teachers, we should all have a vision of where we want to go with our curriculum.

However, as we have noted several times, an inquiry-based approach is messy because it leaves space for students to explore their questions and real thinking does not have one clear end. Throughout these first lessons, we encouraged students to search for answers to their own questions, but we also supplied some guidance in the form of specific questions they

Culture Collage Assignment

Create a collage to represent your culture. As you design your collage, be sure to think about how you define your own cultural background for yourself. While composing this piece, take notes for yourself about your thinking related to your culture.

For your collage, you can use a variety of images, such as clippings from magazines, newspapers, or an Internet search. You can also create your own sketches or use your own photos.

Your collage can be a print or digital text. Some tools to consider for creating a digital text include

- Capzles
- Mural.ly
- Padlet
- Smore
- ThingLink
- VoiceThread

In a paragraph or two, write an explanation about your collage to explain how it represents your cultural identity.

Assessment Criteria

Your collage should identify characteristics of your cultural identity. These characteristics of culture are more abstract and metaphorical; consider them as "thinking about culture." For instance, the United States is often characterized as "individualistic." One way to represent that would be to include a picture of a person wearing a personalized shirt.

When others view this collage, it should be clear that you have identified a culture to which you belong. It should include

- Your identity related to the self and family culture, and/or
- Your identity related to the local community culture, and/or
- Your identity related to the broader American culture
- Specific artifacts of a culture (art, music, fashion, food, traditions, language, etc.)

Your collage will also be evaluated on the following criteria for attractiveness/appeal:

- Excellent use of visual design (which may include font, color, graphics, etc.) to enhance the work
- Thoughtful consideration of the rhetorical situation (mode and media, audience, purpose, situation)

might consider as they worked through the various activities. Specifically, we wanted students to begin to learn how to extend their initial thoughts to form an exploration of larger ideas. As Randy Bomer (2011) describes it, we wanted students to begin "writing toward what is significant" (p. 192). Bomer further argues that "[o]ften a writer starts writing about something that is not, in and of itself, particularly a big deal," suggesting that as they write about a topic, students need to ask themselves, *"What's important about this? How is this significant?"* (2011, p. 192). With this in mind, we planned our activities to guide students toward deeper writing and questioning and, in turn, toward a deeper sense of thinking and discovery.

As we had anticipated, at times Dawn's students, in their efforts to play the game of school, wanted to know if they were doing things right and accomplishing the goals that we set out for them. As this chapter has shown, students shared images and thinking in a Google shared folder, and they commented on one another's ideas. They started collaborating on the wiki with contribution to discussion tabs. They began to post pictures through the class perspectives ethnography invitation. And they collaborated in their reading as they took notes on an article and responded to one another too. All this feedback and conversation served not only to extend their learning but also to make them more comfortable with the messiness involved in genuine research and inquiry.

As we wrapped up this first week of instruction, it was clear that students were starting to think in rich and purposeful ways about culture. Students were considering perspectives and being ethnographers. Students were thinking critically about a variety of texts. And it was natural and purposeful. Even though the type of thinking that we were asking them to do was difficult—both because we began each morning with big questions and because these questions were different from what is often asked in schools— Dawn's students began the process with eagerness.

2 Getting Started With Inquiry Work

Visual Literacy and Literature Circles

> *If students aren't taught the language of sound and images, shouldn't they be considered as illiterate as if they left college without being able to read or write?*
>
> —Filmmaker George Lucas, quoted in *Edutopia*

Across time and throughout various cultures, the manner in which texts take form has changed due to cultural, economic, and communicative practices. Forms of texts have evolved from symbolic to alphabetic. At one time, our Western culture privileged print-based texts. However, when we focus on texts in the 21st century, it is easy to understand the need to expand this mind-set. The National Council of Teachers of English recognizes that current "literacies are multiple, dynamic, and malleable" and notes that

> active, successful participants in 21st century global society must be able to
>
> - Develop proficiency and fluency with the tools of technology
>
> - Build intentional cross-cultural connections and relationships with others so to pose and solve problems collaboratively and strengthen independent thought
>
> - Design and share information for global communities to meet a variety of purposes
>
> - Manage, analyze, and synthesize multiple streams of simultaneous information
>
> - Create, critique, analyze, and evaluate multimedia texts
>
> - Attend to the ethical responsibilities required by these complex environments (National Council of Teachers of English, 2008b)

As we help students embrace the role of various texts in their literate lives, we need to teach them how to effectively analyze both print and a variety of other texts, including visual images. The Common Core State Standards (CCSS) require that students be able to "use technology . . . taking advantage of technology's capacity to link to other information and to display information flexibly and dynamically" (CCSS.ELA-LITERACY.W.9-10.6), which we would argue includes visual communication.

The lessons covered in this chapter build on the work referenced in Chapter 1. Through the activities discussed here, Dawn's students continued to use an inquiry approach and technology tools to develop and refine their thinking about culture, visual design, and the role of images within culture. Specifically, they expanded their questions about identity and culture by creating a culture collage, as well as through their work with literature circles.

Literature circles, as described by Harvey Daniels (2002), are small groups in which students engage in discussions around a specific text. In Dawn's class, students formed literature circles to read through a cultural lens. They did not adopt particular roles within literature circle groups; instead, students practiced close careful reading of texts throughout the inquiry unit by writing in a dialectical journal and questioning their reading.

Again, as we consider how this approach rewires the typical research and writing process taught in high school classrooms, we want to note a few of the moves Dawn made at this point in the unit. First, she purposefully wove in a literature circle study (Lesson 8) to complement the research process that focused on analyzing nonfiction texts related to our unit "Reading Our World and Exploring Perspectives: Identity and Culture," and students' personal inquiry questions related to culture, as well as "self" and "world" questions (see Lesson 1). Second, she paired close reading of text with close viewing and interpretation of visuals. These multiple literacies were interspersed throughout the unit. Finally, she integrated a specific reflection at the end of this week of instruction (Lesson 11), about one-third of the way through the entire unit.

LESSON 6. VISUAL LITERACY AND DESIGN

The purpose of this lesson is to help students

- Define visual literacy and its importance in society today

- Explore aspects of visual literacy and design

- Apply concepts of visual literacy to the design of a culture collage

- Share experiences of being ethnographers

- Engage in peer response to culture collages

A "Crash Course" on Visual Literacy

According to the Association of College and Research Libraries (ACRL; 2011), "Visual literacy is a set of abilities that enables an individual to effectively find, interpret, evaluate, use, and create images and visual media." Moreover, visual literacy skills

> equip a learner to understand and analyze the contextual, cultural, ethical, aesthetic, intellectual, and technical components involved in the production and use of visual materials. A visually literate individual is both a critical consumer of visual media and a competent contributor to a body of shared knowledge and culture. (ACRL, 2011)

The National Council of Teachers of English also recognizes the importance of exploring visual literacy with students:

> To participate in a global society, we continue to extend our ways of communicating. Viewing and visually representing are a part of our growing consciousness of how people gather and share information. Teachers and students need to expand their appreciation of the

power of print and nonprint texts. Teachers should guide students in constructing meaning through creating and viewing nonprint texts. (National Council of Teachers of English & International Reading Association, 1996)

As we engaged Dawn's students in the study of visual literacy, we wanted them to understand the types of communication that happen through the use of picture-based content—from fine art to graphic art to web design. We wanted students to be able to read images and explore their message, as well as to create images with careful consideration of the rhetorical moves involved.

Throughout our very brief "crash course" on visual literacy, students expressed an interest in using it to look more closely at images and think more purposefully about their compositions. In this lesson, students reviewed the slide show "Visual Literacy and Document Design," which Dawn slightly modified based on the work of Dànielle DeVoss. Available as a link from our companion website (**http://resources.corwin.com/ writingrewired**), the presentation reviews additional principles such as color, font, and principles of design. Through this slide show, students explored definitions and examples of elements of visual literacy. At the basic level, we introduced the "rule of thirds," a popular guideline for photographers to consider when framing an image. In this case, "[t]he basic principle behind the rule of thirds is to imagine breaking an image down into thirds (both horizontally and vertically) so that you have 9 parts" (Rowse, n.d.). These parts can help those who are framing a composition to be aware of where the eye is first drawn to a page.

We also introduced the students to design principles from Robin Williams's text, *The Non-Designer's Design Book* (2008). Williams describes how four basic principles—contrast, repetition, alignment, and proximity—can combine to create powerful visual effects. For instance, the idea of contrast can apply to colors, shapes, fonts, or other visual elements in a document. When creating contrasting elements, Williams argues, the contrast should be stark, not subtle. The starkness of black text on a white background is perhaps the easiest example to point out, though DeVoss's presentation shows many others. The repetition, alignment, and proximity of visual elements, too, create opportunities for thinking about effective visual design.

Moreover, we discussed the use of colors (such as red to suggest a dynamic, aggressive product) and fonts (such as Helvetica, a simple, clean sans serif font used on signage around the world). Students were especially interested in the psychology of colors; since many students did not know that reds and yellows prompt hunger, for example, they immediately connected this new information with their knowledge of the colors used by many fast-food chains.

Lesson 6. Visual Literacy and Design

Visual literacy is an important skill to bring to our reading and composing. We must be able to evaluate, analyze, and create images. To more fully understand visuals, there are several concepts worthy of consideration.

Activity 1: Defining Design Concepts

As we review the presentation on "Visual Literacy and Document Design," write a definition for each of the following design concepts in your own words.

Contrast	
Alignment	
Repetition	
Proximity	
Rule of Thirds	
Colors	
Perspective	
Font	

Activity 2: Applying What You Have Learned

Using an image search, find a compelling photograph, drawing, cartoon, logo, or other visual image.

Then, use at least three of the concepts you defined above to describe how your chosen image is an example of effective design.

Please write this in paragraph format and be sure to cite the source of the original image.

Consider the image of the musician here. For this response, you might write about the way the photographer used the rule of thirds, perspective, and proximity to compose the image.

Source: ©AaronAmat, Thinkstock Photos.

watch it here

Video 2.1

http://resources.corwin
.com/writingrewired

Finally, we introduced ideas about how images can (and often do) distort reality. Since students are bombarded with visuals throughout the school day, on the Internet, in the media, and throughout their daily lives, this crash course in visual literacy was especially useful for them. As students integrated their learning with their personal experiences, they began to identify and understand the psychological moves companies make to impact our daily lives and our cultures (Stanger, 2012). Throughout the inquiry unit, we encouraged them to think through elements of design and consider how to be purposeful in their moves as they composed their own visual texts, specifically their culture collages. In Video 2.1, Dawn discusses the specific assignment of the culture collage, which needs to consider visual design.

Extensions and Adaptations for Lesson 6

Teaching visual literacy in the English language arts classroom has become commonplace, and as such, many wonderful resources are available for use in the classroom. We contend that analysis of images, as well as creation of images including image manipulation and remixing images or using various images for different purposes, is an important part of understanding visual literacy. Teachers may also wish to approach visual literacy learning in the classroom by asking students to

- Analyze existing advertisements, comic strips, or photographs to study elements of design

- Create their own image (such as an advertisement, comic, or photograph with a specific message) and explain the intentional moves they made in their composition

- Edit images with software such as Fireworks, Paint, or Photoshop

- Explore the role of images related to argument

- Explore media literacy with resources from the Media Education Lab (http://mediaeducationlab.com)

LESSON 7. CULTURE COLLAGE SHARING

The purpose of this lesson is to help students

- Share collages to validate work, collaborate, and build on ideas

- Reflect upon elements of culture portrayed in each collage, including exploration of identity and self, family, community, and American culture

- Reflect upon the role of design in the collage to practice identifying visual design moves

Sharing and Responding to the Culture Collages

We asked students to share their culture collages so they could collaboratively grow in their thinking and inquiry and embrace the audience of their classroom community. While this move could have been quite simple (talk to your neighbor, share your ideas, etc.), we purposefully crafted a response guide (see page 71) so that students could use the collage to prompt further thinking related to their inquiry work, while the collage and their peer response served to monitor their thinking through this formative assessment.

For this lesson, we intentionally decided to have students write responses on paper versus on a computer so they could quickly take and share notes as they looked at each other's collages. In this case, we wanted students to focus on the discussion and developing inquiry questions without having to navigate any elements of technology (except their collage, if it was created digitally). When making decisions about whether or not a lesson could or should include technological elements, we teachers must consider the learning objectives. Consider the following questions as you explore options for each lesson:

- What benefit would technology bring to the conversation or the learning?

- What might technology take away from the learning?

- How would students engage in the lesson with technology? Without technology?

- Would the lesson still be engaging if students used technology? Or might students use technology to "get off task"?

As Dawn's students examined each other's collages, we asked them to think carefully about the messages conveyed by various images, as well as by the visual design, and the manner in which each collage reflected cultural identity. To carve out a focus on cultural identity, we also invited students to complete a Venn diagram as part of their response guide (page 71) for each of their partners. In the diagram, they included the elements they recognized that were connected to identity related to self and family culture, identity related to the local community culture, and identity related to the broader American culture. While the students did not need to address all of these areas in their collage, we felt the peer feedback from the Venn diagrams would help them see specific ways that other students read the collage. We were pleased to see that, later on in the researching phase of their work, students did return to their notes from this day of collage sharing as a natural part of the recursive thinking, researching, and writing process. Additionally, we kept inquiry in mind and offered students the opportunity to help one another share ideas about inquiry questions.

Supporting Students With Questions

Students shared their work in small groups. The conversations were very rich as students wanted to learn together and share their ideas. When we visited groups, we continued to coach students with questioning by asking them about moves they made as composers of the collage. In this way, we were validating a collage as a visual composition, one that required the author to think critically and carefully about the decisions he or she made. For instance, Dawn asked one group, *"What other possible messages does an image like that send? Would different audiences look at that image in a different way?"*

Dawn looks on as Charlie and Asha review Asha's culture collage made with web-based service Smore and shared on the computer.

Asha had the following to say about her collage:

I'm proud of the voice I put into my collage and also the things I did within it. While I was going through some other people's collages, I found out not only how different they were, but that what they put was different as well. I found that some would put more into their personal life than American culture and some would do it the other way around. I tried to put Michigan, my personal culture, and American culture into one. I tried to make it as even as possible, and I'm proud of it.

First, with my personal culture, I put in my beliefs. After that, I put in teenage culture, then American culture. Lastly, I explained Michigan culture. I feel like it is important to teach Michigan culture to adolescents who live in Michigan for the fact of taking everything here for granted, for example our Great Lakes. People who live next to the ocean would disagree that such a thing could be a lake, but sure enough it is. The colors the leaves change and the smell of the air . . . why else would people tour Michigan?

Mass culture and teen culture have become so important to businesses. Teen culture would probably have more of an impact on them, just because teens are the "guinea pigs" for everything people are putting out (except cleaning supplies). Teens impact Google and everything it owns nowadays plus new electronics, video games, movies, etc., etc. Though adults are watching these movies and getting into electronics, these companies are getting their ideas from what teenagers like and what sells.

Though my personal life should not influence anyone, it influences mass culture. If everyone said "my personal life does not matter," then there would not be any mass culture or teen culture, Michigan culture, or any culture. It is because of you that mass culture is here. Because we are part of something, we all have someone to relate to and with. This fact makes me forget about how I do not have any idea what I want to be when I grow up and makes me feel like I have a place in this world somewhere, somehow. I have learned from this project that even if someone came from somewhere different or is going somewhere else, there will be something that you can always relate to the person with. No matter your age, race, height, religion, or gender, there will be a connection.

Celebrating Ethnic Heritage

Dawn's class was fortunate to celebrate diversity as students embraced learning about one another's cultures. For instance, Thaarini described to Allison the way Indian women put a jewel on their forehead, as this was depicted in her collage, and how in her family they maintain this tradition even after moving to America. The class also discussed how some students embraced being part of more than one ethnic culture. Beverly shared a map of the United States, using a Chinese flag as part of the design (see the photo on page 67). When Dawn asked Beverly about it, she said she was proud to celebrate being Chinese American. However, Beverly also shared that her mother was concerned that some viewers might mistake the image for a communist symbol. This prompted even further conversation about various potential responses from a different audience.

Dawn probed Beverly by asking, *"What would other people say?"* and even *"What if this shows that China is growing as a world power?"* This led to an interesting conversation with a small group of students as they discussed viewpoints of different cultures and perspectives toward people from different cultures. This also led students to think about awareness of audience, as well as how stereotypes are supported or refuted in society. Rewiring research, while focused on student inquiry and questioning, is modeled through moments such as these as teachers prompt students to think about different perspectives by modeling open-ended questions.

As we worked with students, we noted a few important trends emerging in the room. Some students were identifying with their ethnicity, as in the Indian American and Chinese American conversations discussed earlier. Another student spent time talking about being part of the first generation of her family to be born in the United States and the differences between her experiences and her parents' experiences in terms of their understanding of identity based on ethnicity. Another student talked about how American culture was a mash-up of other cultures. At the same time, students were engaging in questioning with one another. At one point, a student asked, "What does *inquiry* mean again?" not realizing that he was practicing inquiry by being curious and asking questions.

Reading Visuals

Some of the students also engaged in specific conversations about how to read a collage. For instance, Asha used the web-based service Smore for her collage, and another student commented that it looked more like a website than a traditional collage. This led to discussion about what makes a collage "qualify" as a collage—that is, how can students most effectively meet the demands of a specific modality? Others embraced conversations about visual design as they explored the use of white space and its effect on modality. Still others revisited each element of design from the visual literacy and design lesson (Lesson 6) to analyze the visual composition for design elements, and others focused on the rhetorical read of author purpose. By spending more time "reading" the visuals, students were able

Dawn discusses Beverly's culture collage with a small group of students.

to think about the intention of a composition. Additionally, considering visual design prompted students to be inquisitive about each visual, which led to questioning and tied into their inquiry.

Discussing "Right Answers" and the Need to Take Risks

Students also engaged in conversations about "one right idea" as they shared the collages. As noted earlier when students worked on defining their initial thinking about culture in the preview lesson in Chapter 1 (page 25), we often have students who want to know the "right" answer. It can be hard for students to take risks, especially with grades on the line. However, if we want students to engage in rich critical analysis and offer new ideas and insights, then we must ensure that risk taking is part of the writing process. We know we need to continue to challenge teens with engaging topics relevant to their needs; still, when asking them to take a risk, timing is also important as students need to trust they can risk thinking carefully and critically.

Although we never said they had to do the collage in a specific way, some students really wanted one clear way to approach their own work and to evaluate the work of others, complete with the number and type of images to include. We wondered if that seemingly unbreakable preference for a predetermined path was simply human nature or something that just happens in school. In short, do we ask students to "play school" too often? Do we, as teachers, set parameters for assignments that students feel they must simply complete without any real investment? We asked ourselves if making choices for a composition is difficult and scary for students. How do we support learners and their work with rhetorical moves in various compositions?

In response to student discomfort, we had conversations about safe classroom communities that give students the space to take risks. When a student complained that the activity was "hard," Dawn encouraged her to identify what made it so. The student then said that it was hard because it required her to think. Other students admitted that they wanted to fill in the boxes with "right" answers, as students are traditionally taught to do in many school contexts. To what extent are students offered and embracing choice about topics for writing? Rewiring the research process requires that students make an investment in their own learning, and this is a difficult, yet necessary, step. Through our conversations, the students began to recognize this work as a different kind of thinking. This led to a student discussion about what makes something "schooly" and how students embrace or reject challenges in academic and nonacademic environments. We reminded students that sometimes they need to take risks in order to move their work to a higher level. We also explained that inquiry work is positioned to help students with just that goal in mind. Our inquiry work continued to draw on students' own interests, as we offered choice for students and explored texts from their lives. This made learning relevant as students engaged in connected learning activities.

Responding to Guided Questions as a Means for Further Inquiry

The students' use of the handout for Lesson 7, "Culture Collage Sharing" (page 71), worked very well, and the activity inspired higher-order thinking. Student conversations were authentic, but they were also driven by the questions the handout prompted them to wrestle through. As noted, the Venn diagram prompted students to think about how their individual cultures— as well as broader community and American cultures—sometimes overlap and at other times diverge sharply. Students found the diagram to be a surprisingly complex but useful way to tease out new ideas. For example, one group used the Venn diagram to engage in major debates about what each image represented in the collage and how the concepts and characteristics of culture could be categorized. These conversations reflected intentional purposeful decisions for the items included in the collage. And one student said, "This [consideration of cultural characteristics] is all about perspective, Mrs. Reed."

Through the conversations prompted from the guiding questions on the handout, students engaged in a rich, dialogic curriculum as they discovered the importance of recognizing other perspectives as well as various arguments related to what characteristics impact culture. For instance, as students grouped ideas related to different aspects of culture (e.g., through the use of the Venn diagram) and explored abstract ideas through characteristics of culture as represented by images and artifacts of culture, they formed additional questions as they worked to figure out how they might classify images. By choosing this activity and guiding students through their discomfort when they could not easily determine one "right answer," Dawn ensured that, even early on in the research-based inquiry unit, students were situated in a position to become curious about a lot of ideas and potential concepts worthy of further exploration.

Through their work with the guiding questions on the handout, students also began to notice that visuals are an interesting composition by which to establish the voice of the author. Some students discussed that they could recognize the person who created the collage simply by looking at the content and arrangement of the images. One student, Allie, explained her decisions for her collage by stating that she was exploring not only culture but also photographic truth as she included images of herself with a Photoshopped blue layover, an image of her mother without any adjustments, and a magazine image of a female model that clearly had been Photoshopped. She additionally set up contrasts in images, including veggies on a burger bun, to reflect different types of healthy food choices as well as "typical" American food. This collage served as a springboard for Allie to explore the question of photographic truth in a world where digital image manipulation is so prevalent, an idea that later developed into her inquiry question. Allie was one of many students who shared that they valued the opportunity to create a visual representation of their thinking through their work on this collage. In this way—as well as in the questioning and challenging of ideas—the students' work was both authentic and challenging.

Assessing the Culture Collage

We decided to approach the culture collage activity as a formative assessment, as this was a step to monitor learning and continue to support students' inquiry. Students received feedback through participation in discussions with their classmates, and they also received a copy of the completed handout "Culture Collage Sharing" (page 71) from each respondent.

Dawn provided feedback on students' writing about their collages, too. Her feedback focused on asking questions or noting ideas that each student wrote about that could inspire an inquiry focus. If students met the criteria of designing a collage that highlighted their culture through various images and explaining how the images represented their cultural identity, they received full credit for the score on the assignment. If their work was not very thorough or clear, they lost a few points on the assignment.

Additionally, if they did not have both the collage and the writing, they received only half-credit for the assignment.

It is important to note that we chose not to evaluate the collage as a summative assessment because we wanted to extend the students' sense of wonder and curiosity throughout the parts of the inquiry unit that followed. A major grade, we felt, could have stopped the process dead in its tracks. At this point, students were eager to find answers to some of the questions they had generated through the collage activity, and we pushed them to consider answers to the question, *"So what?"* In other words, we invited them to ask themselves, *"Why does this collage matter in the big picture of my inquiry? How is it important for me as a reader, writer, and thinker? Why does this all matter as I address my inquiry question?"* With these gentle nudges, we felt students were ready to use the collage activity as a springboard into more careful critical thinking: reading a literature circle book and conducting research.

Extensions and Adaptations for Lesson 7

Teachers will always have a variety of considerations to make when establishing a sharing and peer-responding setup in the classroom. From informal versus formal sharing, to digital versus print responses, even to anonymous versus known authors, students can share work in a multitude of ways. Throughout the year, if students are encouraged to experience a variety of peer-responding situations for various purposes—and to directly share their experiences with peer response—students will learn to recognize that a mere "thumbs-up" does not promote revision or careful critical questioning of a text. Modeling ways to question and observe in a text can be very helpful; after all, students often give a "thumbs-up" response when they do not know what to say. For this collage-sharing activity, we have provided one specific way using the "Culture Collage Sharing" handout (page 71) for students to respond to the text in a face-to-face conversation with guided note taking.

Other approaches could include having students share in Google Drive. While reviewing a collage and related writing, students could, as noted in Chapter 1 (page 28), "ink shed" responses by highlighting and commenting. Students could also respond by identifying specific traits within the writing and collage, or by offering mere wonderings. In this case, students might select five images and write five responses starting with "This image makes me wonder . . ."

Learning goals for peer response generally help establish the structure. Entire-class review could include celebrations and questioning or could provide the teacher time to model questioning and avoiding looking for one "right" answer in a text.

Lesson 7. Culture Collage Sharing

Responding to Culture Collages: Exploring Cultural Identity

Name of collage author:_____

Name of respondent:_____

- What messages do you read from the collage? What prompted you to see it in this way?

- How does the collage demonstrate an understanding of culture?

- What strikes you about the visual design of the collage? Why?

- In what ways does the collage share an interesting perspective related to culture?

- How does the collage reflect cultural identity?

Complete the following Venn diagram to note ways the collage reflects aspects listed in the boxes.

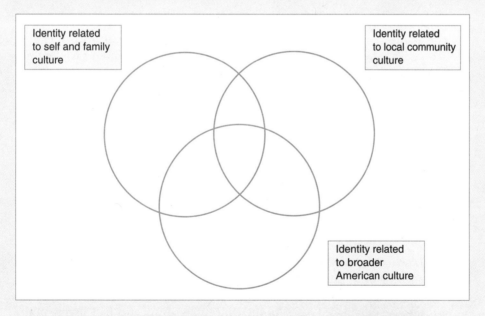

Identity related to self and family culture

Identity related to local community culture

Identity related to broader American culture

As this writer thinks about developing inquiry questions, what recommendations do you have for him or her?

LESSON 8. LITERATURE CIRCLES

The purpose of this lesson is to help students

- Begin exploring a new text for analysis of inquiry questions

- Join literature circle teams

- Establish personal goals for reading and learning

- Establish team goals for reading and a team reading schedule

- Begin reading their selected books with their own inquiry questions as well as the group focus in mind

Following the lesson on culture collage sharing (Lesson 7), we briefly introduced students to the idea of adding on to their thinking through literature circles. We asked students to work in pairs to spend two minutes (one minute per student) discussing the following prompt:

Quick reflection: What have you learned about the role of ethnography and perspective to explore your thinking or inquiry questions?

Following this fast discussion, Dawn shared that each student would be adding a new lens to his or her thinking through work with literature circles. She invited students to select a book and focus their reading not only on plot, characters, and setting but also on culture and identity in fiction. She explained that the literature circle groups would explore their literature circle text, including an examination of cultural characteristics and artifacts.

Student Goal Setting: Putting Ownership in Student Hands

In this lesson, we asked students to establish reading and learning goals for themselves and for their literature circle groups. Through goal setting, we wanted students to take ownership of their reading and learning. After Dawn distributed books (noting that some students were ecstatic while assuring other students that the book they received would, indeed, be just fine), students met in groups to divide the reading sections for each meeting. We established dates for these meetings so students had a sense of the time they had to read the books. To help students form their teams and get used to discussion with their team members, we asked students to share their "self" and "world" questions from their profile on Youth Voices (see Lesson 1, page 34) so they could learn more about each other's thinking before they started the reading journey together.

Literature Circle Assignment

We designed the literature circle assignment to build on work already explored in Dawn's classroom. Prior to this activity, Dawn had explored with her students the use of discussion questions and how to write them when studying a common text. Because students had experience asking deep questions as well as using Socratic discussions, they were able to quickly work together to develop thoughtful questions and engage in dialogue with one another. We focused literature circle meeting preparation on open-ended questioning as a main technique, and practicing skills with close reading. Dawn's students had already worked on developing reading strategies and using dialectic journals; they also quickly engaged in this form of responding to the text. Dawn reminded students that a focus on close careful reading was the goal of the journaling and questioning process. Students set up their journals in a manner that worked for them and supported their reading.

The new feature that Dawn introduced to students specifically for this inquiry unit was the culture log, which she asked them to use to keep track of cultural characteristics ("thinking about culture" or intangible factors of culture) and artifacts of culture (tangible factors of culture, such as identifying language reflective of a culture) that impact the story and potentially the reader. Dawn explained that this log was designed to support students' thinking in their own reading and with their literature circle teams as they engaged in class conversations about culture.

Book Selection

Dawn briefly introduced students to each book option, providing a short summary of the text. Additionally, she explained that students could read more about each book on the class wiki; she had created a link from each book title to its Wikipedia or Amazon description (as based on availability of websites). Students then were able to select five top choices using a Google Form (see image on page 75). We also gave students a chance to note if they had read a certain book already or if there were special considerations they wanted to note about their choices. Special considerations included students' deep desire to read a particular book or preference for a specific type of book.

When selecting literature circle books, we find it helpful to consider students' reading level and ability to wrestle with content, as students would need to be able to work through texts in a more independent manner than with a class text. That said, knowing that students can support one another in their reading is an important part of learning, too, so challenging texts can work for readers ready for this work. In short, we did not limit students by Lexile scores. Furthermore, the literature circle texts needed to complement their culture conversations and provide inspiration for students to work with big ideas for their inquiry-based research essay and media project. While many books fit this need, we also selected books based on their availability. To view a list of book options we had available, along with a brief note about why we selected the texts, visit our companion website at **http://resources.corwin .com/writingrewired**.

To organize book selections, Dawn used a Google Form. After reviewing the form, she made groups based on the following:

- Using student-noted preferences for what they had read before, as well as what book they wanted to read

- Offering appropriate reading materials for students based on reading level and content as based on interest

- Balancing group sizes to three to five students

- Making appropriate groups (based on student behavior when interacting together as well as skill level) for students to work together

In Video 2.2, Dawn introduces literature circles as a way to extend exploration of curiosities and inquiry through the study of fiction.

Extensions and Adaptations for Lesson 8 and Literature Circles

There are many ways to adapt or modify this literature circle assignment to meet a variety of learning goals. Here are some factors you might adjust:

- **Meeting Times.** Adjust the number of meetings and length of time for meetings based on your classroom needs.

- **Reading Assignments.** Not all ways to respond to a reading will be a good fit for your students. Other assignments might be a better fit, and this one can be modified or adapted to fit your students' needs. Check out Wilhelm's *"You Gotta BE the Book"* (2007) and Mitchell's "Fifty Alternatives to the Book Report" (1998) for alternative ways to respond to a text.

- **Group Organization.** Sizes of groups might vary, or you could also do work with several small groups reading the same novel.

- **Literature Selection.** Novels that are accessible for students could work in different configurations. For instance, all students in the classroom could read the same novel, but discuss mostly in small groups. Also, small groups could read and discuss short stories and/ or a variety of other reading selections, such as nonfiction texts.

- **Group Collaboration Space.** As groups got started, we established workspace within our class website using a project space within our Wikispaces for each literature circle group. There are various ways to set up group spaces for work, from Wikispaces to Google Docs, and you can create a system that works best for you and your students based on your school network, course management software, and other needs.

watch it here

Video 2.2
http://resources.corwin
.com/writingrewired

Google Forms

Google Forms, part of the Google Apps for Education collection, allows you to gather information from students relatively quickly and in an organized manner. Through Google Forms, you can make a variety of types of forms. Once students submit answers to forms, the results appear in a spreadsheet for your review. This was a very helpful tool for Dawn to make literature circle groups because she didn't need to flip through papers to figure out which books students wanted to read. The following image shows the first part of the form we created to track students' preferences for their literature circle books.

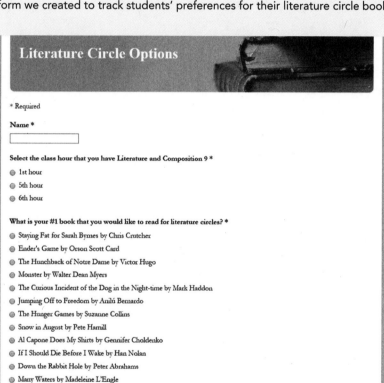

Source: Screenshot courtesy of Google Forms. Content is author created.

HAND
OUT

Lesson 8. Literature Circles

As a part of our close careful reading and analyzing of culture, you will have the opportunity to read a fictional text in a literature circle group.

Identify three reading and learning goals that you have for your work with your book and literature circle group. Be sure to consider your work with critical reading and journaling, discussion, and inquiry questions.

Goal 1:

Goal 2:

Goal 3:

(Continued)

(Continued)

Your group will have four major discussion dates. Divide your book into four sections—one for each of the meetings.

Meeting 1 date: _____   Pages due: _____

Meeting 2 date: _____   Pages due: _____

Meeting 3 date: _____   Pages due: _____

Meeting 4 date: _____   Pages due: _____

For each literature circle meeting, please complete the following:

- Read all the pages assigned in the book.

- Be a careful and critical reader. Mark passages that you would like to discuss. Use sticky notes to mark spots that you would like to review in the reading when you discuss with your group.

- Journaling—there are multiple purposes for your journal:

  ○ It is a place to think about your reading. Remember, writing is thinking.

  ○ It is a place to prepare for your discussions of the reading.

  ○ It is a place to chart your reading and its connection to culture and identity. It is also a place to explore your inquiry questions and chart out connections.

  ○ Your journal needs to be set up for *you*. You may choose to complete a digital journal (you could use Google Drive, our class webspace, or another digital space, such as a blog or Youth Voices). Or you can write out a print journal. Any form is perfectly acceptable.

For each meeting, prepare the following minimum (yes, you can and should do more than this) in your journal:

- **Write out three discussion questions.** Use the questioning strategies we've explored with Socratic discussions, including open-ended questions, to think more critically about the text. Remember:

  ○ Closed-ended questions are for clarifying, as they generally have a "correct" answer.

  ○ Open-ended questions challenge readers to think about the text and additional connections. They may require evidence from the text or outside research to extend beyond the text in connection making.

(Continued)

(Continued)

- ○ Open-ended questions may ask about character motivations or the author's purpose, or they may relate events in the text to the world or a universal theme or an essential question. They may also be a literary analysis or author's craft question. Additionally, they may relate to the cultural connections you are making while reading from a cultural lens. They may also relate to your "self," "world," and inquiry questions.

- **Dialectic journaling.** This is the practice of having a dialogue with the text by arriving at truth based on the exchange of arguments. In two columns, write out notes that are in dialogue with one another. This is the practice of exchanging ideas with the text to further analyze and carve out your understanding.

    - ○ In one column, record quotes and paraphrasing with page numbers.

    - ○ In the second column, record your thinking about this work through a response to the quote, exploring the importance and interesting factors related to the content. Consider some of the ideas noted in writing an open-ended question earlier.

    - ○ Use this journal to specifically address some of your inquiry questions and the big culture questions we are exploring.

- **Culture log.** Keep track of cultural characteristics (characteristics of culture are more abstract and metaphorical; consider them as "thinking about culture" or factors of culture that are intangible yet are often shown through specific culture artifacts) and artifacts of culture (which can be from various parts of culture, from art, to music, to fashion, to food, to traditions, to language, etc.) that impact the story and potentially the reader.

Example Journal Setup

If it helps you, you may set up your reading journal using the following structure:

Discussion Questions

- Question 1
- Question 2
- Question 3

(Continued)

Dialectic Journal

Quotation or Paraphrase	Page Number	Response to Quote
Keep track of compelling passages that relate to you, your inquiry questions, and your analysis of ideas, writing style, and plot.		Response to quote: Consider some of the following ideas in your thoughtful and thorough response: • Why do I find this quote interesting or important? • What does it help me to understand about the text? • How might it help me to relate to the text? • How does this quote relate to my inquiry questions? • How does this idea or quote relate to culture? • How does it relate to my understanding and analysis of the text?

Cultural Log

Identify Cultural Artifacts and Characteristics	Page Number	Reflect on the Cultural Artifact or Characteristic and Its Role in the Novel
Cultural characteristics: abstract and metaphorical representations; consider them as "thinking about culture" or factors of culture that are intangible, such as defining culture as individualistic OR Artifacts of culture: specific representations of a cultural characteristic; for instance, to show an individualistic culture, a picture of a person wearing a personalized shirt, etc. (consider various artifacts—art, music, fashion, food, traditions, language, etc.)		• How does this cultural characteristic or artifact impact my reading? • How does it impact the plot of the story? • How does it help me think about big questions related to culture and identity?

(Continued)

(Continued)

Assessment for Literature Circle Meetings

After the first and fourth literature circle meeting, I will collect your notes to do a spot check of your thinking. Additionally, after the first and fourth meetings, I will ask you to fill out a self-assessment using Google Forms. Combined, these activities will give me a picture of your thinking over the course of your literature circle work. Final grades will be based on the following:

Discussion Questions

- Questions that earn all points encourage strong and sophisticated discussion.
- Overuse of closed questions or questions that do not adequately encourage strong sophisticated discussion earn fewer points.

Discussion Active Engagement

- The student is actively involved in the discussion. This is demonstrated through body position in the discussion, preparation for the discussion, use of and references to the novel in the discussion, and involvement in recording student thinking in notes from the literature circle team meetings.

Dialectic Journal

- The journal thoroughly records thinking based on passages from the novel, and
- responses to the passage show analysis that explores its significance to the text and to bigger inquiry questions.

Cultural Log

- The cultural log highlights both artifacts and characteristics of culture and analyzes these items in relation to the novel and inquiry questions.

LESSON 9. FASHION AND IMAGE IN AMERICAN CULTURE

The purpose of this lesson is to help students

- Analyze an aspect of culture by focusing on the artifact of fashion

- Hold a classroom conversation focusing on questioning the cultural artifact of fashion

- Explore the concept of fact versus fiction in images

- Introduce and explore the idea of images being modified and the ways to critically read images

- Explore the role of visual design in marketing

Cultural Artifact Focus: Fashion

This lesson focused on one artifact of culture—fashion—partially because all teenagers are aware of fashion and partially because we chose to look at fashion as a visual text, or artifacts of culture that reflect particular values. Teachers could easily extend this lesson, which we set up for one busy class day, to a few days depending on adaptations (see "Extensions and Adaptations for Lesson 9" on page 83). After following standard classroom practices of writing to generate ideas and participating in reflective discussion, students looked at several different magazines to analyze images and explore a variety of ways fashion is portrayed in magazines.

Students then shared selected images in small groups and discussed what each image suggested about fashion. Then each group selected one image to share with the entire class. During this time to share, students also discussed the target audience of the magazine and why it would highlight certain types of fashion. Additionally, students noted generalizations about fashion through their careful reading of images.

After exploring the role of fashion in the modality of magazines, students watched the Dove commercial "Evolution" (Piper, 2006). Many videos such as Dove's explore the concept of image doctoring or changing images of models to fit a societal ideal of "beauty." We decided to use this commercial in the lesson to prompt students to build upon their earlier conversations related to images and extend them to explore image doctoring and the role of images as fact or fiction. Moreover, we wanted students to begin to consider how this focus on fashion could be extended to a larger exploration of images in reading our world.

HAND OUT

Lesson 9. Fashion and Image in American Culture

Reflective of our visual culture and as an artifact of culture, fashion reflects cultural values.

- What cultural values do you believe are reflected in the fashion you see every day?
- What cultural values do you believe are reflected in the fashion you see in popular magazines or on television?

Activity 1: Writing Reflection on Fashion

Fashion can be an artifact of culture. Describe American fashion.

- How is fashion important to Americans?
- How is it important to American culture?
- What characteristics of culture are conveyed through fashion? How?

Activity 2: Looking at Images

In small groups, look at various popular magazines based on various types of magazines. Find images that represent American fashion. Discuss the following:

- Why did you choose these images? Share responses with the large group.
- Discuss the audience and purpose of magazines and how the audience impacts the type of fashion that is represented and how it is represented.
- Discuss: What is fact or fiction about images we see in magazines?

Activity 3: Exploring Model Culture

View the Dove commercial "Evolution" (directed by Tim Piper in 2006) and discuss.

- What does this film portray about images in advertisements?
- Are the images fiction or nonfiction?
- What does this film suggest about American ideas related to beauty and fashion?

Interested in more analysis of model culture? Explore Cameron Russell's TED Talk "Looks Aren't Everything. Believe Me, I'm a Model" (2012), available at http://on.ted.com/CameronRussell.

Extensions and Adaptations for Lesson 9

Within this lesson is a link to a TED Talk from Cameron Russell (2012), who demonstrates the power of fashion in how people form opinions of others by literally changing her clothes during the TED Talk. This piece could be the basis for an extension and would open many conversations related to fashion, image, and stereotyping. While students could also analyze more magazines, they might also analyze images from an Internet search, or even children's toys. The cutout doll or Barbie does offer an opportunity to reflect on American fashion and marketing, including how various age groups receive messages about fashion and expectations for society. Students may also analyze fashion within a specific cultural focus, such as sports culture with a focus on athletes and their fashion needs or musicians and their needs. Exploring how musicians need to consider fashion in contemporary society compared to societal expectations for musicians throughout history could lead to interesting conversations about the values within a culture.

LESSON 10. READING IMAGES: FACT OR FICTION?

The purpose of this lesson is to help students

- Learn to continually question text credibility

- Recognize that all types of text—including visual and multimedia texts—can have a bias or agenda from the author

- Reflect upon and determine ways to evaluate web content

- Explore purposes for adjusting or manipulating images

- Explore the concepts of remixing material to meet the needs of real audiences and purposes

When teaching students these broad goals, we focus in on two factors: image manipulation and consideration of the broader context for the visual or the rhetorical situation of the visual (relating the conversation back to MAPS—mode, audience, purpose, and situation—with focus on audience and purpose). Each of these factors has both technical and ethical implications. For instance, many popular magazines that include models or celebrities on their covers all too often use Photoshop to change the images. Some consider this practice ethical and, indeed, necessary. Others, however, consider it misleading, at best, and dishonest, at worst.

The two factors we ask students to consider, then, will help them make judgments about the technical aspects of the editing as well as the ethical implications for viewers. First, image manipulation, or the process of changing an original image through photographic or digital techniques, can entail adding or subtracting elements from an original picture. One technique would be to add individuals from an ethnic minority into a picture of mostly white people in order to demonstrate diversity. Another famous example included in the slide show "Reading Images: Fact or Fiction?" (available on the companion website, **http://resources.corwin .com/writingrewired**) is to alter the shading and color tones of an image, as done in the infamous O. J. Simpson covers of *Newsweek* and *Time* magazines. Other times, images are outright hoaxes. One such case was the altered image of a man standing on top of the World Trade Center with a jetliner superimposed in the background. This image—claimed to be taken by a tourist on 9/11—made its way around the Internet until the hoax was debunked.

Second, we need to consider why someone would manipulate an image in the first place. For instance, the image of a young woman mourning the death of a fellow student during the Kent State massacre was originally changed with no malicious intent. In order to clean up the image, a photo editor took out a pole from the background that, given the camera angle, appeared to be sticking straight up out of the woman's head. This was not done to make the woman appear glamorous, nor did it detract from the gravity of the situation. Yet, it was manipulated. Other images, of course, are altered for more nefarious purposes. This lesson invites students to consider when, why, and how such manipulation is ever justified. In Video 2.3, students wrestle with critical viewing skills.

watch it here

Video 2.3

http://resources.corwin
.com/writingrewired

Extensions and Adaptations for Lesson 10

There are plenty of materials to use to connect to this lesson, including films such as Jean Kilbourne's *Killing Us Softly* (2015). An April 2014 KQED Do Now conversation included a discussion about "How can we address the high costs of fast fashion?" (Green, 2014). While this Do Now conversation is past, rich resources on this question are still available on the KQED blog (see http://blogs.kqed.org/education/category/do-now).

To expand this inquiry unit, teachers might tie in a conversation about civics or even economics of the clothing industry and cheap labor. Students can also explore how the media highlight doctored photos by examining sites such as *Time*'s "Top 10 Doctored Photos" (n.d.). In order for students to further understand the role of image doctoring, students can also modify their own images using a variety of editing tools, such as Fireworks, Paint, or Photoshop.

Lesson 10. Reading Images: Fact or Fiction?

Image manipulation is common practice in our world today.

- How do people change or manipulate images?

- Why are images manipulated? What purpose does image manipulation serve in our society?

- In what ways can we critically read images?

Activity 1: Reading Images

We will read and discuss the presentation "Reading Images: Fact or Fiction?" adapted from Dànielle DeVoss at Michigan State University. As we explore the content of this presentation, use the following chart to take notes on the concepts by writing about specific images of your choice from the presentation.

	In what way(s) do you think that this image has been manipulated? How does this affect your experience as a viewer?	For what purpose do you think this image was manipulated? Was it an acceptable "revision" to the image given its context and purpose?
Image 1:		
Image 2:		
Image 3:		
Image 4:		

Activity 2: Writing Reflection

Consider the following about your beliefs related to images and their impact on culture:

- For what purposes are images manipulated?

- Is it ever acceptable to alter images?

- How does the altering of historical photographs impact history?

- How should images from any source, especially ones shared widely on the Internet, be evaluated?

Discuss: What factors will you think about now when you evaluate images?

It is also beneficial for students to work on establishing approaches to evaluate websites and images for reliability. Some teachers hand out predetermined checklists for students to consider in evaluating websites. Many libraries offer this type of resource as well. Students could also create their own evaluation tools with the teacher's guidance and through careful review of a website.

LESSON 11. PERSONAL INQUIRY REFLECTIONS

The purpose of this lesson is to help students

- Reflect in writing and create their first blog post related to inquiry questions

- Use mentor texts and guides to support their thinking related to writing

Reflecting on Thinking and Questioning: Personal Inquiry

As we prepared students to make a shift in the research process, we wanted to ensure that they were writing and reflecting throughout the process and in public spaces. For this lesson, we asked students to write and post their first blog entry on Youth Voices. We recognized that it would be essential to give students adequate time to write, reflect, revise, think, and post.

Our assessment of this blog post focused on formative assessment, monitoring students' ideas and processing related to their personal inquiry. While we chose to make this part of a participation grade, teachers can assess this work in a variety of ways, including simply responding to the students' blog posts. Students can also respond to one another's posts to share ideas. Models to help students learn how to respond to blog posts effectively can be found on Youth Voices and are represented in the following handout. Additional guides for how to explore and speculate a personal inquiry are found on Youth Voices. We also recommend that students respond to one another and to others in the Youth Voices community, across classes, and throughout the country. Teaching students how to be part of a personal learning network and how to be thoughtful digital citizens includes prompting them to realize that they also need to respond to others in online communities.

Lesson 11. Personal Inquiry Reflections

Today you will be reflecting on your thinking over the past few days. Think about your "self" and "world" questions, our cultural conversations, your collage, your literature circle reading, our class discussions, and all of our lessons. What are you thinking about based on everything we've been discussing?

Activity 1: Explore a Mentor Text

First, let's examine another student's writing to gain ideas for how you might approach your own writing. Read Kendra's blog reflection on inquiry. Highlight, underline, or put a star next to lines in her reflection that stand out to you as important to know or that show her carefully thinking and reflecting related to inquiry.

Can culture be both restricting and liberating? We have always said that culture is a way to connect and express ourselves with others, but are there restrictions from culture that may hinder you from being the best you can be? Does this mean that culture has both positives and negatives?

When culture is expressed by an individual, will it ever be the exact same as another's culture? Moods, attitudes, and ideas might be different from those of others, so even though people may say that they have the exact same culture, don't ideas and feelings change that? It makes me think that every single person has his or her own unique personal cultural identity.

Is our culture how we define ourselves? Culture is usually what makes up how we think of ourselves and others with attitudes, beliefs, and opinions, which affect our personalities and appearances. From this, I also believe that it's impossible not to have a culture when it makes up who we are and how we think of others as well.

(Continued)

(Continued)

- What do you appreciate about Kendra's reflection?

- What would you ask her about her ideas and inquiry?

- What might she explore for her inquiry research?

Activity 2: Review the Writing Guides on Youth Voices

- Navigate to YouthVoices.net and click on "Guides."
- First, review the guide for "Personal Inquiry": http://youthvoices.net/personalinquiry.
- Then, review the guide for "Speculating on an Inquiry": http://youthvoices.net /speculating.
- Choose one of these two guides as a template for forming your reflective blog post.

Activity 3: Write a Blog Post as a Class

As a class, write an example of a personal inquiry blog post.

Activity 4: Write Your Own Blog Post About Your Reflections Related to Inquiry

Individually, write your own personal inquiry reflection and post your first blog entry on Youth Voices!

Blogging

Blogging can have a variety of purposes and be accomplished in a variety of spaces. Our purpose for blogging is (1) to have students reflect on a weekly basis about their learning in a public academic space in order to solidify and share their ideas, and (2) to help students develop effective communication skills through collaboratively sharing ideas and pressing back on ideas though the discussion aspect of the blog.

Blogging is a public forum for journaling, but it is also a different modality of writing for the web. Students should think about paragraphing and adding images to the blog post as they compose.

Students should also consider their purposes for blogging and how they should address their world audience. If they want to inspire a dialogue, and we hope they do, then we should remind them that opening their ideas up to others through questioning can be helpful.

There are a variety of blogging platforms that teachers may want to consider setting up for their students, including Blogger and Edublogs, and there is even a blog feature on websites such as Weebly.

TECH TIP

Extensions and Adaptations for Lesson 11

Opportunities for students to reflect in writing are an invaluable part of the inquiry process. Rewiring research places focus on students' reflecting and thinking rather than finding one right answer or quick citation to fill in a space. Whether engaging students in reflection in a writer's notebook or digitally through a word-processed document or blog post, this part of the process is important. We contend that students need to share these reflections in a community of learners and that the ideal way to do this is digitally. In this way, students can begin to form a personal learning network.

Students can continue to reflect in their own journals and various digital spaces. Their literature circle teams might have a folder within their Google Drive just for reflections. Students may also have various guidelines on how to respond to one another. Students might be assigned another specific student to respond to, or they may respond to one another from their literature circle team. When students blog, that does not mean they will just automatically receive an audience that responds to their work. However, by making their work public, they begin to, as Kenneth Burke (1973) reminds us, "put in their oar" and have the means to start building connections. Teaming up with another class to blog or have students receive comments outside of their own class can be a helpful part of this process.

REFLECTIONS ON MENTOR TEXTS FOR ANALYSIS AND DEVELOPING INQUIRY QUESTIONS

As this week of lessons came to a close, we again reflected on the five *Ts*—teens, timing, topics, texts, and technology. We recognized that providing time for writing to think was an important wrap-up so that students could begin to refine their inquiry focus through reflection. At this point in the inquiry unit, students had added an additional mentor text to their thinking with a focus on fictional texts with their literature circle book. The focus of Lessons 6 through 11 on building student knowledge related to visual literacy—as well as on reading their worlds through exploration of visual arguments—offered students the opportunity to engage in analysis of culture and texts. Additionally, they were practicing critical reading skills.

Formative assessments of this part of the inquiry unit included student work with the culture collage, as well as their reflections in blogging. This work allowed us, as the teachers, to monitor each student's thinking so that we could continue to probe students to further their work with inquiry and exploration of ideas. In this way, we set up the conversations and reflections to help students dig a little deeper into their inquiry and reading.

Rewiring research, as it turns out, is about more than just layering different technologies or steps in the process. Students had very clear ideas of what constituted "research" from their previous school experiences, and what we were asking them to do was not research by that definition. In fact, as students continued to ask more questions about research, we recognized that we were not only teaching them new processes and expectations for inquiry, but also unteaching many of their ingrained tendencies to simply complete assignments to a teacher's specifications, and not develop rhetorically sophisticated pieces of writing. Rewiring, in this sense, was certainly about integrating technology, extending audiences and purposes for their work, but it was even more about rethinking the research process entirely, offering time to question and explore inquiry areas of personal relevance to students.

3 Laying the Groundwork for Research Writing

Developing Close Reading Skills and Organizing Digital Spaces

> *Books are mirrors: you only see in them what you already have inside you.*
>
> —Carlos Ruiz Zafón,
> *The Shadow of the Wind*

As students engage with a text, we want them to use close, careful reading strategies to enrich their reading experience. One of the strategies to promote higher-order thinking involves reading through different lenses (Appleman, 2009; Beach & Myers, 2001; Beach, Thein, & Webb, 2012; Smagorinsky, 2007). For instance, we can ask students to develop critical approaches to reading through the use of these lenses: differential feminist, differential race, new criticism, archetypal, socioeconomic, sociocultural, and reader response theories, among others. Dawn's students applied some of these lenses, as well as their cultural lens, to their reading of their literature circle books and the various media sources we presented in the inquiry unit "Reading Our World and Exploring Perspectives: Identity and Culture." Through questioning and exploring different perspectives based on reading through a critical lens, they were able to critique and analyze texts in new ways, often making connections that were otherwise not apparent. As shown in previous chapters (see the handout for Lesson 8, page 76), the students also used dialectical journals as well as a culture log to note both cultural artifacts and broader characteristics in their book, and as a result, they came to the literature circle meetings with many ideas for discussion and analysis.

> Close reading affords students the opportunity to explore elements in literature that might not immediately be aspects of a novel they would otherwise gravitate toward analyzing.

Close reading affords students the opportunity to explore elements in literature that might not immediately be aspects of a novel they would otherwise gravitate toward analyzing. For instance, Zoya and Allison, who were in the literature circle team reading Victor Hugo's *The Hunchback of Notre-Dame*, read the same book in a very different way. Zoya was intrigued by the way the gypsy Esmeralda was treated and how other characters were drawn to her beauty. This led her to explore the way in which various cultures have different standards for beauty. Allison was curious about the way in which violence was used as a form of entertainment in this novel. This idea piqued her interest, and she ended up exploring entertainment trends and cultural influence on entertainment over the years.

Through questioning, both Zoya and Allison were able to look closely at elements of the novel and extend the connection between Paris, France, in 1482 and their lives in the United States today. Zoya also ended up exploring her topic through a differential feminist critical lens in her analysis of beauty expectations for women. While these ninth graders would not be formally introduced to lenses of literary criticism until their junior year, we found it interesting and valuable that they began to analyze their texts through literary theory. We will explore both Zoya's and Allison's projects in Chapter 5.

Beverly and Raywa both read *The Curious Incident of the Dog in the Night-Time* by Mark Haddon (2004) and analyzed the work with a close reading on culture. Through her reflections, Beverly explored the main character Christopher's life living with Asperger's syndrome, and she extended her reflection to explore how our culture responds to people with Asperger's syndrome. In one of her reflections, Beverly wrote, "And even if Christopher likes being alone, should he just stay cut off from everyone else? In what ways can we help these people to learn how to connect with others?" Like several students, Raywa found her close reading through careful analysis of cultural details in the text. Her work in the culture log focused on finding cultural markers, which allowed her to recognize the cultural setting of the book (see Table 3.1).

Table 3.1 Example Culture Log From Raywa

Culture Characteristics and Artifacts of Culture	Why It Matters and Impacts the Story and Reader
"I put the dog down on the lawn and moved back 2 meters" p. 4	This is an artifact of culture. Everywhere other than the U.S. uses the metric system. This sets up and gives a clue to the location of the story. The metric system is a specific representation of culture.
"lose my rag" p. 9 "... wee on the clothes ..." p. 14 "It's a bloody dog" p. 20	The way we talk is also a direct representation of what culture we belong to. We have developed slang and ways to say things that differ from culture to culture. These are words/sayings that they say over in the U.K. but we never hear.
p. 13 = uses Euro sign "... cost billions of pounds" p. 25	Currency is also a way culture defines where we come from. Nowhere in this book does it say where this book takes place, but we can figure it out due to these little culture clues.
"... wore a fleece with a zip down the front which was pink and it had a tiny label which said Berghaus on the left bosom" p. 19	Berghaus is a U.K. outdoor clothing brand. This also shows locational and cultural belonging with clothing. We in the U.S. also have certain brands we wear a lot, just like in the British culture.
"Scooby Doo" p. 25	This isn't such a defined aspect of culture. There are some things that we can all relate to. Scooby Doo is the entertainment that most people have seen and watched. This is part of a world culture that binds and connects us.

George also created a high-quality reflection as one of his Youth Voices blog posts (see the prompt described in Lesson 11 on page 86) during this part of the inquiry unit. It is clear that the literature circle work with dialectic journals and the culture log has afforded him the opportunity to collect notes on his thinking as demonstrated in this reflection. Additionally, this piece reflects George's use of reading strategies for careful analysis, such as predicting, while also exploring cultural elements throughout his reflection.

Ender's Game is a book about a boy named Ender Wiggin who is a genius. I think the book is very well written and thought out. The culture aspects in the book are very interesting due to the book being written in the 1970s. This influenced the book even though the actual book takes place in the future. I really love how everything is put almost into the future with desks, spaceships, and even the people. The way they talk, the book's setting is almost a new world with different cultures from ours today. Some parts of the book are confusing including how Peter is always angry and even chokes Ender but apologizes in the end. It doesn't clarify that.

The 14th chapter of *Ender's Game* by Orson Scott Card might leave a reader feeling shocked because Mazer, a character in the book, manipulates Ender in a way nobody would ever guess and it shocks you. An example of this is on page 296. Mazer laughed, a loud laugh that filled the room. "Ender you never played me. You never played a game since I became your enemy." This is shocking because Mazer admits that Ender has been commanding the fleets in the "games" to actually destroy the buggers. Mazer when he first meets Ender even admits that he thinks it's due to a miscommunication that they are fighting the buggers, and now he is laughing that Ender destroyed them.

So far, the culture in *Ender's Game* might remind a reader of the story in another book, *Among the Brave*, because both governments are almost run by military powers. Both are set in the future. They have a common child control law only allowing a certain number of children to be born in a family. If families have extra children, they are often looked at as a minority in both books. *Among the Brave*, though, is more strict on extra children.

After this part of the book, most readers probably will be looking forward to reading the rest of this book because you have to wonder what Ender is thinking and what he will do to react to this news. I wouldn't think he would be very happy to hear what he has done. The government was only scared of Ender not cooperating due to him being the savior of the world, but now the government doesn't need him. What will happen? What's probably going to happen next is that Ender might either leave because he is so mad and have mixed emotions or maybe even rebel against what the government is doing.

You have to wonder what Ender is going to do after the book ends. I wonder what people will think of what Ender did and how he kept the Queen to repopulate the buggers.

In addition to supporting the close reading focus for this week of lessons, we asked students to pull their ideas together by organizing their material in digital spaces. Up to this point, students had worked on several ideas related to inquiry and culture, so this week we wanted to move them a step forward to help them see what they had done, focusing their ideas related to culture and inquiry in connection with their literature circle book. As a class, we reflected on past work, and we also began the intentional process of teaching research skills, including reading a variety of texts to inform their thinking.

To help students monitor comprehension of their reading of their literature circle book, as well as to encourage them to dig deeper in their literature circle reading, we asked them to work in small groups to discuss their reading. In this way, students also served as models for one another as they shared their skills in reading, reflecting upon reading practices, and listening.

LESSON 12. LITERATURE CIRCLE MEETING 1: ENGAGING IN ACTIVE DISCUSSIONS

The purpose of this lesson is to help students

- Practice discussion skills and better understand literature circle books through careful, thoughtful discussion

- Analyze their literature circle text through close reading of passages, developing and discussing questions, and exploring culture artifacts and characteristics

- Establish shared space for notes on the class wiki to see examples of others' work and collaboratively build knowledge

Digital Spaces for Group Discussion

Before jumping into the literature circle group conversations, we established a space for students to post notes for discussion. Each group had their own page within our class wiki for taking notes about their literature circle book. This was especially helpful for two reasons:

1. Groups with similar texts could read each other's ideas.
2. All students could use the work of other groups as a model.

After we reviewed discussion skills as a class, including the specific behaviors highlighted on the Lesson 12 handout (see page 97), students were ready to engage in the group conversation. Dawn monitored groups by walking around, observing, and taking notes on group conversations and student comments related to the text, as well as students' work with discussion skills, including engaging all members of their team. When groups appeared to be done with their discussion and notes, we asked them to make sure they had thoroughly discussed their work with questions, dialectic journals, and culture logs. If they discovered that they had not, then we expected them to engage in further conversations.

Most groups took the entire class period to discuss their reading and prepared materials. If groups were indeed thorough in their discussion and completed their notes, they returned to Youth Voices to respond to discussion posts from members of their group. Since students wrote discussion posts prior to this meeting (for full description of this writing reflection exercise, see Chapter 2 (Lesson 11, page 86), all students had plenty to read and respond to from their peer work. George's reflection on page 94 is one such Youth Voices post that his peers could comment on. Additionally, we coached students to check their team notes for accuracy based on their discussion, as well as to make sure each team member knew how to access and add to the digital space. In this way, all team members were required to review the notes that represented the discussion. This ensured that all students practiced use of the wiki and understood the tech skill, although the main focus remained on the discussion itself and not the technology.

Lesson 12. Literature Circle Meeting 1: Engaging in Active Discussions

Discuss the assigned pages of reading with your group. Active discussions involve every member of your group, and they require you to hone your discussion skills. Remember to practice the following:

Body Language

- Visibly show you are listening through leaning in, looking at the speaker, and nodding your head.

- Demonstrate engagement by using your notes and book as reference points.

- Use the computer to type notes, but tip the screen down when talking with your classmates to engage in the dialogue with your fellow readers, not the screen.

- Engage with each person in the team.

- Monitor your own "airtime" so that everyone is able to discuss and share equally.

- Share collective leadership by taking turns within the team.

Demonstrate Knowledge About the Reading Through Your Discussion and Notes

- Engage in conversation related to the book and big ideas in the reading.

- Use sticky notes to mark passages to discuss.

- Use your discussion questions that you prepared for this meeting (Lesson 8).

- Give clear responses and use the materials you prepared for the meeting, including your thinking from the dialectic journal and culture log (Lesson 8).

- Explore the essential questions for our "Reading Our World and Exploring Perspectives: Identity and Culture" inquiry unit.

- Take collective notes on our online class space.

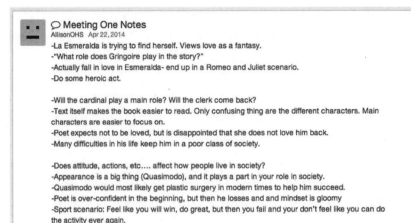

○ **Meeting One Notes**
AllisonOHS Apr 22, 2014
-La Esmeralda is trying to find herself. Views love as a fantasy.
-"What role does Gringoire play in the story?"
-Actually fall in love in Esmeralda- end up in a Romeo and Juliet scenario.
-Do some heroic act.

-Will the cardinal play a main role? Will the clerk come back?
-Text itself makes the book easier to read. Only confusing thing are the different characters. Main characters are easier to focus on.
-Poet expects not to be loved, but is disappointed that she does not love him back.
-Many difficulties in his life keep him in a poor class of society.

-Does attitude, actions, etc.... affect how people live in society?
-Appearance is a big thing (Quasimodo), and it plays a part in your role in society.
-Quasimodo would most likely get plastic surgery in modern times to help him succeed.
-Poet is over-confident in the beginning, but then he losses and and mindset is gloomy
-Sport scenario: Feel like you will win, do great, but then you fail and your don't feel like you can do the activity ever again.
-Personal experience regarding the above topic.

Allison's Notes From Her Group's First Literature Circle Discussion

Source: Screenshot courtesy of Wikispaces.

The image above shows an example of how one group of students managed their literature circle discussion and notes by developing categories and questions surrounding their topics and offering specific content to address questions.

Extensions and Adaptations for Lesson 12

There are many ways to establish discussion in the classroom, from Socratic questioning techniques, to whole-class and small-group discussions, to pair sharing. Depending upon your placement for this inquiry unit, the discussion work you have already done, and your students' needs, you may need to take different steps with your students. If students decide to designate specific note takers for their literature circle discussions, remember to keep each person accountable for the information in the notes. Students can use many different spaces to take notes, from Wikispaces to Google Drive to a pencil and paper. Each medium has a different feel, setup, and focus. Teachers may find it particularly helpful to explore these different capabilities with students to meet the purposes and needs of different classrooms.

LESSON 13. SELF-ASSESSMENT AND REFLECTION

The purpose of this lesson is to help students

- Reflect through self-assessment on their journal process work (dialectic journals and culture logs) and preparation (careful critical reading, note taking, writing of discussion questions) prior to the literature circle meeting

- Identify quality work and areas that need improvement in their work

- Reflect on skills used in discussion

- Practice supporting their self-assessment with evidence and explanation of their work (practice argument skills)

- Review individual journaling and collective notes from literature circle discussion

- Reiterate expectations for work with journaling and close reading of literature circle books

- Use student self-assessment reflections to establish improvement goals as they continue to improve on journaling, close reading, and discussing

- Provide the teacher with valuable feedback related to students' progress and assessment of their own work

Scaled Questions and Written Reflections

Lesson 13 focuses on self-assessment. As students engage in learning, it is important to help them reflect and find ways to monitor their own learning and goals (Wiggins & McTighe, 2005). Setting goals and monitoring learning are important moves for students to take ownership of their learning and become aware of their own progress. Self-assessment is also important to support students' reading, writing, and reflecting, so that students are monitoring their comprehension, writing development, and growth as learners. It additionally honors students' voice and perspectives on their work.

After our first literature circle meeting, we designed a set of scaled questions to help students assess themselves and reflect upon their work to prepare for and participate in literature circle discussions (see the handout on page 102). We also included three written response questions in this self-assessment to encourage students to use evidence to support the accuracy of their scaled responses. This self-assessment approach not only offered opportunity for reflection and self-assessment but also supported practice with argument skills, as students had to explain with evidence why they scored themselves in a particular way. This not only served as a clear explanation or proof of the preparation work they did for the literature circle, but also reinforced argument skills practiced during the school year; as they would also need these skills for their inquiry-based research essay (see Chapter 4), it provided opportunity for continual writing practice.

Before we asked students to complete the self-assessment, we reminded them to think about the goals they had established for their reading, as well as the reading activities they were engaging in with their literature circle assignment (Lesson 8). We also discussed how self-assessment is an important part of monitoring their learning. Moreover, we invited students to be honest and identify both ways in which they were successful with their work and ways in which they could improve. Sometimes students want to rate themselves high to show that they are doing well and to make sure the teacher also rates them high. This is a fair consideration on the part of students, as some teachers do rate students based on how they rate themselves, and there are times and places where this may make sense. However, in this case, we truly wanted students to be honest with themselves and us and to use this self-assessment as a reflection and opportunity to think about how to improve. To address this, we explained the need for honesty and evaluation based on improvement. Since students understood their audience and the purpose for the assessment, they were more honest and clear in their responses for reflection and learning.

Reflecting on their work after the first literature circle meeting allowed students to think about the effectiveness of their preparation and their work within the discussion team. These reflections also gave students the opportunity to consider ways to improve future meetings.

For instance, Raywa, who read *The Curious Incident of the Dog in the Night-Time,* reflected on her experience: "The lit circles were very enjoyable and fun, which is good because sometimes I find them to be boring. I was prepared well, and since our group works well together, we were able to share and discuss our thinking during it. The hardest part was figuring out how to organize our notes, but we figured it out so next time will be even better." In this instance, Raywa shared what was going well in her group, but she also took away ideas for organizing notes, which is important to her improvement.

Beverly, who also read *The Curious Incident of the Dog in the Night-Time,* wrote, "I thought that I prepared pretty well for the first meeting. My culture log mostly included some dialogue (difference between American English and British English) and aspects of British education (A-level exams). The first literature circle meeting went extremely well. We all came prepared and worked well together, and we all very much enjoyed reading the book. I think, for next time, we could write more notes instead of fangirling so much. :)" While these reflections demonstrate that the literature circle went well—and honestly, most students noted their meetings went well because, in fact, they did—Beverly did recognize that improvements can always be made, such as challenging her team to go beyond merely "fangirling," or appreciating the text and one another, and to go even further in depth with note taking.

The majority of the student self-assessment responses were positive like these examples. Still, some noted honestly, "I just didn't get my work done" or "I budgeted my time poorly and took weak notes for the culture log." Others shared where struggles with content were an issue, which was helpful for individualizing instruction in one-on-one meetings with the teacher to help students with comprehension and develop strategies to approach reading and writing.

Student Ownership of Note Taking

It is important to note that we made the deliberate decision to allow students the chance to select how they would take notes. Instead of requiring everyone to use Google Drive (or a notebook or sticky notes), we wanted to honor students' individual goals and give them responsibility over their application of reading strategies that worked for them.

Prior to this inquiry unit, Dawn had provided students with opportunities to try out various reading and note-taking strategies, such as use of graphic organizers to chart thinking or monitoring predictions, questions, and observations with a two-column chart, noting "what happened in the text" and "my response to the text," to determine how they might best compile their notes. As part of the self-assessment for this lesson, we asked students to provide information about how they approached this work and where they were keeping their materials as noted in the Lesson 13 handout (page 102). We also asked students to briefly explain why they were making choices to keep notes in a specific way. In this way, we were honoring student decisions, but also prompting reflection of their note-taking process. In response to this question, students wrote about trying out different approaches and appreciating the opportunity to try different ways to take notes. Some wrote that they read their book at home each night and didn't have a computer beside them; thus, writing their notes was a helpful practice. Others noted that they remembered more when they wrote ideas down. Still others said they felt more organized with the digital notes. All of these responses made sense and reflected purposeful decision making and ownership on the part of students. Yet, it is important to note that some students struggled with setting up this work, and we needed to engage in one-on-one review with these students and help them set up their journals (like the example in Lesson 8 on page 79). This self-assessment and review of student notes directed us to know which students to meet with in order to support in this approach to the reading.

Assessment of Literature Circles

To encourage students to expand upon their reading and reflecting, Dawn did not physically collect their work after each literature circle meeting; rather, she specifically collected work half of the time to review it more closely. She did look at each student's work during each literature circle

HAND OUT

Lesson 13. Self-Assessment and Reflection

Self-assessment and reflection are an important part of the learning process. For this self-assessment, be honest with yourself and with your audience—your teacher. The purpose of this assessment is to reflect on your work and think about how to continue improving your close reading and journaling skills so that you can enhance your reading skills.

Please respond to the following questions using the Likert scale of 1 (*low*) to 5 (*high*):

	Low				High
	1	2	3	4	5
How prepared were you for literature circle meeting 1? Be sure to think about how closely you read your book and prepared discussion questions. Also, think about your work with the dialectic journal and culture log as you consider preparation.					
How well did you participate in discussion? Were you actively engaged? Did you participate in nonverbal cues of discussion? Did you ask follow-up questions and use the text for specific references?					
Discussion questions: Rate your quality of discussion questions. Remember that quality questions encourage strong, sophisticated discussion and prompt exploration.					
Dialectic journal: Rate the quality of your journal. Does your journal thoroughly record your thinking about passages from the novel? Do the responses to the passage show analysis of the passage, including the significance of the passage?					
Culture log: Rate the quality of your work with your cultural log. Does your log include both artifacts and characteristics of culture? Does it analyze these artifacts and characteristics of culture?					

(Continued)

(Continued)

In writing, reflect upon and defend your responses to the focus areas, explaining each of your ratings.

Also, reflect on your experience in literature circle meeting 1. What worked well? What would you improve for next time? Why?

Review how you decided to set up your notes. Where did you complete your journal (Google Drive, the online class space, in a notebook, with sticky notes, etc.)? Why did you decide to set up your journal in this way? What worked about this setup? Why? What didn't work? Why? In what ways does this setup support your reading? Why?

meeting. Moreover, students said that they wanted to keep their notes to review their ideas as they read. This step made sense for two reasons:

- It encouraged students to take ownership over their work.

- It reduced the amount of grading required between literature circle meetings.

Throughout the work with literature circles, Dawn briefly met with student groups and individuals at different intervals to check thinking, look at notes, review materials, and discuss their progress. Since it can be tricky for teachers to find classroom time to talk with each student individually, sometimes Dawn met with a few students each day during other class activities. Additionally, in some cases, she was able to read parts of student work before the student meetings (particularly with notes shared via Google Drive). These strategies helped her with time management.

These mini-conferences were quite positive as students were honest with themselves and Dawn about their progress. In some cases, students didn't realize what they were missing or how they could improve, which was the exact purpose of the conference. In this way, assessment honored student self-assessment and student growth, as well as monitoring instruction to support student learning. Additionally, if students were not doing their work or being honest about their progress, they were open to reviewing this with Dawn.

Extensions and Adaptations for Lesson 13

Teachers can help students focus on self-assessment and reflection in many ways. They can prompt student writing and reflection, such as through discussion and writing. Students can discuss their progress with peers (if the lesson and community of collaboration are constructed clearly and purposefully so they feel comfortable with this type of sharing) and receive feedback from each other about ways to improve. Additionally, students can discuss improvement with the teacher in short conferences. Written self-assessment and reflection can be collected in a different manner too. We used Google Forms, but the handout for Lesson 13 (page 102) would work as well.

To support student thinking and work with analysis, make sure to ask students to justify why they scored themselves in a specific way; this may also be an important conversational point in a mini-conference. Within an English language arts classroom, it can be helpful for students to directly identify what they are doing in their writing and reading, as well as the impact that their reading and reflecting in writing have on their learning.

LESSON 14. LANGUAGE IN AMERICAN CULTURE

The purpose of this lesson is to help students

- Analyze an artifact of culture with a video commercial focused on Americans' use of language

- Explore different ways to learn information, such as through a jigsaw reading and researching on social media

- Reflect upon the changing ways in which people retrieve information and how research is impacted by a society-mediated culture

Activating Prior Knowledge and Building Knowledge With a Jigsaw Reading

A focus on language can clearly take many different forms. Providing numerous opportunities for students to engage in reading strategies, as well as to hone their discussion skills and collaboratively read and pull out key ideas from a text, is a valuable way for teachers to help students develop reading skills. To introduce this lesson, we asked students to view a controversial commercial (*Official Coca-Cola "Big Game" Commercial*, 2014) to activate ideas related to language in the United States, and then engage in a jigsaw reading of an article from the PBS series website "Do You Speak American?" (www.pbs.org/speak). The documentary of the same name (MacNeil, 2005) originally aired in 2005, the series features Americans speaking a variety of English dialects from various regions of the country, and the website offers articles focusing on various aspects of American language.

During the 2014 Super Bowl, a new Coca-Cola commercial aired that highlighted the song "America the Beautiful" (*Official Coca-Cola "Big Game" Commercial*, 2014). In various U.S. landscapes, people with different backgrounds are highlighted engaging in activities they appreciate as part of their culture, from playing sports to eating traditional ethnic food. Additionally, "America the Beautiful" is sung in various languages, while people of different ethnicities are shown. This commercial aired with some appreciation and some controversy (Killough, 2014). We pulled up some of these conversations for students by exploring hashtags such as #Cokecommercial and #SpeakAmerican. The controversy prompted a vigorous whole-class discussion ranging in analysis of the ways the commercial seems to appreciate diversity to the reaction of those upset by the manner in which America is represented, including that the song is performed in many different languages. This discussion served as an effective way for students to begin to look at contemporary conversations and activate their own prior knowledge and opinions surrounding a text or a cultural artifact.

We then extended the students' conversations through a jigsaw reading strategy that involved selecting and reading a text from PBS's "Do You Speak American?" A jigsaw reading is set up much like a literature circle. In this case, students read different articles in small groups, discuss the articles, and then (this is the jigsaw piece) share information from the articles with other students who have read a different text. We designed this jigsaw reading to support student reading development, as well as discussion, and to support students in learning more about language in the United States. The purpose of a jigsaw reading is to disseminate knowledge from a variety of texts. Instead of reading ten articles, students read one and learn about nine others through discussion with the original reader of each selected text. Through the discussion with peers about the text they studied, students will learn if they would like to or should read one of the texts that others read. For our purposes, they did not need to read about each text in order to learn something new about American language. In this way, students were exposed to a variety of issues related to American English and its dialects.

At times, the topic of American language can be quite controversial. Depending on their location within the country, as well as their background experiences, students may or may not have ever considered the many factors involved. The PBS series offers several texts for consideration. Whether you select from this set or offer others, asking students to explore various issues related to language builds context for basic knowledge on this topic and helps students practice close reading and analysis skills.

Research Methods in Our Socially Mediated Society

Our discussions focused on analysis of the PBS text and reactions to the commercial as shared via social networks and reported in opinion and news sources. This allowed us to discuss issues related to language that students had heard about in the news and that were relevant to current conversations. We also used the commercial as a springboard into discussing how people do research in contemporary society. This led to a conversation about social media, including using Twitter and following hashtags as a form of research.

For instance, students noted that researchers who wanted to learn about various reactions to the commercial might use Twitter to find comments in this social media platform. The use of hashtags or #—though sometimes dismissed as simple Internet memes—also can serve the purpose of identifying trends online and finding information through tagging. Tagging, which is essentially providing a descriptor word for a text, is helpful for various

Lesson 14. Language in American Culture

Language is a major part of cultural identity. It is a part of our lives and may vary based on if we are at home or in a work (or school) setting and our audience. Many countries have named a national language. In the United States of America, we currently do not have a national language.

Activity 1: Reading a Commercial

- View "America Is Beautiful" (http://youtu.be/RiMMpFcy-HU), a Coca-Cola commercial from February 2014.

- Share reactions to the commercial in a pair share, then in a whole-class discussion.

- Explore reactions to the commercial (available from http://cnn.it/1fSRbOM).

Activity 2: Sacred Writing Time

- Write about your reaction to the commercial, as well as the reactions of others.

- What does the commercial suggest about American culture and language in the United States?

- What do the reactions to the commercial teach us about American culture?

Activity 3: Jigsaw Reading

- In teams, select one of the articles from "Do You Speak American?" (www.pbs.org/speak).

- Read the article, mark it up using reading strategies we have studied this year (such as questioning the text, making connections, writing your reactions next to the text), and discuss it. Remember that you can put the article in a Google Doc and comment on the text (see the Tech Tip in Chapter 1, page 41).

- Identity at least five key ideas from the reading to share with the class. After our reading, you will be sharing your information with other groups, so be sure to take good notes about the article to share with others.

- In small groups, break into new teams, with each person discussing a different article. Take notes on each article.

(Continued)

(Continued)

Article Name: _____

What are the major points of the article?

Article Name: _____

What are the major points of the article?

Article Name: _____

What are the major points of the article?

Activity 4: Reflection Time

- What ideas did you learn about language in the United States? What reaction do you have to the reading or the commercial?

- What purpose does controversy have in a culture? How do we learn about controversy in American culture?

- In what various ways do we learn about popular topics? How is research changing in our world today?

Available for download at **http://resources.corwin.com/writingrewired**

searches for information. Students recognized that even for people who are not involved with Twitter, understanding the role of hashtags in a culture is important because tagging provides opportunities to participate in online conversations related to pertinent topics.

We know that research is changing in a socially mediated society. Still, researching in databases and finding reliable sources are essential (we will explore this work in Chapter 4), but the shift in learning through social media platforms is now a reality. We need to teach students to search what is trending, as much as we also need to teach them that not everything they read in such platforms is true. Through this brief point of recognizing hashtags, our students began those types of conversations.

This is why we introduced this conversation before we started to discuss the inquiry-based research essay. We knew that the work for the final essay would require more research, which might include following hashtags, but at this point in the inquiry unit, we wanted students to think about various ways in which people gain information in society—and how we choose to gain information in different ways depending on why we need it and how we plan to use it.

Extensions and Adaptations for Lesson 14

This work could be extended to cover a few days. Teachers might ask students to engage in a focused study of language issues within their community, including being ethnographers or interviewing people about issues related to language. In terms of language articles, there are many you might select to use with your students. Others to consider include

- "Mother Tongue" by Amy Tan (1999)

- "The Struggle to Be an All-American Girl" by Elizabeth Wong (n.d.)

- "A Nation Divided by One Language" from *The Guardian* (Crawford, 2001)

- Resources from PBS's "Do You Speak American?" including "Hooked on Ebonics" (Baron, 2005) and "The Midwest Accent" (Gordon, 2005)

As you select articles to share with students, be sure to read and understand them and think carefully about the implications of the content with students. Some of the language texts noted above are narratives, and others are articles. Some are biased and one-sided. Depending on the article, it is important to think about supporting student learning by scaffolding ideas and offering texts that deal with various sides of an issue. Additionally, it is important to use reading strategies to help students understand the content, as well as to provide context for information that may be related to the argument of the text.

You will also want to identify cultural artifacts to explore what will interest your students. As part of our class collaborative researching, we started a resources tab on our class Wikispace to share articles and other resources related to each topic. Teachers may also wish to integrate other social media tools into the inquiry unit, such as Twitter, to help students become more active researchers and search for and follow noted experts or timely and relevant hashtag conversations from leading thinkers. Students might also use curation tools such as Pinterest or Scoop to take on the roles of active curators themselves and to follow existing collections from hobbyists and experts alike.

Other options, such as RSS (really simple syndication) and search alerts, can also allow students to stay on top of their inquiry. RSS is a technology that "pushes" content out to websites and the apps on phones and tablets. Rather than having to visit a specific URL to find information, students can use a tool such as Feedly, Feedspot, Flipboard, or NewsBlur to organize news feeds, blogs, photos, videos, and other web content. All offer free and premium accounts, so getting started is relatively easy. Once students identify key topics, news sources, and bloggers, they can check their RSS reader regularly for the most recent information related to their topic.

Finally, search engines, most notably Google, offer a variety of options to customize searches. Advanced Search allows users to search with specific queries, such as "all these words," "this exact word or phrase," or "with any of these words." Searching can also happen within a specific domain name, and by file type. Google also offers custom search alerts, allowing users to customize search terms and conditions, such as to look through everything on the web, or only the latest news. These custom search alerts can then be saved into RSS feeds, and added to a reader, or they can be delivered as an automatic e-mail. Last, for students later in their high school careers and into college, Google Scholar offers links directly to academic research articles.

LESSON 15. LITERATURE CIRCLE MEETING 2: CLOSE READING OF PASSAGES

The purpose of this lesson is to help students

- Refine discussion skills

- Collaboratively clarify and extend thinking related to a common text

- Critically review passages of a text for close reading and improvement of comprehension

- Refine personal inquiry related to literature circle reading

- Practice making thinking visible through collaboratively sharing ideas and notations

- Identify passages related to big ideas or culture connections

- Practice analysis skills of explaining a passage and thinking about that text

- Hone close reading skills

Close Reading: Text Exploration and Analysis

This second literature circle meeting built upon skills (close reading, purposeful journaling to talk back to the text, question writing, etc.) students were practicing through their preparation for the meetings; it also built upon their discussion skills. While we expected students to continue to explore their discussion questions as they moved forward, here we gave them a specific additional goal of analyzing a few specific passages.

First, we asked students to select five quotes from their literature circle book that they felt mattered to the text and to their thinking. We invited students to reread and discuss these passages together, as well as to share ideas related to why the passages related to the text. In this way, students engaged in a close reading of a text, breaking down a part of the text to analyze the bigger picture. Additionally, this activity built upon inquiry work as students debated which passages were relevant and shared why they found specific passages to be relevant. They also had to determine relevant passages as a team, which required them to explore the text carefully.

> We knew that developing students' close reading skills and their ability to select relevant points in the text would set them up for success with their research.

This activity added to the foundation we wanted students to build prior to launching into the inquiry for the actual research essay. In particular, we knew that developing students' close reading skills and their ability to select relevant points in the text would set them up for success with their research. Through the literature circle teams' work, students had opportunities to practice the skills they would employ for reading research.

In Video 3.1, you will see Dawn remind students about skills they are practicing through literature circle discussions, such as how we engage in discussion in face-to-face meetings and in digital spaces.

watch it here

Video 3.1

http://resources.corwin
.com/writingrewired

Extensions and Adaptations for Lesson 15

Structuring close reading opportunities for students can take different forms through journaling, marking up a text, and analyzing passages they determine or you determine, as well as publishing discussions online.

HAND
OUT

Lesson 15. Literature Circle Meeting 2: Close Reading of Passages

In addition to preparing the journal required for each meeting, for this second meeting, focus on close reading by completing the following. In both your dialectic journal and your culture log, record at least five passages from your book to analyze in your meeting.

Activity 1: Discussion in Literature Circle Teams

Discuss the questions that your team members prepared for this meeting. You should also share insights from your dialectic journal and culture log.

Activity 2: Collaborative Close Reading

Select a few passages to read closely as a team. Mark the text using Google Drive and embed your work in our online space. To get the text in your document, either find an excerpt online, such as from Google Books or Amazon; take a picture; or type the excerpt. Make comments that note specific insights from your reading, including cultural references that explore either artifacts or characteristics of culture.

After your initial close reading of the passage, prepare to share your ideas with others and reread the passage and analyze it again. In review, to create a presentation of close reading related to your book, use the following steps as a guide:

- Start a Google presentation and share it with your literature circle team.
- Record the passage either by taking a picture of the text or by finding the excerpt online.
- Add the passage to a Google presentation.
- Respond to the text with comment features on Google Drive.
- Embed your presentation on your project page of our online class space.

Activity 3: Review Close Reading Passages From Other Literature Circle Groups

Share today's notes and close reading on your online literature circle space. Then visit at least one other literature circle team's notes and close reading. When you read the work of other teams, consider how the team analyzed the passage for insights, connections to essential questions, and cultural references. You should see a variety of approaches to this work; however, you should also see careful and thoughtful connections relevant to our essential questions for study in the unit "Reading Our World and Exploring Perspectives: Identity and Culture."

Integrating this skill throughout the school year was helpful for us because students recognized this as a common class practice and understood our expectations for close careful reading and the importance of extending their understanding beyond plot.

We know students cannot always mark up a school book, so sticky notes can be helpful. Additionally, we had students take a picture of the text, then mark it up within a digital space. Students could also find the passage online or type it out. Additionally, copying articles for students to mark up can be helpful to practice the skill of close reading. Nearly all e-book formats, including Kindle and ePub, have annotation tools students can use for close reading. Even digital books checked out from libraries allow readers to mark up a text, and often those annotations stay in the version of your digital text for the next time you check out that book.

It is important to provide students with opportunities for more than one literature circle discussion. Based on student experience with discussion and potential need for more practice, you might even offer guides for discussion and question strategies, such as sentence starters like "This passage makes me think of ___ because ___" or "This text related to ____ text because ___." In our case, students built their skills through discussion and question writing the entire year. Exploring different types of questions from closed-ended to open-ended, from world connections to literary analysis, can be quite helpful for students. Many resources are available online from various disciplines that support work with student questioning and Socratic discussion. Additionally, several books are available to explore on this topic, such as Matt Copeland's *Socratic Circles: Fostering Critical and Creative Thinking in Middle and High School* (2005).

LESSON 16. QUESTIONING AND SPECULATING

The purpose of this lesson is to help students

- Reflect on reading and cultural questions
- Narrow inquiry questions

Guiding Students to Narrow Inquiry Questions

Guiding students to narrow inquiry questions involves careful coaching through opportunities to write and reflect, as well as to share ideas with classmates and the teacher. Lesson 16 focuses entirely on student reflection as a means for students to write their way into narrowing their inquiry questions, which will ultimately become the focus for their inquiry-based research essay.

HAND OUT

Lesson 16. Questioning and Speculating

Today, you will be writing about your book in connection to your personal inquiry question(s). Think about it: How does your literature circle book guide your thinking about bigger inquiry questions and culture?

Activity 1: Review the Questioning and Speculating Guide From Youth Voices

- In this guide (http://youthvoices .net/node/36247), you are prompted to free write about your book and ask questions based on a close reading of passages and various story lines in your text. Additionally, using quotes from your book can help explain your thinking.

- This guide offers ways to approach this writing, but you may extend beyond the guide in your writing. Think carefully about how your novel of study inspires your questioning and inquiry.

Activity 2: Questioning and Speculating Blog Post

- Brainstorm: How does your literature circle book guide your thinking about bigger inquiry questions and culture?

- Compose your blog post. Remember to include your book and inquiry questions.

- Post your discussion blog on Youth Voices. Don't forget to add an image to your post as this is digital writing and a requirement for posts on Youth Voices.

Activity 3: Respond to Your Peers

Read other blog discussion posts from our class—you might even find posts from other schools!—and respond to your peers. For a few ideas on how to respond to posts, check out the Youth Voices guide at http://youthvoices.net/node/23265. Use the following considerations for responding to peers:

- Address the author by name.

- Be specific in your response. Reference an idea or line from the author's text to celebrate, question, or wonder about.

- Offer constructive responses related to big ideas in the post and raise questions to spark further exploration.

- Keep in mind that this response is designed to share ideas and develop thinking and questioning related to each person's inquiry question.

Activity 4: Narrow Inquiry Questions

After writing and responding to others, explore comments that you received. You might find it appropriate to respond to your responses. In most cases, it is common and expected that you respond to the responses you receive.

Think about your own inquiry questions and start to narrow your focus to one topic or question. Explore resources related to this topic. In this way, you are working on idea generating, gathering resources, and narrowing your inquiry.

Available for download at **http://resources.corwin.com/writingrewired**

So far, students have been engaged in thoughtful questioning for discussion and built connections through reviewing passages, as well as noting cultural references, in their literature circle text. They have speculated related to essential cultural questions through whole-class text analysis from a variety of media focused on different artifacts of culture. As students continue to explore questions, it is also time for them to narrow their topics for further specific research.

The following example of a questioning and speculating blog post is from Allison. In this post, she connects her literature circle novel to her inquiry questions. Allison was exploring the role of entertainment throughout history during the reading and journaling process, and here her ideas for inquiry and research begin to solidify. We appreciate the specificity of Allison's ideas and examples. She weaves her literature circle book in with her inquiry question in smart moves with examples from the text and questions that follow. Additionally, Allison makes her ideas relevant to today as she turns a critical eye to analyze entertainment in contemporary society.

> Guiding students to narrow inquiry questions involves careful coaching through opportunities to write and reflect, as well as to share ideas with classmates and the teacher.

As I read *The Hunchback of Notre-Dame* by Victor Hugo (1892), I notice that there are many cultural aspects that differ from our own culture, but other aspects that are very similar. One question that has popped out at me because of my reading is about entertainment, and it asks: How does the entertainment people have available to them affect their lifestyle and attitudes?

In the book, the people of Paris have to entertain themselves on a daily basis, and when a public event comes up that provides entertainment, everyone seems to flock to that point in order to add some variety to a life that is fairly monotonous. A big event that draws many people is public torture. Like a moth to a flame, the people of Paris all turn out for a display of punishment. They have become so desensitized to public punishment that they make almost no move to stop the action and even partake in punishing the criminal. The author states, "The people, accustomed to waiting for public punishments and executions, did not manifest too much impatience." This cultural aspect of public torture can be recognized by people all over the world as being French, because it is well known that a lot of Western European countries used to publicly torture criminals.

The citizens of Victor Hugo's Paris, however, are not just influenced by public torture, but also enjoy viewing entertainment that is new and different. When the gypsies come to town, everyone is surprised by their acrobatic skills and exotic attitude. La Esmeralda is probably the most attractive to the citizens, drawing big crowds each time she performs in public. The author describes the audience as having their eyes fixed on her, with their mouths hung open. They are fascinated by the unusual, and this makes them curious. This characteristic is something only a Parisian could notice. No one person could say that this aspect is strictly French, so it is not immediately recognizable to the casual visitor.

In our modern-day society, we have many more options available to keep us entertained, such as television, iPads, and desktop computers. This makes us continue to demand to receive information faster, because we have these technologies that allow us to communicate almost instantly. We are also all able to view different categories of entertainment, such as horror, comedies, and romance stories. This alters us individually, whereas the people in Hugo's story have access to the same forms of entertainment, and people were affected together, instead of individually. Entertainment is a big cultural aspect that can affect people in many ways, and with it constantly changing, it is impossible to predict where it will take us next.

As students write questioning and speculating reflections, they start to refine their thinking about their inquiry questions. Some students may need to visit the guide for how to approach this writing more than others, and still others may benefit from looking at a mentor text together. One student may offer his or her blog post writing for discussion for this purpose. When exploring a student text with the class, students could discuss the following questions:

- *What do you appreciate about the ideas in this blog post? How does the author connect his literature circle novel with his inquiry question?*

- *In what way does this author's thinking inspire inquiry? What do you think about her ideas? How does the author make this inquiry relevant to both her novel and the world today?*

- *How would you respond to this author?*

Class discussion such as this would also help foster student examples for how to respond to peers' questioning and speculating ideas.

Extensions and Adaptations for Lesson 16

Structuring students' blogging can happen in different ways, as can formatting responses. One low-tech way to prepare students to use blogs involves setting up chart paper on the walls of your classroom. Identify topics or questions for the chart paper, such as literature circle book titles or major inquiry focus areas. Then pass out sticky notes of a single color and invite students to write about one of the topics. Ask students to place their completed sticky notes on the chart paper. Then pass out sticky notes of a different color. This time, invite students to respond to a post on a topic that they did not originally write about.

This discussion mimics what happens on blogs in how people write and respond to others. You might consider asking students to conduct this activity as a silent discussion, as that is what happens in online spaces, where the written response shows thinking or the voice of the discussion. After students make posts, they will likely want to read responses they have received from others. This exercise can prepare students to move their work with blogging into a fostered discussion for collaboration and support of ideas.

As students start to create their own personal learning networks, they can create their own blogs too. Blogs can also connect with other blogs through a blogroll or a list of links to other blogs.

REFLECTIONS ON DEVELOPING CLOSE READING SKILLS AND ORGANIZING DIGITAL SPACES

The focus of this week of lessons was close, careful, critical reading and reading through a cultural lens. This week also began to lay groundwork for research reading and synthesis through skill development and practice for careful reading, which is important for reading literature as well as researching. Additionally, students focused on gathering resources, exploring learning opportunities in a socially mediated culture and contemporary world, and narrowing the focus on an inquiry question with thoughtful, reflective writing. Integrating research skills into the reading opportunities offered students a chance not only to practice their skills but also to refine their thinking on their topic. This additionally reflected the *Framework for Success in Postsecondary Writing*, as students engaged in habits of mind, such as curiosity, engagement, and creativity (Council of Writing Program Administrators, National Council of Teachers of English, & National Writing Project,

2011). Moreover, students continued to construct thinking through collaboration with peers and teachers and interaction with various texts, as well as writing for various opportunities and purposes.

Rewiring research makes the move of practicing research skills and finding relevant texts for analysis and support of ideas, not only for one paper but also as a way to develop and construct knowledge, explore curiosities, and even enter conversations in socially mediated contexts. We also established this process as a collaborative one, which helped students begin to form learning networks with one another. In this way, students were helping each other as they began to find resources and share ideas related to their inquiry questions.

As students wrestled with various ideas, they constructed knowledge, enhanced their analysis skills, and practiced persistence. This work is no easy task, and we took steps to challenge students so that they would begin to ask important questions. While students can sometimes be overwhelmed by ideas from others in class or from the teacher, we knew that our approach and constant questioning would also help them learn to embrace the messiness of learning, even when some of their questions and responses did not make sense.

We designed the activities in the lessons in this part of the inquiry unit to encourage students to explore as they figured things out and were challenged, such as through a "wobble." At the same time, we were priming students for their next steps of research and writing, which we explore in the following chapters. Students were clearly ready for the next step.

4 Embarking on the Inquiry-Based Research Essay

Collaboration, Citation, and Credibility

> *All inquiries carry with them some element of risk.*
>
> —Carl Sagan, *Broca's Brain: Reflections on the Romance of Science*

One of our key goals for this inquiry unit, "Reading Our World and Exploring Perspectives: Identity and Culture," was to make research a more natural process for students—a process that

- Was filled with curiosity and questioning

- Included collaboration and reflection

- Encouraged students to gather sources and ideas throughout the inquiry process

In this week of lessons, we formally introduced students to the inquiry-based research essay assignment.

KEY FEATURES OF THE INQUIRY-BASED RESEARCH ESSAY ASSIGNMENT

The inquiry-based research essay assignment built on the essential questions of the research unit on cultural awareness and analysis, as well as on personal inquiry. In this way, students recognized that this assignment served as a natural extension of the work they were already doing. It also offered students further opportunities to practice their thinking and reflection related to the rhetorical approach of the writing assignment, MAPS (mode, media, audience, purpose, situation).

Mode

We invited students to create an inquiry-based research essay. We expected students to explore the role of claims, evidence, and warrants to build on the essential skills of developing and structuring a logical argument, which they had practiced throughout the school year (Hillocks, 2011; Smith, Wilhelm, & Fredricksen, 2012).

Just as students had been working with various types of text for analysis throughout this unit, we expected them to explore both their own original research and additional primary and secondary sources in the inquiry-based research essay. Students would include information from published sources and experts related to their topic. In addition, through synthesis of this research, students would connect these sources to their arguments and acknowledge the background of the sources. In this way, students were constructing knowledge from various sources, providing context for their original and synthesized research, and exploring issues related to credibility and reliability. As ninth graders, most of these students were exploring original research and the concept of personal interviews and surveys for the first time. We knew that this active research approach, which required students to use direct sources, would be of great value to them as they continued to do the work of real research-ers throughout their school years and beyond. It also introduced them to the value of thinking about a concept with ideas that do not necessarily come from "experts." By asking students to include both primary and secondary sources, as well as their own research, we built upon the conversations students had been having throughout this unit about texts and analysis, including following trends and hashtags on contemporary research and honoring the conversation and research already published on their specific topic.

Media

Inviting students to write an inquiry-based research essay allowed them to synthesize information and practice writing for a print-based modality. The role of media here included writing a print-based text, while also thinking about the various other features of the rhetorical situation, such as consideration of audience and purpose based on the content of their writing. Further consideration of media for an essay included whether charts or graphs from students' personal surveys or from their secondary research might complement the essay format.

Audience

Through their previous reflections on inquiry and their literature circle books, Dawn's students had started to use writing to construct their own knowledge, to discover and explore what they thought—and to share some of those thoughts with an outside audience through blog posts on Youth Voices and in other venues and discussions, such as on our class wiki, and in their own discussion with peers and adults in their lives. Now, as we asked them to expand this work and to consider possible approaches to their inquiry-based research essay, we invited them to continue to think about audiences beyond just their teacher.

In *Within and Beyond the Writing Process in the Secondary English Classroom*, Dornan, Rosen, and Wilson (2002) address writing as a process, including writing to learn, and prompt writers to think about the role of audience, including the teacher. The authors note that "students should mull over their readers' backgrounds" and that this is important to help writers think about "how their argument might be received" (Dornan et al., 2002, p. 133). It is important to teach students to identify audience as part of the research process so that they can draw feedback from their beginning experiences in a personal learning network and to consider reactions to their ideas thus far.

It is important to teach students to identify audience as part of the research process so they can draw feedback from their personal learning networks.

Specifically, it is important to point out to students from the beginning of the assignment that, as they make the move from invention through inquiry to writing for clarity of ideas, they will need to think critically about audience. We agree with Dornan et al. (2002), who also note that, as students move from discovery writing to a final product, they must "develop from doubt to confidence in meaning-making" and that "content has to be organized in a form that is clear to the reader" (p. 133). In this sense, we were preparing students to make meaning through their inquiry-based research essay and eventually in their media project (see Chapter 5, Lesson 23, page 160).

Purpose

Students frequently identify one of the major purposes for writing as "to get a grade," and honestly, that *is* one of the reasons why they write. However, if students leave their writing experiences at that, then they miss some of the intellectual moves of being a real writer. We reminded students that the inquiry-based research essay was designed to serve several purposes, including building upon the work they had accomplished throughout this unit (including practice with writing and research skills). In particular, we asked them to

- Add to the intellectual conversation surrounding their topic through engagement with an audience that is invested in their question

- Engage in real-life and real-world questions that they are interested in and that relate to their life

These two purposes built upon our learning goals of this inquiry-based research unit and focused on making the work authentic and purposeful for our students. In particular, students built upon ideas that had prompted engagement in public conversations as they explored big ideas, and they continued the real-life inquiry that had served as an essential part of the conversations they had been having over the past few weeks. In addition, we provided minimum requirements for research as a guide for students (as outlined in the assignment; see page 129) but again aimed to focus students on development of ideas and writing to analysis and synthesize those ideas.

Situation

The situation of the writing in this case continued to build upon skills addressed throughout this unit. While we wanted to keep the rhetorical focus of the argument-writing approach centered on the need for students to create an argument using clear claims, evidence, and warrants to meet specific purposes and audiences, we also recognized that some students would be more comfortable if we designated a minimum number of pages required. We decided to set the minimum at three pages but to keep the students focused on developing ideas and proving a claim. Basically, we wanted to ensure that students made a shift away from requirement for length to richness of thinking.

Assessment

We set up assessments to highlight work that students engaged in during this unit, as well as experiences from the entire school year, including argument writing, as well as the use of citations. We wanted students to practice and review these skills throughout the writing process. It is important to recognize that we did not include a standard checklist type of rubric in this assignment. Instead of singling out specific "points" for students to "score," we wanted to encourage self-reflection and create a broad assessment based on evidence of the students' growth and learning, including the skills and habits of mind they used to create their final projects. In addition, this approach supports the concept of writing analysis being about rhetorical decisions in writing. More details on assessment appear in Chapter 6 (see "Assessment: A Flexible, Rhetorical Approach," page 201). To prepare students for the additional skills we would be using in the inquiry-based research essay, we added another layer to the third literature circle meeting with students finding additional sources that relate to their literature circle text (see Lesson 17).

LESSON 17. LITERATURE CIRCLE MEETING 3: INTERTEXTUAL CONNECTIONS

The purpose of this lesson is to help students

- Practice discussion skills through work in another literature circle group discussion

- Better understand their book through careful thoughtful discussion

- Start building connections between their literature circle book and outside texts and their inquiry question

- Reflect on their literature circle book and their inquiry question by blogging about their thinking in a post on Youth Voices

- Explore the inquiry-based research essay assignment and begin gathering resources and focusing ideas

Building Upon Previous Lessons

At this point in the unit, we pointed out to students that they had already begun several important steps toward beginning the inquiry-based research essay, including

- Topic brainstorming through inquiry question development and further reflection of ideas through blog post writing focused on questioning and speculating

- Formulation of ideas related to their potential topic and inquiry question

- Close reading of their literature circle novel

- Analysis of various resources (related to the culture focus) we explored as a class

In particular, we pointed out that the inquiry-based research essay assignment would be grounded in the same cultural conversation we had started during previous lessons, including identifying artifacts of culture and exploring their meaning and how they reflect cultural characteristics (see Lesson 8, page 72). Additionally, students could select questions related to cultural artifacts we studied together, such as the role of images in culture, fashion, media, language, food, and consumerism. Table 4.1 lists some of the initial questions students developed and their literature circle novel, which—in addition to their ongoing writing and research—also fueled their inquiry process.

As we built on students' thinking, reading, and writing related to their inquiry question, we also reminded students that the work of close reading with literature circles was set up to provide practice with the skills they would need for their inquiry-based research essay.

Table 4.1   Student Inquiry Questions and Their Literature Circle Novel

Inquiry Question	Literature Circle Novel
How does image manipulation impact culture? What images do different cultures idolize? Why?	*Ender's Game*
How does the entertainment people have available to them affect their lifestyle and attitudes?	*The Hunchback of Notre-Dame*
What is beauty?	*Staying Fat for Sarah Byrnes*
What role does personal improvement have in our culture?	*The Curious Incident of the Dog in the Night-Time*
Are multiracial people disadvantaged in society?	*Ender's Game*
How have feminine gender roles impacted our culture?	*Doomsday Book*
How is beauty defined in different cultural groups?	*The Hunchback of Notre-Dame*
How do subconscious stereotypes influence human interaction?	*Many Waters*
Can culture be both restricting and liberating?	*The Curious Incident of the Dog in the Night-Time*
How do medical outbreaks prompt mass hysteria?	*Doomsday Book*

We explained that, throughout the new week, students would refine and narrow their questions and practice research skills by exploring

- Reliable sources

- Various types of sources

- Primary sources

- Approaches to interviews and surveys

- Secondary sources

- Fiction (literature circle novel) and nonfiction texts

- Citation tools to help with the research process

The lessons for this week began with a literature circle meeting that asked students to build upon previous lessons by continuing their work with discussion questions and sharing passages from their dialectic journals and culture logs (begun in Lesson 8, page 72). We also built in a research component by inviting students to bring in outside texts—articles from newspapers, magazines, and online sources; videos (including videos from YouTube or even commercials); and images (including art or advertisements)—related to literature and potential inquiry questions.

The day before the third literature circle meeting, the class discussed what sort of material students might bring in. From our previous analysis of food wrappers (Lesson 4, page 44) to various conversations we held in class, students knew they were welcome to use a broad definition of text as they explored materials related to their books and inquiry questions.

By allowing students to share texts with classmates prior to diving into the research essay, we prompted them to

- Engage in research and collaboration as thinking partners with their peers

- Begin to build their research base with their reading

- Build personal learning networks within their literature circle groups, as well as through the Youth Voices community, as they could also share thinking in that space

- Work on being recursive in their exploration of texts and through their reflections, especially those shared through the blogging discussion on Youth Voices

- Put ideas out into the world by posting on the literature circle team wiki page

These opportunities provided a natural start for students to embrace the chance to enter the spirit of genuine inquiry, to examine their own literature circle book more closely, and to dig deeper into the process of writing their inquiry-based research essay. Video 4.1 highlights students building connections between outside texts, their literature circle novel, and inquiry questions.

Introducing the Inquiry-Based Research Essay

After students had a chance to discuss their literature circle book and share outside resources, we felt this was a natural time to introduce the inquiry-based research essay, so Dawn brought students together for a class discussion. We invited them to briefly identify some of the texts that they had brought to the discussion, as well as share how the texts helped inform their thinking. Some students shared that they had brought in interviews with the author; others had found images that helped illustrate the text for them; still others had found research articles that impacted their thinking.

watch it here

Video 4.1
http://resources.corwin
.com/writingrewired

One student, Ricky, who was reading *Doomsday Book* by Connie Willis (1993), was interested in the mass hysteria that happens during medical outbreaks. The article he had brought to class included information about the Black Death, or bubonic plague, and the psychology of mass hysteria.

Another student, Anna, who was interested in Orson Scott Card's personal beliefs impacting his writing of *Ender's Game* (2010), shared articles focused on interviews with Card about his approach to the book.

Still another student, Allison, who was interested in the history of entertainment practices based on reading *The Hunchback of Notre-Dame* by Victor Hugo (1892), collected information about entertainment and the role of social media in society today.

When introducing the inquiry-based research essay assignment, Dawn referenced that students were already engaged in rich work with their inquiry questions, literature books, and exploration of outside texts that related to their questions and novels. In this way, the inquiry-based research essay was a natural extension of their learning. Without having the specific detailed requirements, students had already been engaged in this research and analysis. Students recognized this to be true, particularly since this introduction followed their opportunity to share outside texts.

Dawn then shared the assignment with students both in a printed handout (see page 127) and online. Students appreciated these options so that they could choose how to mark up the assignment as they reviewed it. Throughout the year, students had practiced marking up assignments with highlighters and colored pencils, in both print and digital texts, so they knew that they must carefully read an assignment upon receipt to identify the expectations placed upon them and the requirements to succeed.

Lesson 17. Literature Circle Meeting 3: Intertextual Connections

In addition to preparing your discussion questions, dialectic journal, and cultural log required for each literature circle meeting, for this third meeting, complete the following. Identify and bring in at least two outside texts that relate to an analysis of the novel and your cultural inquiry questions. Remember that texts include print, images, film, and other forms of media.

Activity 1: Literature Circle Discussion of Text

You will discuss the questions that all team members prepared for your meeting. You should also share insights from your dialectic journal and culture log.

Activity 2: Cultural Inquiry Questions and Outside Texts

Share your culture inquiry questions with your team. Then, share your outside texts that relate to your analysis of the novel and your cultural inquiry questions.

Provide a brief overview of the texts that you brought today.

- Why did you select these texts?
- What did you learn from these texts?
- How do the texts relate to the novel?
- How do the texts relate to your questions?

Share your group discussion notes on our online class space.

Activity 3: Reflecting Through Blog Discussion on Youth Voices

Post an individual blog entry on Youth Voices to share your thinking about inquiry questions, your novel, and outside texts.

Activity 4: Introduction to Inquiry-Based Research Essay

Review the handout "Inquiry-Based Research Essay: Cultural Awareness and Analysis." Remember this assignment builds on everything you have been doing with inquiry, including your work with your literature circle book.

As you read the inquiry-based research essay assignment, in the margins, jot down questions you have about what you are being invited to do.

Using either a highlighter on print text or a highlighting tool for a digital text, mark the assignment to draw your attention to key aspects of the assignment.

As homework, review your questioning and speculating reflections and all of your notes on the development of your ideas related to your own inquiry questions. Determine what inquiry question you will explore for your inquiry-based research essay. That is, clearly identify your focus question and topic.

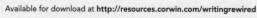

watch it here

Video 4.2

http://resources.corwin
.com/writingrewired

Additionally, the beginning of this assignment intentionally revisits language from the introductory handout on page 9, "'Reading Our World and Exploring Perspectives: Identity and Culture' Essential Questions," so that students can see the connections throughout this unit and recognize that they were already engaged in this work. This move was a decision to support scaffolding, as we directly explained to students that we were building on knowledge throughout this unit. In Video 4.2, Dawn introduces both the inquiry-based research essay assignment and the media assignment.

Extensions and Adaptations for Lesson 17

To invite students to explore outside texts, teachers might encourage collaborative research in class or assign partners or teams to find materials. Further support of personal learning networks may include having a common place in your physical or digital classroom for students to share their topics, so that students can share information they find in their research relevant to various topics. In addition to highlighting and annotating an assignment, students might write out the steps they need to take to start the research process. In each lesson, we guide students through the work of each day; however, breaking down steps with students is also beneficial. In Video 4.3, Dawn unpacks the inquiry-based research essay assignment with students by focusing on the role of audience and purpose for the writing.

watch it here

Video 4.3

http://resources.corwin
.com/writingrewired

LESSON 18. RESEARCHING SKILLS AND TIPS: EXPLORING SOURCES

The purpose of this lesson is to help students

- Activate prior knowledge regarding research skills

- Review research skills

- Explore credibility and reliable sources

- Explore primary and secondary sources

- Learn helpful research tools, such as Citelighter

Collaborative Research

As teachers prepare students for college, careers, and life, it is essential to help them focus on communicating and the changing nature in which communication and learning happens. Digital collaboration in compositions is without a doubt a shift that has happened in terms of communication across the globe. To accurately prepare students, we need to embrace

Inquiry-Based Research Essay: Cultural Awareness and Analysis

For all of human history, individuals and groups of people have worked to form their identities. Some elements of our identity are unique and specific to each of us. Other elements are shared and help us feel like part of a group. These elements are all part of our culture.

Yet, we don't often pause to ask, "What is culture, and how does our culture influence the way we view our world?"

Throughout this unit of study, we've been exploring the following essential questions:

- What is culture? How do various individuals, communities, and groups describe the characteristics of "culture"?

  - What are characteristics of culture? How do these characteristics influence and contribute to culture?

  - When are cultural characteristics seen as positive, and when are they seen as negative?

- What is cultural identity? How does my culture influence identity?

  - What is my own cultural identity in relation to my family and community?

  - How is American culture described through various forms of media, in my school, and in my community?

- How do these visions and elements of culture influence my life?

  - What are the artifacts of my culture (imagery, music, food, clothing, ceremonies, pop culture icons, etc.)?

  - How do I imagine these artifacts and characteristics of culture will continue to influence my life in the future?

Personal Inquiry

To further explore these big ideas, you will be narrowing the focus of your personal inquiry question related to cultural awareness and analysis. The following rhetorical situation offers the focus for this inquiry exploration.

Mode: You will be writing an inquiry-based research essay.

This piece will include the following:

- Insights related to culture and identity with a focus on your own inquiry question, through which you will develop an intellectual conversation surrounding your inquiry question

- Argumentative thesis statement about culture and identity formed from an inquiry question

(Continued)

(Continued)

- Clear subclaims used to support the thesis statement
- Evidence from multiple sources used as part of the support of subclaims and ultimately the thesis statement
- Warrants used to explain how the evidence supports the claims

You will need to use a variety of evidence in support of your claims. You need to have enough sources to back up your argument. At a minimum, use your literature circle book and three other texts (including various media and print texts). Include your own original research, as well as several primary and secondary sources to support your ideas. You can use sources we've explored, but you'll also need to do your own research to find other sources to support your ideas too.

Your Original Research	Primary Sources We've Explored	Secondary Sources We've Explored
• Your own surveys and interviews • Your original blog posts • Your culture collage	• TED Talks or commercials • Data sets • Literature circle book	• Articles and presentations that analyze or report on existing data • Book reviews

Media: You will be writing a print-based text.
You can turn in your work in either print form or through Google Drive.

Audience: You are writing this piece for a variety of audiences.

Your audience includes the following:

- You

- Teacher

- Your primary audience (identified by you and based on your topic), which may include Youth Voices, our online class space, readers of a magazine, or an audience that might be exploring similar questions in various professional learning networks (both digital and print-based)

- Other potential readers that you invite to read your work, such as family members and friends

Purpose: You also have a variety of purposes for your work.

Your purposes include

- Examine your own thinking about your inquiry question and the unit essential questions

- Engage in real-life and real-world questions that interest you and relate to your life

(Continued)

(Continued)

- Analyze literature, including fiction, nonfiction, and other research
- Explore your own original research, as well as primary and secondary research
- Practice argumentative writing skills
- Delve into research and synthesis for analysis
- Consider a variety of evidence to support your ideas
- Hone research, analysis, and synthesis skills
- Develop a debatable and defensible claim to address your inquiry question
- Add to the intellectual conversation surrounding your topic by engaging with an audience that is invested in your question
- Understand that because you are a researcher, your writing fits into a larger intellectual conversation

For this piece, you need to think about how your audience and purpose are related.

Situation: As part of your work, you should consider the following situations.

Writing: A successful inquiry-based research essay will

- Pay homage to essential questions about culture and identity
- Tease out some characteristics of culture, using artifacts as examples
- Embrace an audience and purpose relevant to your topic and beyond just your teacher
- Be long enough to develop your argument with adequate support and evidence (at least 3 pages)
- Cite resources according to guidelines from your teacher with both in-text and works cited lists

Writer: As a writer, be the best you can be. Plan ahead and stay on top of deadlines.

Brainstorm for peer response due _____

Introductory paragraph for peer response due _____

Body paragraph for peer response due _____

Body paragraph for peer response due _____

Draft 1 for peer response due _____

Draft 2 for peer response due _____

Final draft turned in to teacher and published _____

(Continued)

(Continued)

Assessment: Your paper will be evaluated based on the following:

- Writing addresses the rhetorical situation (on the due date, you will have time to write a reflection identifying your rhetorical situation and reflecting on your work).

  ○ Writing is shared with an audience identified by the author.

- Writing includes an argumentative thesis statement about culture and identity formed from an inquiry question.

  ○ Writing includes clear subclaims used to support the thesis statement.

  ○ Writing includes evidence from multiple sources as part of the support for subclaims and ultimately the thesis statement.

  ○ Writing explains how the evidence supports the thesis statement (warrant).

  ○ Writing includes a variety of evidence used in support of your claims. You need to have enough sources to back up your argument. At a minimum, use your literature circle book and three other texts (including various media and print texts). Include at least one original research primary source, as well as several other primary and secondary sources.

- Writing teases out some characteristics of culture, using artifacts as examples.

- Writing includes a list of references, including primary and secondary sources as well as your own original research.

the role of collaboration, as well as independent thought, and choices that happen in digital spaces.

Throughout this unit, collaboration to foster knowledge has been important. By sharing outside texts, writing and reflecting together and in response to one another, and engaging in collaborative reading such as through discussion, collaborative annotation, and jigsaw reading, students have been engaging in approaching their work together.

Collaborative work is essential to today's classrooms to help students

- Build critical thinking and questioning skills

- Synthesize ideas across texts

- Learn how to work with others

- Support learning through the writing process, as well as reading and synthesis of research material

When we're talking about collaborative work, we don't mean the negative experiences we've all had at one time or another where students form groups but only one person does the work. Fortunately, today's digital spaces create more accountability, particularly when students are required to post and the site credits content creation back to a student account. For instance, Google Drive and Wikispaces Classroom are two tools that make tracking student participation quite easy in most cases. Teachers can easily determine when students have made changes because those changes are automatically associated with their username and often will also include a time stamp.

We started our focused work with research by inviting students in this lesson to collaboratively find resources related to cultural artifacts. This move included three important purposes:

1. It encouraged students to set up personal learning networks through collaboration both in class and by posting in digital spaces.

2. It prompted students to revisit valuable resources posted on the class wiki cultural artifact page by Dawn or other students.

3. It sparked ideas as students performed "fast searches" in teams, which helped them identify potential resources, get involved in research, and start activating their prior knowledge of their topic.

On our class wiki, we set up pages for students to share resources as they found them. For our focus, we made pages for artifacts of culture, and on each page of the website, students could add links to articles. For instance, we had artifact topics identified by the teachers, such as language, food, and

HAND OUT

Lesson 18 (Part 1). Researching Skills and Tips

Research includes reading widely. In support of your efforts as a researcher, we will explore resources together. Then, we will look at other skills involved in the researching process.

Activity 1: Collaborative Research

In teams of two, add at least one resource to the cultural artifact resources page on our online class space. Explore various websites, including research databases, always keeping in mind the context of the content. By sharing work through the collaborative gathering of resources, we will have several resources that you may be able to use in your research process and potentially in your inquiry-based research essay.

Activity 2: Reviewing Research Skills

In your team, make a list of research skills you already know and use. As a class, we will share our lists to make one master list, which we can also add on to as we discuss some of our approaches to research.

Considerations When It Comes to Research (what we already know)	Other Considerations (add to the list throughout class discussion)

When it comes to research and seeking sources to further our thinking and support our arguments, there are some key considerations to think about:

- What makes something a reliable source?
- When should I use print (vs. digital) texts?
- What are databases, and why are they valuable?
- Is it appropriate to use social media in an inquiry-based research essay? When and why might I use it?
- What about Wikipedia? Is it a credible source? Why or why not?

Lesson 18 (Part 2). Researching Skills and Tips

As we reviewed when discussing research skills, primary and secondary sources are an important consideration of the research process. But, what are they, and why do they matter?

Activity: Primary and Secondary Sources

What are primary sources? What are secondary sources?

In what ways can we use primary and secondary sources to support our own arguments?

According to the library at Yale University (2008), "Primary sources provide first-hand testimony or direct evidence concerning a topic under investigation. They are created by witnesses or recorders who experienced the events or conditions being documented."

It is important to carefully analyze the source as a reader and as a writer to provide context for your source so that you are presenting the ideas accurately, as some primary sources are less reliable than others. Finding a balance with sharing different types of sources is essential to develop a sound argument.

Also, you are collecting your own original source data through research methods that might include conducting a study, survey, or interview or even ethnographic observations. In a sense, you are the person responsible for witnesses, recording experiences, and data.

Secondary sources are sources that others have composed based on their research. These sources are an analysis of other research or a compilation of ideas about society. Additionally, many database articles that focus on analysis of other research are secondary sources, which are essential to back up your ideas and build credibility.

Review the following sites to further explore the role of primary and secondary sources:

- Yale University, "What Are Primary Sources?"
  (www.yale.edu/collections_collaborative/primarysources/primarysources.html)
- Borough of Manhattan Community College, "Primary vs. Secondary Sources"
  (http://lib1.bmcc.cuny.edu/help/sources.html)

Based on our study of various texts, here are a few original, primary, and secondary sources.

Your Original Research	Primary Sources We've Explored	Secondary Sources We've Explored
• Your own surveys and interviews • Your original blog posts • Your culture collage	• TED Talks or commercials • Data sets • Literature circle book	• Articles or presentations that analyze or report on existing data • Book reviews

What additional primary and secondary sources have you gathered so far? What else do you need to gather? What keywords and topics will you search for?

Available for download at **http://resources.corwin.com/writingrewired**

HAND OUT

Lesson 18 (Part 3). Researching Skills and Tips

Wikipedia as an open-source website is often debated as a valid source. Let's explore that argument for our own research purposes.

Wikipedia: A "Credible" Source?

First, we will listen to a story from NPR's *On the Media*: "Get Me Rewrite" (July 8, 2005). In this piece, you will hear media scholar Clay Shirky discuss how Wikipedia functions, both in a technical sense and as a community.

Audio and transcribed text are available from www.onthemedia.org/story/129250-get-me-rewrite/.

Activity 1: Listening, Reading, and Taking Notes

As you listen and read the story, take notes about the following features of Wikipedia:

Talk Page	History Page	Neutral Point of View

Clay Shirky says that "what makes a wiki good is not the technology but the community." What does he mean by this? How is Wikipedia written and edited? Do you think that Wikipedia is a credible source?

Activity 2: Determining Credibility

Examine one Wikipedia page about a topic in which you are interested. Try to determine the following:

- When was the page created?
- When did the most recent edit occur?
- How many total edits have occurred on the page?
- How many discussions about the page have occurred or are currently going on?
- How many references are available to outside sources?

Based on the information above, do you think your Wikipedia page is "credible"? How would you defend or refute the credibility of this page to a teacher who wants to know why you may or may not use Wikipedia as a source?

fashion, as well as student-generated topics, such as architecture and cultural icons. On those individual pages, students then shared links to articles, infographics, videos, and even poems related to the artifact topic.

Reviewing Research Skills

As we prepared this unit, we recognized that students should consider many essential research skills. We designed the questions on the Lesson 18 handouts to jump-start their thinking, but we knew that we would also need to conduct in-class discussions and provide students with many opportunities to practice these skills.

Determining Reliability of Online Sources

When the two of us were in our own K–12 careers, the Internet was not a daily fact of life. We spent many class periods of English, even in elementary school, in the school library learning how to use the card catalog, touring the reference and nonfiction sections, and studying specific guidelines for how to manage piles of material on note cards, which we would then transfer to the outlines we formed to guide our rough drafts. Even when we finally had access to word processors, little room for variation existed. Encyclopedias, magazines, and newspapers—all professionally edited—were viewed as the authoritative sources, and we could draw only from them.

Then, in the mid-1990s, as we finished high school and entered college, the Internet, specifically the graphical interface of the World Wide Web made possible by HTML, happened. And, to the horror of librarians and English teachers, anyone with adequate access and technical skill could publish his or her work to the world. At that point, teachers still admonished students to use only "reliable," print-based sources. Information from websites had to be verified by cross-checking with reputable, edited sources.

Fast-forward to the present. The web is now dominated by just a few search engines, and many searches generally lead users to Wikipedia and/or a blog within the top few hits. What are teachers to do?

Most teachers we know seem to rely on a definition of "reliability" that comes from a pre-Internet era. They demand that students never use Wikipedia and cite only print-based sources. Even when an article appears on a "trusted" website, they may require students to cross-check it with other sources. On one hand, this makes sense, as we do not want students to blindly accept anything that comes up in a search. If there is anything that we have learned about using the web, it is that many people are good at placing hoaxes or outright lies online. Careful, critical reading of the web is an essential skill, and being able to spot items that are patently false is important.

However, when teachers tell students that they must use only this or that type of source—rather than inviting them to consider a variety of sources—teachers can instill a particular, fixed mind-set about the entire research process in students. If we require that students only find peer-reviewed information from databases, for instance, and do not allow them to find and examine blogs and other media outlets, then we are likely preventing them from seeing the wide scope of information related to their topic.

Also, there can be many benefits to introducing students to sources such as Wikipedia. While it remains true that nearly anyone can change a wiki, Hicks and Perrin (2014) describe the nature of writing on Wikipedia as an example of both "focused writing" and "writing-by-the-way." That is, "as a space for focused writing, Wikipedia provides the world with a public view of almost any topic that contains relevant and up-to-date information, as well as links to outside sources" (p. 234). Individual authors become part of a broader team, led by editors, who work to ensure a "neutral point of view" on thousands of topic pages.

Additionally, Hicks and Perrin (2014) describe how writing on Wikipedia happens quickly and collaboratively, and how this process is documented on "talk" and "history" pages for each topic:

> The talk pages are the heart of the Wikipedia community, allowing writers and editors to have discussions about the topic, determining what information to present on the main page and how best to share it. The history page, too, offers insights into the writing process as it happens. Every time a user saves a new version of the page, the history page saves a snapshot of the previous version, allowing anyone the ability to compare the current version of the page with past versions. (p. 234)

Professional in tone and practice, this "writing-by-the-way"—both the product and the process—makes Wikipedia a unique space for students to explore how knowledge is constructed in a connected culture. If we are asking students to be collaborative researchers, then what better way to encourage them to embrace collaborative research? Both because a Wikipedia entry is likely to appear in the top few hits of nearly any Internet search, and because Wikipedia itself offers readers an inside view of its own creation, we included an exploration of Wikipedia as part of Lesson 18 (see the Part 3 handout on page 136).

When we talked about Wikipedia with our students, they referenced going to the original source but getting that source from Wikipedia. This is a solid practice to find original sources. Additionally, students referenced needing to know their audience in academic spaces, as some teachers allow students to use Wikipedia as a source while others do not. We suggest that teachers encourage students to understand and use it, perhaps even adding to it as they pursue their own inquiries.

Most teachers we know seem to rely on a definition of "reliability" that comes from a pre-Internet era. When teachers tell students they must use only this or that type of source, they may instill in them a fixed mind-set about the entire research process.

Along the same lines, teachers may want to open up more general conversations with students about what constitutes a reliable online source. That is, in addition to the traditional markers of web credibility such as the domain name, author credentials, the site design, and a page identifying the author(s), what other determining factors can students use to look for markers of credibility? For instance, what language does a particular news outlet use to describe a topic vis-à-vis other news outlets, such as "school choice" versus "privatization"? If the source is a blogger, how long has that person been writing about the topic at hand? If the source is Wikipedia, how many authors have contributed to a page, and how many editors monitor that page? When was the last revision?

By reframing our insistence on "reliability," we can provide our students with opportunities to think critically and carefully about the sources they have researched, and we can offer them insights into how to conduct their own original research too.

Here are some additional issues to consider as you discuss the concept of reliability with your students:

- Remind students to use common knowledge and common sense when researching because many false stories circle the Internet.

- Discuss the fact that anyone can put information online. Seeing a .org or .edu and assuming it is fair and accurate is no substitute for critically analyzing a web resource.

- Suggest that students use multiple sources to support their research, including work from experts that is peer-reviewed in a database.

- Ask students to provide context for texts (e.g., they should note that blog posts present a single perspective, and consider the qualifications of the blog author).

- Discuss how different types of social media can be a reliable source for different types of information (e.g., lawyers may use a Facebook entry as a major piece of evidence in court cases)—but not in all cases (e.g., a Facebook entry about the merits of a favorite political candidate may not be based on fact).

Using Printed Texts

Like us, you might remember going to the library to lift the big encyclopedia to a desk for research. While this move is a lot less common today, print texts continue to have value. Is it essential that all students include print material in their research? Not necessarily, as much of this will depend on the student's topic. Also, depending on students' eventual field of work or study, their research may or may not include print texts. Still, helping students recognize the legacy and history of books, magazines, and newspapers is important. After all, older texts do hold value as we explore histories and development of thinking over time. We value these types of publications and spend at least a full class period in the library and working with our school librarian to help students identify additional materials that they can use.

Including Original Research, Primary and Secondary Sources

Why primary and secondary sources? If we want students to be real researchers and think carefully about various perspectives on a topic, situating themselves in conversations that are relevant to their daily lives and their culture, then both primary and secondary sources matter.

With Dawn's students, we shared two perspectives on primary and secondary research. The first is similar to typical academic discussions about primary and secondary sources, such as the examples offered on the Yale University (2008) and Borough of Manhattan Community College (2015) websites we reference on the handout for Lesson 18 (see page 135). In this sense, primary sources are original research pieces—such as scientific data presented in a journal article, an interview with an eyewitness, or an original work of art—whereas secondary sources interpret or analyze those original sources. Secondary sources include books or other reviews of the arts, syntheses of other research, and biographies. These distinctions are, indeed, sometimes difficult to draw, yet we worked with students to think about the difference between "original" work or research and "interpretations" of that work or research.

This was a core distinction for our inquiry unit because, as we have noted throughout this book, we wanted students to *become* researchers, not just report on the work of others. Thus, we talked with them about doing their own original research in addition to finding primary and secondary sources. As suggested on the inquiry-based research essay assignment handout (see page 129) and through instruction and review of primary research, students' own research could take many forms, including a reflective analysis of their blogging and culture collage, an original survey or interview, or an ethnographic observation. Several students cited their own original thinking from previous blog posts on Youth Voices, while others shared concepts from their culture collages in their final inquiry-based research essays. Others shared observations they found from looking at the world from an ethnographic perspective.

One student surveyed random students in the cafeteria at lunch about her inquiry question by asking one focused question about appearance. In her final essay, she was able to share the percentage of students based on her sample who felt they would change something about their appearance. Another student conducted an informal survey with paper and pencil in our classroom. Another student created a survey using Google Forms and shared this survey in the Youth Voices community. Other students explored interviews for their original research. One student studying Asperger's syndrome interviewed a classmate who openly shared his experiences with having autism.

Still others e-mailed other teachers or professionals who had insights related to their inquiry question.

We wanted students to take ownership of their research process with their original work, such as with their writing, and we also worked with them to develop research tools, such as surveys and interviews that they could conduct as they worked on their inquiry-based research essay and media project (described in Chapter 5). The exploration of using surveys and interviews was discussed with the review of primary sources and was further supported in group and one-on-one coaching work with students. We did not go into extensive detail about all the techniques available for doing such surveys and interviews, and we recognize the informal nature of this work and potential for extensions; however, students recognized the value and role of reading their world through conducting original research to extend their inquiry. As you will see in some of the final essay examples (in Chapter 5), they took up this task with interest, with most of them conducting surveys and interviews of their peers.

Managing Citations

Many wonderful digital tools allow researchers to keep track of information, including NoodleTools (www.noodletools.com) and EasyBib (www.easybib .com). While some teachers liken the use of such tools to "cheating," we believe that bibliographic management tools are a key part of success in academic writing, and we teach our students how to use them. Citation tools can be compared to calculators, a useful staple of mathematics teaching once students have a conceptual understanding and a moderate amount of practice with, say, algebraic equations. Just as allowing students to use calculators does not negate or replace initial teaching or student thinking, allowing students to use citation tools *once they have learned the concepts surrounding the need for citation* does not interfere with their learning.

> We wanted students to *become* researchers, not just report on the work of others. Thus, we talked with them about doing their own original research in addition to finding primary and secondary sources.

In fact, without citation tools, many students can get lost in the nuts and bolts of completing the formula to make a citation "correct," when instead they should be seamlessly integrating the ideas of others into their own writing. Citation is a rhetorical move, not just an exercise for filling in the blanks and matching a particular citation style, such as APA or MLA style. It is much more important for students to understand why they are citing a source than to spend time worrying about quotation marks, italics, and other minutiae.

For this project, we taught the students how to use Citelighter (www .citelighter.com). When students use academic databases—entries that have metadata about each article embedded in the code of the web page— Citelighter allows them to save citation information and mark texts to save passages or quotes that may be relevant to their argument. With just a few clicks, they can have the article title, the publication title, the author's name, the publication date, and an exact quote saved in their Citelighter database, as well as space to add their own comments and questions. While this tool is not quite as useful with websites lacking appropriate metadata, Citelighter can still be used to create an entry from scratch, even for a print source such as a book, magazine, or newspaper article. Most important, Citelighter can connect with Google Drive to import material from the research space to the writing space.

Extensions and Adaptations for Lesson 18

Collaborative Researching. Depending on how you approach the research process with students, there are many ways to establish collaborative research. In addition to sharing on a wiki or Google Doc, or using Citelighter, students might also use Diigo (www.diigo.com), a collaborative social bookmarking tool. Diigo allows students an opportunity to save web spaces and annotate them. You can also set up groups to share research.

When using Diigo, students can mark a text with a digital sticky note and then reply to others if sharing a resource or if students are in a group within Diigo. In this way, Diigo includes spaces for annotation of a text and collaborative conversations about a text, as well as ease in sharing resources. Additional collaborating could include a web-based scavenger hunt to find resources or small-group sharing based on topics that students have selected in the room.

Organizational Approaches. There are many different ways to help students organize their research. We used Citelighter and Google Drive, and can imagine Diigo or Evernote as options, too (Hicks, 2014). All are great tools to help with research organization.

Reliable Sources. To help students develop their skills at identifying reliable sources, you might ask them to analyze several materials and determine if the work is reliable. For instance, you might present students with articles from a database, hoax messages sent across the Internet, tabloids, newspaper articles, or other texts. Fake websites would be helpful to explore with students, too. Through practice, students can develop skills for analyzing a text and exploring features that help cue in a reader to the reliability of that text.

Establishing Guidelines to Evaluate the Web. Work with students to establish a checklist or guidelines for evaluating web content; this can serve as a helpful tool as students wrestle with many big ideas.

Online Filter Bubbles. In our information society, we all have "filter bubbles," often ones that are invisible to us as we navigate the web. See Eli Pariser's TED Talk and book (Pariser, 2011) to begin exploring this conversation with students.

LESSON 19. RESEARCHING (ONLINE AND IN THE LIBRARY MEDIA CENTER)

The purpose of this lesson is to help students

- Research their inquiry question through use of various tools, including print documents, databases, online articles, and multimedia

- Work with reading, writing, and researching

- Practice the recursive nature of research thinking and synthesis

- Engage with both print and digital texts

- Experience the importance and value of the library

- Share ideas with others to further their thinking

- Confer with classmates, the teacher, and the librarian over research ideas, including finding resources and their thinking related to their findings and inquiry question

In Video 4.4, students visit the library for a day of research.

Colleagues and Collaboration: Community Mentorship

As teachers support students throughout the research process, it can be useful to help students connect with "experts" in their own school. Encourage students to ask questions of other teachers, and talk at faculty meetings about the work your students are engaging in. For instance, depending on the focus of each student's inquiry, we might invite students to discuss the manipulation of images with a photography teacher, the celebration of cultural heritage with a world language teacher, and so forth. As we support students' reflection about critical thinking and big ideas that span across disciplines, the role of mentorship across fields is important.

watch it here

Video 4.4
http://resources.corwin
.com/writingrewired

The Changing Nature of School Libraries

We love the school library. As schools deal with information shifts in the 21st century, libraries too are making the shift. Sandy Fields (2014b), the librarian at Dawn's school, shares her blog post in response to this shift: "The School Library in an Informational Renaissance" (access this piece at **http://resources .corwin.com/writingrewired**). While we still value print texts, e-books have become an important part of receiving information, as have online sources, and students can now access some of these materials through the school library. Teachers need to expose students to the school library so that learners can discover more about the various resources available. Unfortunately, with budget cuts impacting schools, all too often school libraries are not a sustained and rich learning environment that honors the rich thinking readers, writers, and thinkers do. However, Dawn's students had the great fortune of having access to a school library that embraces learning in an informational age.

HAND OUT

Lesson 19. Researching (Online and in the Library Media Center)

Today, we will be researching in the school library. You will have various resources to use, including computers with Internet access, as well as print resources such as nonfiction texts and magazines, and the opportunity to work with our librarian, who is a master researcher.

Activity 1: Research in the Library Goal Setting

Goals for today: Find sources you might use in your inquiry-based research essay and add them to your Citelighter notes. Be sure to capture all of the bibliographic information in the Citelighter entry. Remember, your goal is to find additional sources that will support your research. Don't forget about finding various sources. Find the following different types of sources, as potential support material for your essay:

- Nonfiction book

- Database article from a research-based journal

- Current article that was published within the last 6 months (this could be from a journalistic news source or magazine, online or print-based)

Activity 2: Research Workshop

As you look for materials to support your ideas and further your thinking, your ideas should grow and develop. Researching is recursive in that you will be exploring answers to your questions though reading that may redirect your thinking. So, today, you will be researching, reading, and writing with both print and online resources. You will also have time to conference with your classmates, teacher, and librarian. Before you leave today, write a reflection on the following:

- What new or surprising information about your topic did you learn today?

- What information did you find that confirms other information you have already discovered? Did you find information that contradicted a previous discovery?

- What are your next steps in the research process?

The library at Okemos High School, the Library Media Center (LMC), offers students opportunities to engage with print and digital texts. Additionally, support staff—including the librarian—help students not only find great books to read but also research and think through writing questions, as well as explore technology capabilities of various programs. During the class research project, Dawn embraced the opportunities to bring students to the LMC for the resources available and the mentorship that takes place within this learning space from student to student and from student to librarian.

Extensions and Adaptations for Lesson 19

Teachers may find that setting up specific conference times with each student during the research process is very effective. Asking students to share their thinking on their research, to review their sources, to talk about their writing process, and so forth is a beneficial way to help them map out their thinking and writing.

Depending on time and the structure of the research, teachers may also want to foster a guided peer response. Students could respond to others' ideas, sources, and even written responses to various sources, as well as drafts of their writing. While many teachers wait until nearly the final draft to engage students in peer response, this approach is certainly successful earlier and more often during the process, perhaps by asking students to focus on just an opening paragraph or even a thesis statement (see the handout "Inquiry-Based Research Essay: Cultural Awareness and Analysis" on page 129).

LESSON 20. WRITING AND RESEARCHING WORKSHOP

The purpose of this lesson is to help students

- Review explicit writing instructions they have worked on all year

- Explore various writing strategies for invention

- Provide opportunities to read, write, and research

- Use opportunities to work with their peers and collaborate

- Provide the opportunity to conference with the teacher

A Workshop for Writing and Researching

Providing class time for students to work constructively is important. As you might note throughout this unit, we continued to challenge students with mini-lessons or warm-ups to focus their work for each day.

Lesson 20. Writing and Researching Workshop

As you compose your inquiry-based research essay, remember that this work is a recursive process of reading, researching, rethinking, and writing. As a writer, you have a variety of strategies you can use in the writing process. Let's review some of the skills we've studied this year.

Activity 1: Writing Strategy Review

In teams, review one of the following writing strategies we've worked on all year:

- Brainstorming and mapping out your writing
- Organizing your ideas
- Developing an argument
- Writing a thesis statement
- Creating an introduction
- Using claims to focus organization
- Embedding quotes for evidence
- Using evidence to back up claims
- Using warrants to explain how the evidence relates to the claim
- Creating a conclusion

Write a team response to the following, to review writing strategies, and share this review with other classmates.

- How do these strategies work? Why are they important?

Post your review of these strategies in our online class space.

Activity 2: Workshop Time

During this class period, you may use the workshop writing time as follows:

- Research your topic
- Draft your inquiry-based research essay
- Critically read your literature circle novel
- Conference with classmates and/or the teacher

Additionally, workshop time provides students with an important opportunity to ask questions of their classmates and teacher. For instance, some students chose to work with literature circle teams to discuss their questions and findings in research. Others conducted interviews with peers and shared results from their informal surveys with one another. During this workshop time, students also reviewed notes they collected all year in their writer's notebook about ways to approach writing, such as ways to set up an introduction.

Still other students were able to clarify questions or workshop writing and revisions with one another and both of us, as their teachers. Students met with us individually or in teams to talk through their ideas or written drafts, to receive support with researching effectively using various sources, or simply for a quick review of citation details. While we were working with a team reading *The Hunchback of Notre-Dame,* conversation about obsession with the beauty of Esmeralda led to considering different cultural representations of beauty and then reviewing specific sources related to the impact of beauty in different cultures. After meeting with a team to discuss ideas, we then headed to a one-on-one conversation with another student about where to find the best sources and record them in Citelighter. Throughout this unit, it is possible to add more workshop dates depending on time and your students' needs.

Extensions and Adaptations for Lesson 20

There are many ways to review the writing skills that students have worked on throughout the class. Students might try a specific strategy for a draft of their work. For instance, as a class, you might review strategies for introductions and then have students try writing introductions in a few different ways. Or students might focus on one sentence and share it to workshop with their peers. Dawn often uses erasable sentence strips in her classroom for students to post drafts of sentences or paragraphs as mentor texts or for comment for review purposes. Use of the writer's notebook in Dawn's classroom and the importance of posting writing in the room are inspired by Jeff Anderson's *Mechanically Inclined* (2005). To help students get used to sharing in this way, it can be helpful to start with sharing one sentence, such as attention-getting sentences or thesis statements for feedback and inspiration.

This workshop time was designed to honor the recursive nature of the reading, writing, and researching process but also to review the many writing strategies students practiced all year and would need to employ in their essays.

REFLECTIONS ON THE RESEARCH PROCESS

At the end of this week, students were moving along with each aspect of their work in rich, thoughtful ways. Specifically, students were engaged in

- Reading, journaling, and analysis for literature circle books
- Close reading and researching related to inquiry questions
- Critical analysis of cultural artifacts and characteristics
- Composing drafts of their inquiry-based research essay
- Rethinking and reflecting on inquiry ideas

It was clear to us that students had a lot going on. At this point, the student focus was on finishing their literature circle work, researching, and composing material for their inquiry-based research essay. Throughout this week, students continued to ask questions and seek sources to inform their thinking. In this way, research was rewired to focus on the process of thinking, reading, researching, writing, revising, and re-seeing ideas.

In this part of the unit, students explored rich research processes of collaboration with their peers, as well as with mentors within the school, including the librarian and other teachers. Additionally, students improved their research skills by exploring their own research, primary sources, and secondary sources. In some cases, students began to shift their thinking about research and the reliability of sources as they became active producers of their own research and participated in the conversations related to using a source such as Wikipedia. These ideas of rethinking source credibility and being producers and makers of meaning reflect a rewired research approach. While still honoring credible sources and conventions of traditional research papers, such as the use of citations and building an argument with actual research, students were engaged in connected learning with a focus on the questioning, thinking, reading, writing, revising, and collaborating rather than basic checkboxes noting concepts such as where a period falls in a citation or how to format a note card to keep track of research information. Rather, students embraced the messy process of research because they were thinking, they were curious, and they were engaged in a purposeful research process.

Students also developed an understanding about the importance of context in writing regarding sources as they worked to purposefully voice their analysis, along with using evidence to support their claims. They gathered this evidence from a variety of sources, including their literature circle book, their own research, and their own ideas, as well as additional primary and secondary sources. Students were fully engaged in the reading, researching, and writing process. Next, students would be wrapping up their work with literature circles, revising their essays, and expanding their thinking related to their inquiry question with the media project, as we discuss in Chapter 5.

5 Writing Workshop and Media Projects

Responding, Revising, and Reflecting

> *Revision is one of the exquisite pleasures of writing.*
>
> —Bernard Malamud

The final week of the inquiry unit, "Reading Our World and Exploring Perspectives: Identity and Culture," focused on workshop time, which students spent composing, responding, revising, and reflecting. We also explored media literacy through the role of media projects. During this week, we expected students to

- Complete work with literature circles, with the final meeting, reflections, and final self-assessment of journaling work

- Continue to write and revise their inquiry-based research essay

- Complete and publish their inquiry-based research essay

- Reflect upon their inquiry-based research essay

- Compose their media project, which includes sharing ideas from the research essay in a new format for a media composition

- Publish and share their work

In this chapter, we will include in the span of this week two days of the following week, one to wrap up the work and another to celebrate through sharing the work. Over the course of these lessons, students pulled together all of their work for this inquiry unit and reflected on their growth of ideas and experiences.

The activities we designed for this part of our unit reflected our own background in the theory and practice of writing center work (Childers, Fels, & Jordan, 2004; Hicks, 2010; Inman, 2006; North, 1984; Stock, 1997). The main point that we take from our writing center work is that we must aim to help writers grow over time, not simply to fix a single piece of writing.

> We must aim to help writers grow over time, not simply to fix a single piece of writing.

Thus, similar to the guiding principles of writing center work, our perspective on peer review centers on the need for teachers to enhance and deepen students' understanding of helping a writer, not just fixing a piece of writing. We, as teachers, need to help our students understand how to talk about writing, including rhetorical choices, and differentiate between higher-order concerns such as organization and lower-order concerns such as spelling and punctuation. Also, we need to scaffold the process of providing effective feedback, inviting our students to understand the kinds of comments and questions that will help their peers move forward toward revision. Finally, we agree that students—when providing substantive feedback to other writers—can grow as writers themselves, both by identifying the moves that effective writers make and by offering suggestions for revision. Ultimately, in peer response, the writer maintains ownership of the work, and must make decisions about the advice the reviewers have offered and how best to move forward with the writing.

LESSON 21. LITERATURE CIRCLE MEETING 4: FINAL THOUGHTS AND REFLECTION

The purpose of this lesson is to help students

- Engage in final discussion about their literature circle book

- Discuss final thoughts about the novel and how it impacted their thinking about their inquiry questions

- Share dialectic journals and culture logs to explore their final analysis on the common literature circle group work

- Compose a reflective blog post synthesizing their ideas about their literature circle book and their inquiry work and respond to one another's blog posts

- Move between discussion spaces from the classroom, to Youth Voices, to Wikispaces

Students— when providing substantive feedback to other writers— can grow as writers themselves, both by identifying the moves that effective writers make and by offering suggestions for revision.

Connecting Big Ideas

Students began this week of lessons for the inquiry unit with the final literature circle meeting. We invited students to connect big ideas from their books with the arguments that they were beginning to formulate in their inquiry-based research essays.

This final literature circle meeting gave students an opportunity to talk about their reading and final reactions. Additionally, through work with their culture log, as well as through questioning and the dialectic journal, students engaged with a final close reading and discussion surrounding the text. In their discussions, some students shared that they felt they were going deeper with their reading because of the cultural lens. They also shared this rich thinking surrounding their books and inquiry questions through their blog discussion posts on Youth Voices. The following blog discussion post is from Kendra.

As someone who is a huge bookworm and reads every single day, The Curious Incident of the Dog in the Night-Time (2004) by Mark Haddon was a book that I highly enjoyed. I came into the project feeling really disappointed and uninterested, seeing as it was an assigned reading and not a genre that I'm usually interested in. That changed, however, when I opened the book to the first page and my attention was immediately snatched with the

HAND
OUT

Lesson 21. Literature Circle Meeting 4: Final Thoughts and Reflection

In addition to preparing the journal required for each literature circle meeting, for this final meeting, also complete the following. Write a final reaction to the novel, its relation to culture, and your ideas related to your inquiry questions. For this final reflection, write a blog post on Youth Voices. Check out http://youthvoices.net/node/36253 for how you might get started.

Remember to write how reading your novel has impacted your thinking related to your inquiry question. Consider our culture-focused big questions in your final response:

- What are elements of culture?
- Why are elements of culture important to a cultural identity? How do these elements influence culture?
- When are cultural elements positive and negative?
- How does culture influence identity?
- What is a cultural identity, and how does it impact the world around us?

Activity 1: Literature Circle Group Final Discussion

Discuss the questions that all team members prepared for your meeting. You should also share insights from your dialectic journal and culture log.

Activity 2: Responding to Blog Posts

Read and respond to individual group members' blog posts on Youth Voices related to their final reaction.

Activity 3: Sharing Final Notes Online

Share your group thinking on our online class space. Include both ideas from discussion and ideas from your work responding to one another's blog posts on Youth Voices.

Available for download at **http://resources.corwin.com/writingrewired**

blunt introduction, "There was a garden fork sticking out of the dog," and it never wandered after that. Throughout the book I relished Haddon's marvelous writing from the quirky perspective of a 15-year-old boy with Asperger's syndrome. I laughed and I cried and my brain got an exercise trying to understand the working of young Christopher's mind.

Christopher's mind was another story altogether. Through his eyes, I gained a whole new perspective and grasped the true meaning of how hugely our friendships and our connections depend on culture. As I read the book, I noticed how Christopher remained totally disconnected from other people because of how greatly his cultural identity clashed with those around him. It showed me how people connect and relate to each other by the similarities that they share within their own cultures. Because Christopher shared no similarities with other people, he remained detached from them, and alone.

This book brought to light the fact that culture isn't always a wonderful and beautiful thing, like I had previously thought. Christopher was always alone and ridiculed because of the things that made up his cultural identity. It was too different from everyone else's, and so he suffered the criticisms and the confusion of trying to fit into a society that totally clashed with who he was. He also had opinions and beliefs that constantly hindered him from being completely comfortable, like hating the colors yellow and brown, or freaking out whenever anyone touched him. Because of these things, he lived a life that was always very complicated and stressful, and he really couldn't do anything about it because culture is something that you just can't control.

Here is Beverly's response to Kendra.

Your Post Makes Me Feel Inadequate (In a good way :))

I like your reaction to the book. I had similar feelings, and the book was amazing. I really loved the voice that Mark Haddon used for Christopher. It was simple and to the point, but not so much that it made you feel as though people with Asperger's don't have as complex of thoughts. Reading *The Curious Incident of the Dog in the Night-Time* helped me realize a lot about how culture can separate and divide people, but also (if indirectly) bring people together.

Through this reflection from Kendra and response from Beverly, it is clear that both students made rich connections in their collaborative reading. The reflection from Kendra highlights much more than a simple "The book was OK" response. Rather, it shows that the lenses through which she read the book clearly impacted her thinking.

Based on these blog posts and the discussion in the room, it was clear to us that the students were engaging in smart, critical thinking related to their novel and the focused reading and writing they were doing. Additionally, the connections that they made reflect the recursive thinking students were engaging in.

Extensions and Adaptations for Lesson 21

There are a variety of ways to have students respond to one another. For instance, students could also respond to classmates from different reading groups. Students might review one another's project pages on Wikispaces, providing feedback on similar cultural themes across the different texts. After reviewing their own journals and culture logs, students could also write collaborative responses to the novel as a final post about their literature circle book.

LESSON 22. WRITING WORKSHOP AND PEER RESPONSE

The purpose of this lesson is to help students

- Engage in a final self-assessment that focuses on their work and thinking from literature circle groups

- Review assignment requirements and qualities of the mode of writing an inquiry-based research essay

- Reflect in writing on the role of audience for their inquiry-based research essay, revisiting goals of the assignment and considering structure based on audience

- Identify the type of feedback student writers need from others on their current draft

- Explore one another's work for multiple purposes, including

  ○ Reviewing other models of inquiry-based research essays

  ○ Supporting peers by providing feedback related to the requirements of the assignment

Literature Circle Final Self-Assessment

Through a final self-assessment, we invited students not only to respond to their experiences with literature circles but also to reflect on how the work was grounded in their inquiry. Here are a few examples of the students' responses.

My dialectic and cultural journals were related well to the book. I pulled out key ideas that sparked thoughts within my group. The cultural log especially helped to organize my thoughts about what we were talking about in class and relate it to my book. I think I could continue to improve my careful reading; sometimes I speed through a paragraph in a text that I find confusing.

—Zoya

Literature circles help me make predictions about the book through foreshadowing that I or someone else found. We express our feelings on a character's opinion or something one did and debate if we would do the same thing or if we would do something different. I feel like I enjoy literature circles more than I did when I was little, and sometimes I wish I had actually read the books so that I would have become a better reader.

—Asha

The lit circle group I had worked really well together. We challenged thinking and had some really smart discussions. I grew as a reader because of the new and different ways I learned to think about something.

—Raywa

Lesson 22. Writing Workshop and Peer Response

Pausing to reflect and make connections across your literature circle work and current progress of the inquiry-based research essay is an important part of monitoring your learning and identifying next steps for your writing.

Activity 1: Literature Circle Final Self-Assessment

Write a final reflection on your work with literature circle close reading and discussions using the following questions as a prompt:

- How did literature circles help you to focus on being a careful, critical reader?

- How have you grown as a reader?

- How have you grown in your responses to reading both in writing and through discussion?

- How has your reading helped you to formulate and explore inquiry questions?

- How did your reading inform your writing?

- How did your reading inform your chance to wonder?

Activity 2: Review Inquiry-Based Research Essay
Assignment and Qualities of Inquiry-Based Research Essays

Individually, review the assignment. Put a check mark next to aspects of the assignment's rhetorical situation (MAPS) that you are doing well within your writing. Star areas you need to consider further as you revise.

Activity 3: Writing Reflection on Audience

- Quick write (in your writer's notebook or a Google Doc): Who are the audiences that care most about your topic? Who are the potential audiences for your work? What conversations are you entering as an academic reader and writer?

- Pair share your writing about audience for your inquiry-based research essay.

- Review questions about the writing assignment.

(Continued)

(Continued)

Activity 4: Peer Response to Inquiry-Based Research Essay Draft

- Identify two or three specific questions addressing areas that you would like feedback on for your work. Put these questions at the top of your current draft.

- Put your paper in your Google Drive peer response group shared folder.

- Carefully read and respond to your assigned writer in your team on his or her current draft.

- Be sure to be specific in your response to the writer. Be sure to address the following:

1. In-text responses: Offer feedback within the text to note areas that make sense and are strong and why they work. Also, note areas where you are confused or need more clarity as a reader.

2. Final response to your peer's writing:

- When you finish reading this essay, what do you understand to be the inquiry question and the analysis of that question?

- How does this essay address assessment criteria?

- In what ways could this work further meet the requirements of the essay?

3. Address the author's specific questions identified at the top of the writing:

- After responding to your partner, review your feedback and create a revision plan for your writing. Identify at least five specific aspects of your writing that you can work at revising.

- You may work on revisions to your writing with your peers. During our work time today, writing conferences with other peers and your teacher will also take place.

These responses demonstrate how students engaged carefully and critically with their books and peers in their literature circle team, making connections to their broader inquiry questions.

The Qualities of Inquiry-Based Writing

We know that writers often do not revisit their assignments. However, as writers review requirements partway through the project, they can make sure that they have met all of the requirements, and they can think about why certain requirements work in specific ways for their writing situations. Dawn approaches this task quite simply by directly revisiting assignment requirements with students and modeling this approach to writing assignments. For our unit, we intentionally scheduled the review of the essay assignment for the day that students reviewed some of their classmates' work. At the same time, we also reviewed the qualities of effective inquiry-based research essays. In this way, students prepared to respond to others and practiced reviewing requirements for themselves.

As the class reviewed the assignment, many students were not surprised by its content, but others were surprised to discover (or, really, to remember) that they needed primary research—sources that are considered primary as well as their own original research—and to use their literature circle books.

Reflecting on the Role of Audience for the Inquiry-Based Research Essay

We asked students to reflect on the audience for their research paper to help them understand that writers also need to provide context for research material and the conversation related to their argument. For instance, since some members of their audience might not have read the literature book the students discussed in the essay, it was necessary for students to place their statements about the book in a clear context.

One student wrote:

Audience: Peers, teachers, family, friends

I will provide context for my literature book and explain how Staying Fat for Sarah Byrnes led me to research body image and its connection to being an outsider. I will need to give background information on Sarah and Eric. Every audience member didn't read my book.

The reflection on audience also helped students think about the structure of an inquiry-based research essay to build ideas in a logical sense and clearly articulate how their evidence supports the argument of the essay.

Peer Response to Inquiry-Based Research Essay Draft

In "Peer Review in a Digital Space," Holmes and Reed (2014) argue that

> the digital environment creates unique opportunities for composition and revision. Digital peer review—a regular, ongoing process of posting student work online for peer evaluation—improves student writing, sharpens literary analysis skills, and fosters critical thinking. . . . Given the structure of the modern workplace, it is probable that students will work in a team at some point in their careers—and with digital communication becoming more and more prevalent, digital peer review is a skill students are likely to use throughout their lives. (p. 193)

In this way, peer response serves multiple learning goals. It helps students model good writing for one another, it provides students practice with identifying characteristics within writing, it encourages critical reading and writing, and it helps students develop higher-order thinking and analytical skills. Moreover, receiving feedback on writing is helpful for writers as they consider their audience and work to revise. Students appreciated their peer response time. Some students received feedback identifying the inquiry question for the author, while others received statements such as "I don't understand how this paragraph supports the idea of body image being a challenge in American culture." Students offered questions for one another, identified specific traits of writing they recognized or that they felt the piece lacked, such as use of quotes for evidence or a clear argumentative thesis statement. And students explained when they were confused about the author's writing and what prompted this confusion in their reading. Students were specific in their responses not only because they had to review the assignment requirements and address those aspects in their peer response, but also because their peers asked for specific feedback on their writing. Working within digital spaces made sharing and commenting on documents a seamless process.

In our classes, we often repeat peer response workshops to focus on the editing stage after addressing some higher-order concerns. Lower-order concerns, such as edits for run-on sentences or sentence fragments and use of colons versus semicolons, are also important to the writing process. While we did not have a specific day focused on editing for this paper, that was a decision solely based on time. However, because time to focus on editing was a common practice in Dawn's classroom, students were reminded to engage in this process, and they did so on their own by collaborating with their peers.

Extensions and Adaptations for Lesson 22

Setting up peer review for students can happen in multiple ways and spaces. Besides using Google Drive, teachers can ask students to use blogs for peer response, as well as such academic networks as Spruz, GroupSpaces, Ning, or Wiggio.

Teachers may also want to check out Eli Review (elireview.com), a tool designed by Jeff Grabill and Bill Hart-Davidson, professors at Michigan State University, and their colleague Mike McLeod. This tool allows teachers to set up peer review and focus on various types of reviews. Additionally, the system can collect data based on peer review, which teachers can then use for educational purposes. In interest of full disclosure, please note that while Eli Review is an excellent program that we have both been involved with in terms of research and development and that we both highly recommend, it does have a subscription fee.

When students first practice peer review, it is important for teachers to model approaches to peer review and the level of questioning and sophistication expected. Students need to be explicitly taught differences between higher-order concerns, which include the major features of the writing, such as organization and argument, and lower-order concerns, which are more a part of the editing process, such as grammar, usage, and mechanics, in order to help students go beyond only offering editing comments.

LESSON 23. MEDIA WORK

The purpose of this lesson is to help students

- Understand the media assignment requirements
- Review the rhetorical situation (MAPS) of the assignment
- Brainstorm ideas for the media assignment
- Begin crafting ideas and gathering information for the assignment

Introducing the Media Assignment

It's important to note that as we considered the many ways that students could compose their final media project, we wanted to be mindful of both their digital writing process and their final product. For the next stage of the inquiry unit, we asked students to create a media project that addressed their inquiry question(s) in a compelling manner, using principles of visual and media literacy and demonstrating their analysis of cultural artifacts and characteristics. Essentially, we were asking students to repurpose ideas from their inquiry-based research essay and turn them into a digital writing composition. We allowed students to choose from a list of possible formats for this project, including a documentary, an advertisement, a TED Talk, a website, a podcast, and an infographic.

We recognize that students were already engaged in critical careful thinking and that they were very busy in their work. While students could tackle this project after their essay, we determined with our group of students that they were ready and engaged in their inquiry and so could handle this work. Additionally, the range of this media project can vary based on the time frame and resources available. The media project assignment follows on page 162. In this assignment, reference to the rhetorical situation with mode, media, audience, purpose, and situation (MAPS) is made for students, to support their continual development in considering these elements of writing—and, quite honestly, they expect this, and they should as they work out their plans for their composition.

Additionally, this media project is designed to have students share their arguments from the inquiry-based research essay in a different format based on a different mode, media, audience (though this could be the same as for the essay), purpose (this too could be the same), and situation. Further, the role of "media" is focused on students selecting different options for sharing their work; however, the focus on the rhetorical situation is essential to our conversation so that students are intentionally selecting media for their audience and purpose. Additionally, our mentor texts of study throughout this unit are models for students to think about their media work. For instance, we had students explore TED Talks, commercials, visuals in print magazines and created with photo editors, design of food wrappers, and so on. In this way, we scaffolded models of media work to prepare students for this assignment. Students were already familiar with many models for their work, and they were provided with ideas to explore various media options for their response. In some cases, the projects could be extensive, such as a detailed documentary, while in others, a vine (a short video on a continual loop) or an infographic (a graphical representation of material) might not take as much time. Because of the range of time needed for such projects, this assignment lends itself to the student choice in the depth of the project, but, of course, teachers can put more parameters on these features of the work.

Media Project Assignment: Cultural Awareness and Analysis Inquiry

To extend your thinking beyond one rhetorical situation (MAPS) for your research, you will have the opportunity to engage in synthesis related to sharing your work in a media-based format. You have multiple purposes, as explored below, but you will also need to describe the purpose of the work as based on your identified mode, media, and audience. For this work, you will be informing an audience (your class and ideally a larger audience of your choice—an online audience would work too) about your research.

- **Mode:** a media text exploring intellectual conversations stemming from your inquiry question
- **Media:** a media composition (video, web design with images and text, audio composition, etc.)
- **Audiences:** you, your teacher, and an online audience (Youth Voices, KQED Do Now, our online class space, another personal learning network, etc.) interested in your topic
- **Purposes:** all the same purposes that apply to your inquiry-based research essay, including the following

You have a variety of purposes for your work:

- Examine your own thinking about your inquiry question and the unit essential questions
- Engage in real-life and real-world questions that interest you and relate to your life
- Explore primary and secondary research
- Practice argumentative writing skills
- Delve into research and synthesis for analysis
- Consider a variety of evidence to support your ideas
- Hone research, analysis, and synthesis skills
- Develop a debatable and defensible claim to address your inquiry question
- Add to the intellectual conversation surrounding your topic by engaging with an audience that is invested in your question
- Understand that as a researcher, your writing fits into a larger intellectual conversation

The difference is that you also have additional purposes, as follows:

- Synthesize learning through use of media
- Consider different audiences and purposes for research work

(Continued)

(Continued)

- Develop your own project related to your inquiry conversation
- **Situation:**
  - Writer: You may work with others who have similar inquiry questions.
  - Writing: Your composition should
    - Explore your inquiry question
    - Address a clear audience and purpose for the work
    - Synthesize your research in interesting ways
    - Purposefully embrace a digital component to your work (and select something for a real purpose)

A few ways you can approach this assignment include, but are not limited to, the following:

- A documentary or other film modality
- An advertisement with clear consideration of visual design
- A TED Talk or Ignite presentation
- A website/wiki/blog
- A podcast or radio program
- An infographic (for data sets, see www.tuvalabs.com/datasets)
- A short video composition

Assessment will be based on the following requirements:

- A media project that addresses your inquiry question(s) in a compelling manner that employs principles of visual and media literacy, and demonstrates your analysis of cultural artifacts and characteristics.
- A complete description of the MAPS criteria related to the project. You will define your own mode, media, audience, purpose, and situation (~100–300 words).
- A reflection that describes the context of your project, an analysis of how well you feel you have met your MAPS criteria, and the ways in which your thinking about your inquiry topic has changed over the course of the unit (~300–500 words).

HAND OUT

Lesson 23. Media Work

Throughout the unit "Reading Our World and Exploring Perspectives: Identity and Culture," we have explored a variety of different types of texts including media compositions. Now it is your turn to repurpose some of your explorations from your inquiry research and writing to create a media response to your inquiry question(s).

Activity 1: Review Media Assignment

- What are the major components of the assignment?
- What expectations do you have for yourself and your own work?

Activity 2: Brainstorm and Outline Media Work

- Write out the MAPS plan for your media work.
- Work on brainstorming, outlining, and drafting media work.

Remember to think about your rhetorical situation (MAPS):

- **Mode** refers to what the writer understands about the type, or genre, of writing, including the conventions of writing that make up the modality.
- **Media** refers to the tools with which we compose, such as a collaborative word processor, a video-editing program, or an online space. Each of these media forms has technical conventions that guide it but is not necessarily rhetorically focused in and of itself.
- **Audience** refers to what previous experiences and knowledge of the intended reader the writer can assume, as well as recognition of what the audience may be interested in hearing.
- **Purpose** refers to the action that this writing will take, such as to inform or argue; it involves the reasons the writer is composing this text.
- **Situation** refers to the personal context for the writer (e.g., experience in the genre, comfort with the topic, preferences for writing) and the writing task (e.g., deadline, length, formatting requirements).

Mode	
Media	
Audience	
Purpose	
Situation	

Available for download at http://resources.corwin.com/writingrewired

Supporting Students' Thinking

When we require students to consider factors that move a media project beyond a lone artifact, we give them more thoughtful and thorough learning opportunities that rely on both their digital composing process and the outcomes achieved in their final products. In this inquiry unit, we designed the media project to help students think through their own MAPS of the composition. As such, students thought about different messages to convey based on their inquiry and research.

Additionally, students would have the opportunity to write a reflection to explain their rhetorical situation or MAPS of their media work for two reasons:

1. It offered clarity of student aims for the text.
2. It prompted students to reflect on their work and make purposeful decisions in their compositions.

Through discussion and by assigning a reflection with the media project assignment, we emphasized that students needed to think about the decisions they made as they created their composition.

For this initial brainstorming, Allie wrote the following for her plans:

Mode & Media: I am making a collage to visually represent the different types of photos and videos I talked about in my essay.

Audience: My classmates and teacher.

Purpose: Conveying my ideas and showing different aspects of my topic.

Situation: It needs to be creative and intriguing.

My media project suggests that different types of photos and videos can be used for different purposes. For example, you can use Photoshop to make someone prettier and in a way almost fake, or you can use it for artistic purposes to create an interesting image.

This response would later be refined when she explained her final project.

Zoya's reflection on her media project assignment identifies the MAPS she had in mind for her assignment, the argument, and her experience in sharing this argument.

> When we require students to consider factors that move a media project beyond a lone artifact, we give them more thoughtful and thorough learning opportunities that rely on both their digital composing process and the outcomes achieved in their final products.

The argument that my media project suggests is that there is no set definition for beauty. The variety of different faces and cultures in the collage portrays that there is a variety of ways people think of beauty in different parts of the world. The way you define the word may be completely different from the way someone sitting next to you defines it. I selected this media because when thinking of "variety" I automatically wanted to use many different images that would easily show the topic.

M/M—Multimedia/collage/visual

A—Teachers, students, Youth Voices audience

P—To portray the importance of variety in beauty

S—School assignment

Today when I brought my media project to school, I was able to almost do a second study on my topic of cultural beauty. When some of my friends saw my poster, they quickly pointed out the faces that they found most beautiful. They were surprised when I told them that all the faces would be considered beautiful in different parts of the world, but because we live in American culture, we tend to put certain characteristics under our own category of "beautiful." It reflected exactly what I researched.

In Video 5.1, students review their brainstorming ideas about the media project assignment.

watch it here

Video 5.1

http://resources.corwin
.com/writingrewired

LESSON 24. CULTURAL QUESTIONS AND MEDIA LITERACY

The purpose of this lesson is to help students

- Explore cultural fads

- Reflect on big ideas using visual arguments for a response

- Learn about how easy it can be to create and post material for a website

- Look at the actual HTML code to explore the concept of how material online might not always be accurate

- Explore another media tool that could be used for the media project

- Begin to explore media literacy and media responses to big questions

Media Literacy: Talking About Celebrity

Celebrity obsession is an aspect of American culture that students are interested in. We designed the activities in this lesson to encourage students first to read critically and then to consider the reliability of online sources. At the same time, we wanted to pull in the role of visual argument, asking students to use images to support a point, which built in scaffolds for the media project.

As part of the lesson, we also asked students to construct an argument based on their response to a question from the KQED Do Now site: "Is celebrity obsession bad for us?" We asked students to ground their answers by considering the question in the particular contexts of our nation. KQED Do Now offers weekly conversations about relevant topics for students to discuss. As a part of KQED Do Now, topic background information in print and multimedia texts is shared on the website. To support the conversation, the background information provides an opportunity for students to gain a better understanding about this topic before chiming into the conversation via the KQED Do Now blog or via Twitter. We started our conversation with students by using the KQED Do Now resources, including a film and print texts. While these are represented in the Lesson 24 handout (page 169), variations of content or another KQED Do Now prompt (including current topics) may better fit your needs.

In addition to joining the conversation with written text, we wanted students to think bigger than a yes or no answer in response to this question with a media argument. Therefore, not only did we invite students to respond with developed written answers and examples, but we also invited them to create some visuals to accompany their argument. These visuals combined an original website image with a modified version of the same website image changed to demonstrate the student's argument. For instance, some students, who believed obsession with celebrity can be an issue, changed headlines on a website. One original image showed Princess Kate Middleton with a headline describing her fashion, and students changed the headline to reflect that celebrities wear expensive clothing every day. As such, students created a visual argument to show that following celebrity fashion extensively could indeed be over the top and an obsession. Students created these images using Mozilla Webmaker X-Ray Goggles.

The Mozilla Webmaker X-Ray Goggles help users to, as the name suggests, "see through" a website. That is, when users install the X-Ray Goggles extension in their web browser, they can use this tool to see the source code for elements on a web page such as the location of an image file or the text in a headline or paragraph. Then, they can change the reference point for material on the website in their web browser. In this way, the source code for the website is temporarily changed on a student's specific machine, and the page appears different.

For instance, we demonstrated how a student could find a celebrity photo on CNN.com, specifically in the entertainment section, and replace the original with another image of the celebrity found elsewhere on the web. We also changed the headline and the introductory paragraph of the article. In this case, we were teaching students how to change the way a website looks on their computer to make an argument. If students take a screenshot of their modified image, they can share the "new" version based on the content that they changed. Of course, the students have not fundamentally altered the original website content—the modifications appear only on their computer, and once they hit "refresh" in the web browser, the image will return to normal.

Yet, in this way, students are able to create one form of media argument. They can use their own media literacy skills to think about parody and critique while at the same time seeing how easily information can be falsified. These are not typical skills we think of when assigning research projects. However, as students are "prosumers" of media, their need for critical reading and careful review of content becomes even more real, especially as they recognize the ways that they, too, can create new media messages.

Throughout the lesson, we invited students to work in teams to help one another with both the content and the technology. Many skills are involved in this work, from formulating a shared response to the question to considering what images might work for the argument. This lesson also taught students the value of connecting a media piece to their research work.

Remixing an Image for Critical Reading

While most students have a general awareness of what it means to analyze a website, we asked our students to change a website using X-Ray Goggles. The purpose of this activity was to show them once again how easily the information online can be manipulated yet still look "true." This work is also often called "hacking," though not in the sense of a security breach (students are not changing any websites beyond what is on their screen); rather, the Mozilla X-Ray Goggles fall under the Mozilla Labs Hackasaurus, which is all about remixing content. Formerly housed at hackasaurus.org (and now

Lesson 24. Cultural Questions and Media Literacy

We live in a prosumer society, in which we consume information and produce it. We need to be critical readers of the world around us. We will explore a relevant question, information about this topic, and our responses in print and visual texts.

Activity 1: KQED Do Now

On the KQED Do Now website, one discussion considers the question, "Is Celebrity Obsession Bad for Us?" (see http://blogs.kqed.org/education/2014/05/20/is-celebrity-obsession-bad-for-us/) and includes the video "Why We Worship Celebrities" (also available from www.youtube.com/watch?v=9l76OX0b2fo&feature=youtu.be). While this weekly conversation has passed, it remains relevant to our lives today.

Write your initial thoughts on the following:

- Given the context of income inequality and changing demographics across the country, is the American obsession with celebrities good or bad for our culture?

  - Consider this question in a few different ways. For instance, how does it impact people's thinking if they idolize a celebrity who later turns up in the news for criminal behavior? Or, as we think about the role of income, are celebrity bank-rolls reasonable for the average American?

  - A few other considerations:

    - Name a celebrity who is involved with charity work. How does this model help support our culture?

    - Name a celebrity whose various homes or other forms of economic wealth are represented in the media (or even think about which celebrities are shown attending the Super Bowl). How does the representation of their wealth impact our view of culture?

- Share and discuss responses.

Activity 2: Exploring the KQED Do Now Question With a Media Response

One tool that we can use to explore the concept of media literacy—and repurpose existing media with a critical lens—comes from the Mozilla Foundation, the makers of the Firefox web browser and advocates for understanding how the Internet functions. Mozilla's X-Ray Goggles allow a user to "see" the component parts of a website such as links, image file storage, and formatting tags for text such as those for bold print, emphasis (italics), and various levels of headings.

(Continued)

(Continued)

- Visit https://webmaker.org/en-US/goggles/install and install the X-Ray Goggles in your web browser. Steps in this process are on this website.

- Choose a website about your topic and create a remixed version of that site using the X-Ray Goggles. For instance, if your project is about the role of beauty in culture, perhaps you can find a website devoted to beauty products and then change the images, film, or text to show the Dove "Evolution" video, or images of everyday people enjoying normal activities rather than models at a fashion shoot.

- After visiting a website and making a plan for adjusting an image, you can use the X-Ray Goggles to make changes. It will appear as though you've changed the actual website; however, only the specific page on your screen has been changed, as you are actually altering materials on a website that is only on your computer. To share your changes, you will need to take a screenshot of the image on your screen.

- Share your image and a written reflection of your image in our online class space.

- Share your work with the class.

- Discuss:

  ○ How do the X-Ray Goggles allow you to understand the way that a web page is structured? What do they allow you to do?

available from https://webmaker.org/en-US/goggles/install), X-Ray Goggles were originally described as a tool for "learners [to] see the Web as something they can actively make instead of just passively consume, becoming co-creators and taking charge of their own learning" (Mozilla Labs, n.d.). Thus, the term *hacking* was originally employed by Mozilla and, in turn, by us as well.

The need for this exercise became clear to us during the third literature circle meeting (Lesson 17). Despite the fact that students had already explored image doctoring and said they understood that Internet sources aren't always reliable, students abruptly stopped a heated debate about Suzanne Collins's *Hunger Games* (2008) when a student found a news source that supported her point. None of the students thought to question the reliability of the source or to try to confirm or discredit it; they simply took it as the truth and ceased their valuable conversation.

The role of media literacy, which involves the careful, critical reading of media as well as the creation of media, is an important skill for students. Through this lesson, we invited students to think about how easily they could change a website. This was an effective way to remind them that people do change the Internet and even news sources may not always be correct or reliable.

The example in the following image shows how one group of students effectively manipulated a celebrity photo and headline as part of their argument about how society glorifies the actions of celebrities. This post (as well as other examples) appears on the KQED Do Now website in the comment section after an article titled "Is Celebrity Obsession Bad for Us?" (Farr, 2014).

This example shows how the students were able to explore the concept of celebrity in interesting ways through a few simple modifications of a website. Additionally, this activity gave students the chance to practice referencing original texts and creating remixed or "hacked" images. In their blog posts responding to the KQED Do Now question "Is Celebrity Obsession Bad for Us?" students shared their images and in writing provided context for their visual argument. (See page 172 for their post.)

Extensions and Adaptations for Lesson 24

While there is value in asking students to manipulate images in print format—through a process of, quite literally, cutting and pasting—or create their own images, asking students to think about how image and text manipulation may happen online can broaden their critical reading skills. In particular, you can ask students to explore how a composition works through a variety of mentor texts, such as commercials, news clips, and user-created videos, and how they might recognize ways someone could change the argument through manipulation of those texts. In this way, students are

Example of a Remixed Website Using Mozilla's X-Ray Goggles

Source: Bottom image ©Feverpitched, Thinkstock Photos; Screenshot courtesy of KQED.

revisiting what it means to remix and remake content, while also exploring argument and critical media literacy skills. In addition to trying X-Ray Goggles, they can use another Mozilla tool, Popcorn, to remix videos.

Additionally, sites like Know Your Meme and Memebase can provide students with up-to-the-minute links to current Internet phenomena, such as content from a commercial or movie, that turn into memes. Like X-Ray Goggles, the Meme Generator (http://memegenerator.net/) can provide students with another option to focus more on words and images through use of a meme.

Media work can be purposely integrated into various curricula. For example, students in some expository writing classes at Okemos High School begin the research process by conducting original research, including interviews with experts on their topic, and they use the interviews to create documentaries to show various information about the research topic before even composing the research essay.

LESSON 25. WORKSHOP: INQUIRY-BASED RESEARCH ESSAY AND MEDIA PROJECTS

The purpose of this lesson is to help students

- Review ways to integrate quotes in their writing

- Practice building context for quotes to support their ideas in writing

- Use drafts of inquiry-based research essays to explore inspiration for media projects

- Explore key elements of the media project composition

Integrating Quotes: Writing Techniques and Resources

Throughout their work writing the inquiry-based research essay, students reviewed writing techniques they had previously studied in Dawn's class. At this point in the inquiry unit, we also recognized that students specifically needed to review ways to integrate quotes and to cite sources to build credibility in their writing and avoid plagiarism. We used Graff and Birkenstein's *"They Say/I Say": The Moves That Matter in Academic Writing* (2006) as an opportunity for students to explore templates as guides for integrating ideas from others into the context of their argument. Additionally, students reviewed how to cite sources using the Online Writing Lab at Purdue. The OWL is an excellent resource for writers as it offers information about writing, research, grammar, and mechanics, as well as style guides. Students regularly refer to this site to review how to format citations in the style recommended by their teacher. As noted in Chapter 4, we also encouraged students to use Citelighter to save time formatting citations so they could concentrate on other elements of their work.

Students were curious about how to cite the materials that they found for their media project, making the point that they do not often see lists of citations at the end of commercials, music videos, or other popular media texts. This is a rhetorical move on the part of the media creators, and students did not want to clutter their own projects with lists of URLs or with captions on every picture. Thus, for the purposes of this project, Dawn asked students to keep a list of websites that they accessed, but she did not require a formal list of citations for their media sources. While they did create a list of formal citations for their inquiry-based research essay (using Citelighter), it was more important to Dawn at this point that they simply document their media sources, as this also made sense for the rhetorical situation of the media composition.

Peer Response and Media Inspiration

During this part of the inquiry unit, students worked with their literature circle teams to again share ideas and respond to one another. This time, the peer response focus was on reviewing brainstorm ideas and drafts for media work. Various ideas circled the room as student conversations included a focus on ideas, media options, and visual literacy, as well as audience and purposes for their work. Conversations ranged, exploring various ideas, such as

- The impact of a collage

- Reviewing the concept of visual argument from the "Visual Literacy and Document Design" slide show (see Lesson 6, page 60)

- Creating their own TED Talk or video, or a short Vine or looping video, or a Prezi, which is a creative presentation slide show (http://prezi.com)

- Debating the role of printed images versus digital images

Throughout this peer response time, students were exploring media options with a rhetorical approach.

Extensions and Adaptations for Lesson 25

Providing students with opportunities to work on developing academic language as well as workshop ideas and revise is important to the writing process. Dawn builds in practice with using text as evidence throughout her classes. One digital reading activity that supports this includes students selecting passages for close reading and to make a point about writing style or other literary elements, such as motifs. This work is highlighted in *Connected Reading: Teaching Adolescent Readers in a Digital World* (Turner & Hicks, 2015) and is much like the dialectic journal writing and practice students engaged in through literature circle work described in this book (see Lesson 8, page 72). Multiple opportunities for students to practice supporting ideas with textual evidence could also include students responding to one of their texts from their research and explaining how that one text relates to a claim.

Peer response for media work could look just like the peer response that students do with writing. Clearly, students might not have an entire project

Lesson 25. Workshop: Inquiry-Based Research Essay and Media Projects

In our workshop today, we'll review ways to enter academic conversations through integrating quotes into your inquiry-based research essay. We will also explore current work (brainstorming, notes, drafts, etc.) with media projects.

Activity 1: Writing Tip—Integrating Quotes Into the Context of Your Writing

As you work with integrating quotes, there are wonderful models for ways to integrate other ideas in the text. Another template for support comes from Graff and Birkenstein, *"They Say/I Say": The Moves That Matter in Academic Writing* (2006). Check out various models from this book online, including www.csub.edu/eap-riap/theysay.pdf.

- Choose one of "The Most Important Templates," such as "Her argument that _____ is supported by new research showing that _____."

- Adapt this template to include one fact that you have found in your research that connects with a new finding. For instance, you might write, "Professor Smith's argument that beauty differs in various cultures is supported by other research showing that cultural needs can impact what is recognized as 'beautiful.'"

- Review the ways that you currently integrate quotes in your writing. Try various templates as you revise to integrate research, make connections, and provide context for your sources throughout your writing.

Activity 2: Peer Response and Media Inspiration

1. Identify one solid paragraph from the current draft of your essay to share with your literature circle team.

2. In teams, read your paragraph. Team members should listen closely and write some notes down for the author. Address the following questions:

   - From this section of the inquiry-based research essay, what images come to mind that can help represent the information presented?

   - What do you notice in the writing that can be presented through media?

Remember to think about the role of visual literacy and various media we have been studying throughout our culture study.

3. Share brainstorming for your media projects in teams.

(Continued)

(Continued)

Activity 3: Brainstorm Media Projects as a Class

Review brainstorming of ideas as a class.

Activity 4: Share Ideas/Drafts With Peers

Discuss the following moves as you share your ideas for crafting your media project:

- What argument will this media project suggest?

- What are the claims in the project?

- What is the evidence?

- What parts are clear? What parts could use further clarity?

ready; in this case, they could share ideas or map out their plans on paper. This writing process is much like that of filmmakers creating storyboards to map out their ideas.

Additionally, some students may need more support with their media work. Actually providing storyboards (which visually map out plans for a video project) might be helpful. This type of planning is akin to graphic organizers used in writing. For any mapping tool, students can work in print or digital spaces. Students might explore mind-mapping tools to draft out their work, such as

Gliffy (www.gliffy.com)

Google Drawings (www.google.com/drive/using-drive/#drawings)

Mindomo (www.mindomo.com)

LESSON 26. REFLECTION AND PUBLICATION OF THE INQUIRY-BASED RESEARCH ESSAY

The purpose of this lesson is to help students

- Reflect upon learning throughout the reading, researching, and writing process

- Reflect on the final product of their inquiry-based research essays

- Celebrate student writing

- Publish their inquiry-based research essays and celebrate writing

Reflecting on the Work

Dawn began this lesson by giving students time to reflect on the process of creating their inquiry-based research essays. As students looked back at various learning moments, they assessed their own learning and demonstrated their critical thinking. The following reflections indicate how much students were learning.

As we worked throughout the unit on our study of culture, my thinking became much broader, incorporating many more ideas rather than honing in on one singular idea. As I questioned all these various ideas, my research was enhanced because I was able to view all these other topics and realize which ones I liked and which ones were not as interesting for me. This allowed me to focus on a topic I really enjoyed, and I think because of this, a very strong paper came out of it. As I researched for my writing, I realized that you need a good number of citations to back up your paper. Primary sources allow readers to hear from actual people, and I feel as though they add a certain bit of credibility to the paper. I am really happy that I figured out how to use in-text citations in a basic sense, but they are still something to work on, because they have so many different rules. I am also proud of how I used primary sources. I think those were very fun to get, and I enjoyed seeing what different people thought about a topic.

—Allison

Writing and responding to essays of others has helped me reflect on not only one single topic, but many different ideas. My thinking has definitely evolved and become more professional, and questioning my research made it more accurate and understandable to read. I developed my writing by comparing it to that of others and taking factors of their process that I liked. I am probably most proud of the main idea that I came up with and the way in which I portrayed my topic; I took a topic that a lot of people discuss, and then added new information that most don't know about. I myself benefited the most when being able to talk to my peers and let them critique my writing, and also when I was able to hear about completely different topics, which expanded my awareness of multiple different things. My topic, beauty, is extremely beneficial to know about since it concerns so many every day. The information I shared portrayed how there is no set definition for such a controversial topic, and wherever you go, you'll see a different aspect/opinion of beauty portrayed. I hope the one thing that people will keep with them after reading my essay is how all beauty is beautiful, which is definitely what I got out of writing my essay.

—Zoya

Both of these responses show that the students were very engaged with their topic; they knew it well and used their work to describe their learning. In Allison's response, she noted not only the expanded ideas that came from this work, but also the role of sources, including primary and secondary sources, in her writing. In Zoya's response, she explored the concept of adding on to a conversation by exploring a common topic, but bringing new information and a new spin to the work. In their reflections, not only did students demonstrate learning, but many also identified what they would continue to work on, which reflected their embracing the transfer of skills in learning situations.

Extensions and Adaptations for Lesson 26

Celebrating their writing with music as the students enter a classroom provides recognition of the hard work that happens when we engage in real critical reading, researching, and writing. There are many ways, of course, to celebrate student work. This is also a time when review of skills learned could be a part of the conversation, as students could collaboratively create print posters of skills learned or infographics highlighting key research skills.

Students could also write letters to someone who helped with their essay, such as a person they may have interviewed for their original research or a librarian who helped them conduct their research. Additionally, students could collaboratively reflect on their learning by writing about the research process for a future class. In this way, students can engage in recognizing their learning and also celebrate just how far they have come in their own learning process.

Publishing student work for authentic audiences is an important part of the writing process. Beyond publishing digitally, it can be inspiring to publish a student collection of work for the class or even for parents/guardians and community members.

Sharing Inquiry-Based Research Essays

We offered students the opportunity to publish their work, specifically through publishing on Youth Voices and/or their student profile pages on Wikispaces, but we did not require them to do so. While we encouraged all of them to publish their work on our class wiki or on their own blog, we recognized that even some of the students who took the most pride in their work would still find the process of sharing it too nerve-racking. Fortunately, many students, including Allison, did choose to publish. The introduction to her inquiry-based research essay follows on page 181.

HAND OUT

Lesson 26. Reflection and Publication of the Inquiry-Based Research Essay

Congratulations on all you have accomplished with your inquiry-based research essay. Let's stop and reflect on our writing context or rhetorical situation as well as our learning. We'll also share and publish writing today!

Activity 1: Identifying Your Inquiry-Based Research Essay Rhetorical Situation

Using your notes regarding mode, media, audience, purpose, and situation (MAPS) for the inquiry-based research essay, identify the MAPS for your writing, as they are unique to your essay. For instance, what audience would benefit from hearing about your work? What disciplinary field would like to hear about your work? Explain in a written reflection how you used this rhetorical situation in your writing process.

Activity 2: Reflect on Your Learning

Think back over your learning this year and especially throughout the inquiry unit. Reflect in writing on your work for yourself, your teacher, and a public audience (such as Youth Voices or your profile page of the online class space) if you would like to publicly share your thinking. For your reflection, consider the following questions:

- How did your thinking evolve over the course of this inquiry unit?
- How did questioning impact your research?
- How did you extend your understanding about using research when writing?
- How did you develop in your writing and thinking?
- What are you most proud of in your writing?
- What will you continue to work on in the future?

Activity 3: Celebrate and Publish Your Work!

Congratulations on the completion of your work for your inquiry-based research essay. You are a researcher! You are a writer!

1. Share your paper with your literature circle team.

2. As a team, share a few specific celebrations from your papers and learning process.

3. Publish your work to share with others. Post your work on your profile page of the online class space and/or Youth Voices.

4. Consider other potential audiences that you could share your work with. For instance, if you interviewed people for your original research, would you like to share your work with that audience too?

That's Entertainment!

"This is the Fox 47 evening news." "Can't fall asleep?" "Must be the coffee." "#sleeplessinSeattle" "Off with their head!" These phrases all appear in some form of entertainment. We may hear a television reporter introduce the local news, or a restless traveler complaining on Facebook. All of these media provide entertainment for people, and they have been affecting our culture for years. Even before the arrival of modern-day technology, people found ways to occupy their time. But one question that can be asked is: How do different forms of entertainment affect people's lifestyle and attitudes? Since the beginning of time, the way people entertain themselves has affected the way they behave. From the viewing of public torture and the practice of alchemy in the Middle Ages, to social media and video games today, entertainment is like a double-edged sword, both benefiting and harming us.

To read the rest of Allison's essay, visit the companion website at http://resources.corwin.com/writingrewired.

While not all the students' essays were as strong as Allison's, we would argue that nearly all the students had gained a new sense of appreciation for questioning, researching, and writing, as well as citing what they had been reading, using examples from both their literature circle book and the nonfiction pieces they discovered through research. As we have noted throughout the book, students composed their essays while simultaneously creating a media composition. To put the finishing touches on that piece, we wanted to introduce them to a variety of concepts related to copyright and fair use.

LESSON 27. EXPLORING BASIC COPYRIGHT ISSUES: COPYRIGHT, FAIR USE, CREATIVE COMMONS, AND THE PUBLIC DOMAIN

The purpose of this lesson is to help students

- Explore basic issues of copyright

- Learn strategies to be responsive with advanced searching of content under a Creative Commons license

- Practice exploring copyright with a fair use reasoning guide

Exploring Basic Copyright Issues

In this final lesson before the media projects were due, we wanted to reiterate the ideas about copyright and fair use that Dawn had introduced the students to earlier in the year, including insights about Creative Commons and "copyleft"—or copyright-friendly—materials. Over the past few years, we have returned again and again to resources created by Renee Hobbs and her colleagues at the Media Education Lab, including *Code of Best Practices in Fair Use for Media Literacy Education* (Media Education Lab & Program on Information Justice and Intellectual Property, 2009) and *Copyright Clarity: How Fair Use Supports Digital Learning* (Hobbs, 2010), which includes a reasoning guide for fair use.

Let's face it—copyright information is confusing to many people, not just students who are still learning to give credit to sources. The videos in this lesson provide student-friendly ways to get at the basics of copyright, and they even help teachers better understand and explain copyright. "User Rights, Section 107" posted by Renee Hobbs (2009) offers a catchy music video to teach the basics of fair use of content for the repurposing of material. This film also offers a model of fair use because all of the visual content in the film is repurposed under fair use.

While some students found the video silly, they understood the message. Some of our students reviewed the lyrics as noted in the lesson, while others decided to just listen. Students who used the lyrics found them helpful to refer back to and clarify main points about copyright explained in the song. And, even for those who didn't study the lyrics in detail, many students embraced their auditory learning skills—the next day, some came in singing the "User Rights, Section 107" song because it was stuck in their heads!

The guiding questions given in the Lesson 27 handout for Activity 2 (page 183)—What is "transformativeness"? What are the "four factors"? Why do context and situation matter when considering fair use?—were essential to help students narrow their focus on the content of the video. While most found the video helpful, some students found the song with the video a bit much to follow in one viewing (we posted a link to this video on our class wiki so students could review it later, and some students did go back to it). The focused questions on the handout helped students make sure they understood the message. In short, U.S. copyright law allows users of copyrighted material to repurpose existing words, pictures, pieces of art, songs, films, TV shows, and other pieces of intellectual property so long as they meet four conditions related to the nature, amount, and purpose of the use, as well as the effect on the potential market for the original copyrighted work.

Lesson 27. Exploring Basic Copyright Issues: Copyright, Fair Use, Creative Commons, and the Public Domain

HAND
OUT

> *Copyright law has several features that permit quotations from copyrighted works without permission or payment, under certain conditions. Fair use is the most important of these features. It has been an important part of copyright law for more than 170 years. Where it applies, fair use is a user's right.*
>
> —Code of Best Practices in Fair Use
> for Media Literacy Education, p. 5

Activity 1: Brainstorm and Free Write

- What do you know about "copyright"? What have you heard in the news? What have you seen in copyright notices for movies, books, games, and music?

- Under what circumstances is it legal, and academically appropriate, to use copyrighted material: never, always, or sometimes? Why?

Activity 2: Better Understand Copyright and Fair Use

- Watch "User Rights, Section 107" at http://youtu.be/8tWhKeb-fUQ.

- To watch with the lyrics in front of you, check out http://bit.ly/usersrights.

- Discuss key issues addressed in the video. What is "transformativeness"? What are the "four factors"? Why do context and situation matter when considering fair use?

Activity 3: Apply What You Have Learned

- Explore *Copyright Clarity* by Renee Hobbs (2010) and the reasoning guide "Document the Fair-Use Reasoning Process" at http://bit.ly/fairusereasoning.

- Use the reasoning guide on material you plan to use in your media project.

Activity 4: Creative Commons

- View video on the history of Creative Commons at https://creativecommons.org/videos/get-creative.

- Discuss the major points of the film.

  ○ What is Creative Commons?

  ○ How does it help with searching for information?

  ○ How can you use a license for Creative Commons?

(Continued)

(Continued)

- Explore the Creative Commons website to discover what Creative Commons is and how it functions.

- Try a Creative Commons search at http://search.creativecommons.org.

Activity 5: Public Domain and Other "Copyleft" Materials

- Visit the Copyright Friendly Wiki to find other sources for public domain and "Copyleft" materials with open or generous copyright terms at http://copyright friendly.wikispaces.com/Home.

Reflect and Plan

As you look at the current draft of your media project, what considerations do you need to make related to copyright and citing your sources?

After reviewing the role of "transformativeness" to add value and repurpose, students understood a little more about remixing. One student simply defined transformativeness as "to make something new." Students embraced the role of innovation and creativity through repurposing, and one student wondered, "Why wouldn't we make something new?" Another put it this way: "We have to make something new because it is *our* project, and if we didn't make something new, we'd be dealing with plagiarism."

When we discussed the four factors to determine fair use, we did need to talk about each factor for clarity purposes. For instance, some students asked what it means to consider "the nature of the use," and we needed to discuss the various ways works could be used. We talked about how students, as digital writers, must consider these four factors—nature, amount, purpose, and effects on potential markets—with intention. We also discussed thinking about context for why a composition is created, distinguishing educational purposes from for-profit uses. These conversations were easy to have with students because of the context of rhetorical situations, as described in our approach to teaching this unit, so students were already primed to work through the lens of considering moves they make in their compositions, such as thinking about their own audience and purpose, as well as considering specific content to reuse. Moreover, students talked about modality of a composition in determining what to use and why to use a particular text for a composition. Students recognize that a "works cited" page does not go at the end of videos that they see. Through examination of models, students are able to see different forms of citations for media work.

Following the review of copyright information, students used Hobbs's *Copyright Clarity* (2010) and "Document the Fair-Use Reasoning Process" handout (Hobbs, n.d.) that takes students through specific questions to practice considering fair-use requirements when creating a project. Students found this helpful to complement their thinking about copyright and to apply their learning to the drafts of their projects.

Creative Commons began as a way to solve a problem: "The idea of universal access to research, education, and culture is made possible by the Internet, but our legal and social systems don't always allow that idea to be realized" (Creative Commons, n.d.). The history of Creative Commons film explains how it is a licensing feature that allows others to know that the author of a text finds it acceptable to reuse and share his or her work. Through examples from reuse in the music industry, the film helps explore the role of Creative Commons for permissions. When discussing the Creative Commons search, it can also be helpful to explore Google's advanced search settings. Through advanced search features, settings for Creative Commons are established so that it is clear if a work has been specifically licensed for reuse or not, as well as if it is safe for commercial use. To add on to the conversation, we invited students to explore the Creative Commons website and Copyright Friendly Wiki to read a bit more broadly and develop their understanding about copyright. Through discussion, we knew that students understood the basics of copyright to apply to their work. As a class, we also discussed an important feature of context, that educational use of material is much more open than commercial, for-profit use.

Extensions and Adaptations for Lesson 27

Lessons about copyright could encompass an entire school year. Copyright conversations are important to media work, but they could also be a part of the conversation when teaching students how to cite information. Giving credit to other sources is clearly an important part of building credibility in our own writing as well as being ethically sound in a composition. To address this, exploring various types of citations, as well as how they shift based on the rhetorical situation, could be very helpful. There are many ways to extend work with copyright. Explore the various links on the lesson handout with students. Many of the websites we shared here have much more depth of information related to copyright. Additionally, modeling our thinking processes as we, as writers, think through fair use by using the fair use handout would be valuable for students. We reiterate the work of Renee Hobbs and her colleagues at the Media Education Lab as important voices in this sometimes complex copyright conversation.

LESSON 28. REFLECTING, SHARING, AND CELEBRATING THE FINAL MEDIA PROJECT

The purpose of this lesson is to help students

- Reflect and give context on their media project

- Publish their media project and celebrate their learning

Reflecting on the Work

Just as we invited students to reflect on their inquiry-based research essays, we asked them to reflect on their final media project. We designed this activity to help us better understand the full context for students' thinking, which was essential for our evaluation of their media work. Providing students with an opportunity to explain their planned rhetorical situation, explain decisions they made in their work, and reflect on their learning based on process and product can be helpful for teachers to better understand the aims of the work. Additionally, this honors the process that students engaged in over the entire unit; students explained how their work demonstrates their learning and thinking (which may not always be as clear in the project alone). It also

Lesson 28. Reflecting, Sharing, and Celebrating the Final Media Project

HAND
OUT

Congratulations on your media project work. Reflect and explain your process for this work. Today you will have a variety of opportunities to share and celebrate your work.

Activity 1: Please write a brief reflection about the process and project of creating your media project.

Be sure to address the following:

- How did you define the MAPS of your media work? (Yes, you can just revise your original plans.) Defining the MAPS is part of the criteria for assessment of your work.
- What contextual information would you like your audience to know about your project? (You should already have some information on this, as part of the required assessment information.)
- What did you learn from this project in terms of your composing process?
- What did you learn from the creation of a final product?
- What is your reaction to your media work in terms of process and product?
- How did the media work impact your thinking about your inquiry topic?
- What argument does this media project suggest?
- What are the claims in the project?
- How does the media influence the message?
- Why did you select this media to present your research?

Activity 2: In literature circle teams, share your projects, providing any context needed for your work.

Respond to your peers. Identify the following for each composition:

- A compelling idea expressed in the work
- What you understood about the argument of the work
- Something you learned
- A compelling move in the creation of the piece (the role of color, visual design, audio, etc.)

Activity 3: Publish your work!

You can share your work on Youth Voices and/or our online class space. Be sure to revisit your reflection above to see if you would like to explain any aspects of your work to your audience.

Activity 4: Informally share projects with the class.

Celebrate your ideas, creativity, and innovation!

reinforces learning goals as it demonstrates students' understanding of their learning, while providing ownership of student learning through reflective self-assessment.

Publishing and Celebrating the Final Media Project

Students were invited to publish the final media project as well. To celebrate their work, students shared their projects, not as a formal presentation that was rehearsed and evaluated, but rather informally by simply sharing their work and discussing it. Sharing their work without a formal evaluation led to students focusing on celebrating their work and sharing questions or ideas that the media work prompted for the audience. It also allowed students to discuss process and ideas they gained from being composers of the work without worrying about the added pressure of a formal presentation grade. First, students shared in small groups (and they were excited to do so the moment they walked into the room); then, they shared with the entire class. In this way, sharing insights from the composition itself was the heart of the celebration. Some projects dictated a need to share based on the rhetorical situation of the project. For instance, students that designed presentations that were not stand alone, or an Ignite speech, delivered those to the class as part of their media plan.

For her media project on entertainment (see page 181), Allison created a video called "That's Entertainment," which looks at the role of entertainment throughout history. Her work can be viewed on our Wikispaces page (see http://culture-study.wikispaces.com/Allison+B). Here is Allison's reflection to her media work.

As I worked on my media project, the use of MAPS has definitely helped with organizing my thoughts and the steps needed in order to create my project. As someone views the project, the object was to display the different forms of entertainment over the years, and how they have changed. The use of videos alongside pictures was to create a different feel than a plain video featuring exclusively pictures. I felt that the process that went into this project was very smooth and well executed. There were a few hiccups as I worked on the video, yet it turned out in a way that is professional and interesting. The use of this media allowed me to think more about my inquiry question by giving me a visual to view, instead of just giving me text, which can only offer so much. I could see how these different entertainment forms I mentioned in my paper actually looked, and realize just how popular they actually are (were). Sometimes it is nice to see how someone visualizes a project, and this media allows me to show how I visualized my inquiry question.

Mode/Media: PSA-style video using multiple images of entertainment culture

Audience: Peers, teachers, online viewers

Purpose: Writing for myself, teachers, to earn a grade

Situation:

1. Organize outline

2. Gather clips related to project and other entertainment forms

3. Gather pictures related to project

4. Organize and put it together in iMovie

5. Edit and finalize

Argument: The way people have viewed entertainment has changed dramatically over the years.

Claims: The different pictures and video clips illustrate the changing forms of entertainment. Some examples are a movie trailer, football, chess, storytelling, and musical bands.

My choice of media is able to display these claims in an equal and efficient manner, while also providing more interest than a stationary piece. Along with stationary pictures, this form of media also allows videos, which adds movement and excitement to a piece that would otherwise just be a bunch of pictures.

I chose this media because I felt it would be a lot more interesting than just posting a bunch of pictures on a piece of cardboard. With this media, you are also able to include video footage, and I feel like that is a big form of entertainment, so it is important to include videos. In a normal presentation, this could not happen or would not flow as smoothly.

Allison's reflection and media work clearly reflect the goals we established for the inquiry-based research essay and media work. The thinking processes addressed in her reflection show careful critical review of audience and purpose, as well as how to use media to make a claim about the inquiry focus.

George chose to create a "hacked" or remixed website (see page 191). Here is his response to the media work.

Mode/Media: The mode is a poster/picture with web designs of the same website. I edited the website on one side and kept the website the same on the other.

Audience: This paper could be written to anyone who might be involved with multiracial kids or adults. This can include teachers and parents. This could also be written to people in general because with the multiracial population growing this is starting to be a big deal.

Purpose: My purpose to create this project is to analyze my book, *Ender's Game*, and to engage in real-life and real-world questions that interested me. Lastly, I developed my project related to my inquiry conversation.

Situation: My situation was to synthesize my research in an interesting way and to show a clear audience and purpose for my work.

My media project argument suggests that multiracial people are at a disadvantage in the real society and how it is a big problem in society right now.

My claim is that people are at a disadvantage because people in our society will bully you if you are different to other people. You will be put as a minority and often called racial slurs, etc.

My media suggests that often people are biased in their opinions. The girl, just because she was multiracial, automatically became a target for racial slurs and name-calling even though the commercial was actually funny and really thought-out. If the girl was white, for example, and the family wasn't multiracial, my media shows how news and society would have probably portrayed that as well due to the fact it was a good commercial.

> I selected this media to represent my research because it does a great job showing people how multiracial people are treated in society, in the news. It does a good job giving you a visual about how people might have interpreted the Cheerios commercial differently if the child was white and/or not multiracial.

When George shared his work with the class by informally presenting at the front of the room, students were silent as they contemplated the arguments he was creating. Immediately, students responded with comments from "The argument about race is very interesting here—you got me thinking about who is represented in media" to "I never would have thought of that." Some students also offered responses to the visual, noting that they liked how he put the two images side by side for comparison, and that they had to really think about which image was the original one. Both in writing and through his presentation to the class, George purposefully reflected upon the choices he made for composing. His final project successfully highlighted an interesting argument about the role of perspectives related to multiracial backgrounds.

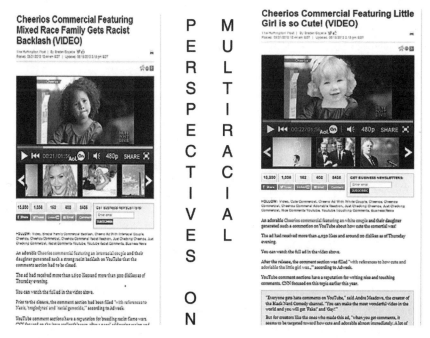

George's Hacked Website

Source: Screenshot courtesy of YouTube and Mozilla X-Ray Goggles.

Zoya wrote a paper on the role of beauty. Her context and reflection on the MAPS of her work is noted on page 166. As she thought about her learning and media work, her choices were very thoughtful. Her media project was not digital because she made the purposeful choice to create a text that could be shared in print format with images printed out on a poster instead of portrayed digitally. And her content and format sparked lots of conversation. When her work was sitting under a front table in Dawn's classroom, seniors in another class huddled around it to think about the message.

Zoya's project cannot be included in this book due to copyright concerns; however, she was mindful of citing her images and copyright for fair use as per Lesson 27. Her project included 15 different pictures of women from different cultural backgrounds. The pictures (five columns across and three rows down) included a woman with a lip ring that extended below her skin, Marilyn Monroe, and a Barbie doll, as well as women with different piercings, hairstyles (straight to curly afros), teeth, colors of skin, and ethnic backgrounds. In the middle of her poster, Zoya included the definition of beauty as follows: "beau·ty /'byo͞odē/ *noun* a combination of qualities, such as shape, color, or form that pleases the aesthetic senses, especially the sight." This text was followed by larger words, with the phrase "Beauty: How do YOU define it?" Zoya's media work, "Define Culture Multi Media," can be viewed on her Youth Voices page at http://youthvoices.net/discussion/define-culture-multi-media.

Days after Zoya shared her media project, she continued to receive questions related to her work with the media piece, and that led to interest in her research essay. For instance, another student, Kendra, asked Zoya where her research paper was posted so she could read it and respond to it. Zoya's intentional work with rhetorical moves in both her media project and her written research essay was quite compelling. Here is the introduction to her paper.

What in your opinion makes a woman's smile beautiful?

A) Shiny white teeth

B) A huge plate in her lip

C) Shark-like teeth

D) Crooked teeth

The world as a whole does not live by the same standards or ideals. One of the most clashing and contrary aspects of culture is the way we see beauty, how we define it, and for what purpose certain beauty standards are set. Most living in American culture will most likely side with answer A as portraying typical beauty, but depending on where you go in the world, every one of these aspects is seen as beautiful. Obviously, these are all extremely diverse and different characteristics, but somehow they all designate and relate to the same word: *beauty*. How is this possible?

To read the rest of Zoya's paper, visit the companion website at **http:// resources.corwin.com/writingrewired.**

When we examine Zoya's media work and essay together, it is clear that these two texts complement one another and echo rich, thoughtful thinking. Zoya's work exemplifies the learning objectives and goals of this unit, including students refining skills through work with analysis of cultural elements, composition of an inquiry-based research essay and media project based on student reading of fiction and nonfiction as well as research, and intentional work within various rhetorical situations. In her reflection on her inquiry-based research essay, Zoya clearly addressed various moves we made in this unit as being effective for her learning process as noted in class and in her reflection about her essay shared earlier in this chapter (page 178).

Another student, Annie, also explored the role of beauty as inspired by a different novel, *The Curious Incident of the Dog in the Night-Time* by Mark Haddon (2004). In Annie's media project, she explored various responses to the role of beauty and the importance of being OK with yourself. When Annie shared her movie with the class, students discussed the consequences of the fact that in her final project, she unintentionally cut off the heads of some of the people she interviewed. The class agreed that while Annie may not have intentionally made this move in her composition, it actually added a layer to their thinking about how in general we represent and think about beauty. In addition, at the end of the video, Annie put a message on her hand that included a misspelled word. However, this unintentional move was also praised by classmates, who felt it supported the concept of being OK with not being perfect, which was the actual argument of her media project. Readers can view Annie's video at http://youthvoices.net/discussion/would-you-change-culture-video-project.

Here is Annie's response to her video.

The mode of my presentation is a video. The claim I'm making is that the modern young woman lacks confidence, and feels the need to meet the unachievable standard of beauty in our culture. I was following in the tracks of my inquiry-based research paper where I inquired about the idea of improvement. I'm well aware that this message of having confidence has been a recurring one, so I wanted to make a project that would resonate with people and not be boring. This is why I chose to make a video. I'm hoping that when those who watched it saw their fellow students talking intimately about their insecurities, it would somehow affect them and make them think more closely about the role of beauty in our culture. At first unintentionally, there are small parts of my video that require deeper thinking. For example, when I first put the video clips together, the faces of the young women were cut off because of how the video was positioned in the program. I decided not to go back and replace the videos because I saw an opportunity to add a deeper layer to my project—this being that it doesn't matter who the girls interviewed are; they are representing much more than their own opinion. I really hope these different elements aren't lost, but from discussion, I think many students understood without me trying to explain why I chose not to show faces in the end. I think the video really showed these elements in an impactful way. I could talk and talk about how everyone is insecure, which may be true, but at some point talking doesn't get the message across, and I think this video did achieve the message I was hoping for to some extent. If I was to present again, I would explain more of my ideas before it was presented, to make sure everyone was paying attention to the message.

Allie's reflection on her thinking throughout the unit and on her inquiry-based research essay follows.

My thinking evolved over this unit because I began to ask more questions. I would start off with one question and then in researching it would come up with different thought-provoking questions, and it became a cycle, which really got me thinking. I think I extended my understanding about using research in my writing by using some of my older work as references, and I realized the different types of research I could use. By that I mean I would find statistics, examples, and different people's personal opinions, and I bettered my ability to analyze photos for the purpose of my paper. All this helped me to better my writing and thinking. I am most proud of all the ideas I came up with and the good questions I asked. In the future, I will continue to work on my research so I can get more statistics and perspectives on my topic.

Allie's paper explored the role of truth in society, a topic that she had been pursuing for the entire unit. Note the way in which she integrates her discussion of altering images and videos with the ideas of truth in her introduction that follows.

Truth in Society

Can images and videos change aspects of truth? In reading *Ender's Game*, this is the question I found myself asking, but is this question relevant to life as well? In researching this question, I ultimately found that yes, it is. The so-called truth in one place may be different in another. Different perspectives like opposite sides of a war may hold different truths depending on news and media shown with different videos and pictures. Now, one of the biggest things that everyone uses every day is the Internet, and who can put information, videos, and pictures on the Internet? The correct answer is everyone. Images and videos can be altered by anyone, including the media, government, and ordinary people, to change public knowledge and opinions.

To read the rest of Allie's paper, visit the companion website at **http:// resources.corwin.com/writingrewired.**

Allie's media work built upon these ideas and even paid homage to the culture collage she had developed earlier in the unit (Lesson 5, page 50). Clearly, the rhetorical moves Allie made in her work were sophisticated and interesting, and she reflected on them in a thoughtful way. While her final

watch it here

Video 5.2

http://resources.corwin
.com/writingrewired

collage cannot be printed here due to copyright concerns, Allie's images were printed on a poster, like Zoya's. Allie included images that were placed in constrast to one another, as one image was an original and the other a manipulated image either from another source or by Allie herself. For instance, Allie included a model photoshoot image with the original and the manipulated image. Allie also took an image of her mother and manipulated the image to change skin tone colors and blemishes. In this way, Allie described her work as challenging ideas about truth in society.

Mode/Media: I made a collage that relates to the question, "How do pictures and videos effect truth in society?"

Audience: My audience was my classmates and teacher.

Purpose: To show the different aspects of truth in various images.

Situation: I needed a well-made project with thought-provoking pictures.

The arguments in my media project basically were that different pictures may be staged or edited to serve different purposes in manipulating people's opinions, and we should be aware of that. I used a collage to show the images I was talking about and visually give people an idea of different types of photos in different contexts, which may or may not be acceptable and how the images they may have before taken as truth may only be partially true. The process in which I made this allowed me to come up with tons of different types of photos, staged, edited, or simply appealing to the human eye, which served different purposes such as advertising, creating an interesting piece of art, or even creating something completely false. I found there seemed to be an infinite amount that I could put on my project, and it allowed me to analyze each photo and come up with more ideas as well.

In Video 5.2, Zoya and Allie share their media projects.

Celebrating Learning and Student Success

It is important for teachers to set aside time for students to celebrate their work. As students celebrate their achievements, they recognize the value of their efforts, identify their progress, and appreciate their major learning. Throughout this inquiry unit, Dawn reviewed the students' work to add comments to challenge ideas and offer praise. As this section has shown, students shared and applauded one another in their work as well.

Dawn also decided to e-mail every parent or guardian (as well as the individual students) to note how the student was engaging in smart critical thinking and, in some cases, what big concepts the student was still working on. Most school communications are limited to point values and do not focus on the actual learning, but these e-mails gave Dawn a chance to praise the students' thinking even if their writing still contained some flaws. Many parents, guardians, and students replied, thanking Dawn for keeping them up to date and expressing a hope that the student would share his or her writing. Some students requested a conference with Dawn to better understand areas for future improvement.

The responses Dawn received also showed that the parents, guardians, and students in her class recognized the value of the learning even when the student did not receive a perfect grade. For instance, one mother told Dawn that she and her son were celebrating his progress instead of focusing on the final grade. Together they had discussed that not receiving an A does not mean that smart ideas are not happening, but rather means that there is still more learning to do. In this way, a community approach to learning was beginning to unfold.

Some students chose to share and celebrate their work in a big way. One student, who had written songs and performed them for our class earlier in the school year, finally took the plunge and published her first song online for her media project. She also created her own YouTube channel. Another student decided to make her first TED Talk, and she not only published it online, but she also delivered it live to the class. Through choices like these, students created far more than we had imagined they would do. It was clear that the careful timing and design of the lessons had set students up to experiment and take risks. As we approached the conclusion of the unit, we were delighted that the students had taken such great advantage of the various opportunities to work as genuine readers, writers, and researchers.

Extensions and Adaptations for Lesson 28

While there are many ways to celebrate student work from music to treats to applause and praising work, a major project like this could also benefit from a formal presentation for students to share and publish their work. Every student could give a formal presentation for the class, but the class could also invite guests (other classes, family members, etc.) to view student work or establish a place, such as your online space or physical spaces in the school, such as the school library or a display board in the hallway, to share the collected media work. Clearly, all of the work cannot be shared

> It is important for teachers to set aside time for students to celebrate their work. As students celebrate their achievements, they recognize the value of their efforts, identify their progress, and appreciate their major learning.

that way, so various types of sharing may be needed. A night to share projects also offers a showcase opportunity through an open-house setup with projects—both printed and digital—open to students, parents, guardians, and community members. Student formal presentations could be a part of a celebratory night like this as well, of course.

REFLECTIONS ON THE WRITING PROCESS

As we shared the rich work of students through their informal presentations, we shared responses to celebrate as a class and to analyze their work even more deeply. This week was very full as students responded to peers for feedback, revised, completed final products of both their inquiry-based research essay and media project, and reflected on both their process and their products. In their final reflections, the students demonstrated the sophistication of ideas they had developed in terms of their thinking related to culture. For instance, Annie said,

> Over the course of this lesson, I think I have grown more in my understanding of our American culture, and the idea of culture as a whole. The questions we asked had me thinking more closely and have allowed me to explore my own thoughts and thinking and led me to see things related to culture in a new way.

This theme was echoed by Beverly, who wrote,

> This unit really helped me realize the importance of culture and how much of an impact it has on everyone. It has opened my eyes to the diversity of today's society.

Reflections from students that note learning about the content are important; however, the transfer of how to learn is even more important here. Annie notes that the questions had her thinking more closely. The role of inquiry and questioning when rewiring research allows for transfer to other critical reading, thinking, and researching opportunities. Through this unit, students explored a topic that is transferable to other texts and life contexts. This is shown, for instance, as Beverly notes that she realizes the impact of culture and how it is an important lens through which to read the world.

Moreover, this work was recursive in nature as the process of the inquiry-based research essay and media work focused less on product and more on process, a topic we explore more in the final chapter.

6 Final Reflections and Conclusions

> *We delight in the beauty of the butterfly, but rarely admit the changes it has gone through to achieve that beauty.*
>
> —Maya Angelou

At the heart of teaching is the desire to help students learn and grow more than they ever thought possible. In the work of the classroom, teachers see the students' need for change and the actual changes they go through. As we help students recognize their growth, their progress in skill development, and their advancements in thinking about how they view the world, we encourage them to continue to monitor, value, and recognize their learning in the future.

When we first set out to create an inquiry-based research writing unit in the context of helping our students develop 21st century skills, we recognized that the approach to many of the traditional steps of the research process (e.g., note cards, outlines, rough drafts, and final copies) had shifted. With this in mind, our goal for each lesson became to engage and support students in activities that would be purposeful, authentic, and relevant. Throughout the "Reading Our World and Exploring Perspectives: Identity and Culture" inquiry unit, we embraced a practice of invention with students because that is how real research occurs. It is worth revisiting Table P.1 on page xxviii to reflect on the changes we considered related to inquiry, process, format, audience and purpose, and assessment.

While supporting invention in the classroom can sometimes seem impractical—perhaps even impossible—given time constraints and the need to meet criteria such as the Common Core State Standards (CCSS), we argue that this balance can in fact be achieved. We know teachers face challenges and tensions related to curriculum and assessment and being told what counts in the classroom. However, staying true to authentic, engaging learning is, after all, something teachers must advocate for to best serve their students. Kelly Gallagher (2015) also reminds us of this need and to "remember that good teaching is not about 'covering' a new list of standards—good teaching is grounded in practices proven to sharpen our students' literacy skills" (p. 7). Through purposeful work with literacy skills, many standards, such as in the CCSS, are in fact met. Specifically, as the previous chapters have shown, we designed the inquiry unit to have a path that matches the curriculum with learning objectives and the CCSS, but also provides students with many opportunities to wonder and question. In this way, we met requirements and stayed true to authentic, purposeful learning for students to engage in reading their world. Throughout the lessons and activities described in these pages, students were engaged in

> As we help students recognize their growth, their progress in skill development, and their advancements in thinking about how they view the world, we encourage them to continue to monitor, value, and recognize their learning in the future.

- Multiple writing opportunities that focused on critical questions and argument, aimed at an audience beyond just the teacher, and had the purpose of developing critical perspectives

- Exploring ideas from various texts

- Critically examining both primary and secondary sources

- Developing their own original research, such as through use of interviews and surveys

- Creating blog posts to foster discussion and responding to others
- Synthesizing reading and research into an argumentative essay and media project
- Reflecting on their learning process, as well as the final project

This work met several literacy goals, as well as unit objectives and the CCSS. Moreover, with the focus on culture for this inquiry unit, we were able to support the students' personal goals and inquiries.

In *Reshaping High School English,* Pirie (1997) notes that his "frustration with English as it has been taught amounts to this: the subject hasn't been big enough," and he recommends a curriculum that is "rethought and rebuilt with broader and hence sturdier foundation" (p. 95). While we do understand the need for students to read various types of literature, including fiction and nonfiction, we contend that curriculum can be bigger and sturdier when we integrate it into rich questioning and contexts for critical reading, as we did with this cultural focus.

> We embraced a practice of invention with students because that is how real research occurs.

In the pages that follow, we briefly summarize our thoughts on assessment and technology. Finally, we conclude with a few takeaways related to our guiding principles of inquiry-based learning, including the need to provide students with a variety of writing experiences and to engage them in connected learning.

ASSESSMENT: A FLEXIBLE, RHETORICAL APPROACH

While we tout the success of the process for all of our students and assessed students throughout the unit, we know it's still important to think about how the end products turned out and how we assessed them. When we first considered assessment for this unit, we reviewed the "Habits of Mind" listed in the *Framework for Success in Postsecondary Writing* (Council of Writing Program Administrators, National Council of Teachers of English, & National Writing Project, 2011), including creativity, persistence, and flexibility. We reminded ourselves that students progress as writers in different ways and at varying paces, so our primary goal as the teachers of this unit would be to continue facilitating their path forward.

We then turned to the National Writing Project's multimodal assessment framework (National Writing Project Multimodal Assessment Project Group, 2013), which provided us with five domains to consider when assessing this type of work:

- The artifact itself, which "incorporate[s] elements from multiple modes, and [is] often digital, but do[es] not have to be"
- The context of "the world around the artifact, around the creation of the artifact, and how the artifact enters, circulates, and fits into the world"

- The substance, which includes "content and overall quality and significance of the ideas presented"

- The process management and technique, which consist of "skills, capacities, and processes involved in planning, creating, and circulating"

- Habits of mind, which include the same types of concepts as articulated in the *Framework for Success* and "can also include an openness to participatory and interactive forms of engagement with audiences"

With these principles in mind, we established the assessment of the final inquiry-based research essay and media project and included these assessment descriptions in each assignment. With each assignment handout, Dawn included a description of what a solid composition would include through a rhetorical explanation of requirements explained through use of MAPS (see the handouts from Lesson 17, page 127, and Lesson 23, page 164); this description helped keep students on track, set up specific elements for evaluation, and served as the basis for the work. In this way, Dawn's response to the final products maintained a rhetorical approach.

Dawn intentionally did not set up a specific point system or rubric to evaluate the students' work because the context varied for each student's composition. In general, if students did not include a required element, then Dawn deducted a certain amount of points based on the impact to the entire composition. For instance, students who produced essays without including their own original research—one of the requirements—lost some credit from their score. However, we intentionally took a flexible approach even to "rules" such as this. When a student wrote in his reflection that he did not include his own research because the topic did not lend itself to this type of research for a specific reason, we determined the explanation made sense and the student was taking ownership as an author. Consequently, he did not lose credit for not including his own research. In this way, students were owning their moves as writers and embracing the rhetorical situation of their work.

Still, as mentioned earlier, students care about grades, and their assessment needs to be clear to them throughout the learning process. To allow for this, as students turned in papers to Dawn via Google Drive, she commented on each one, both throughout the writing process and at the end of each draft, where she provided a holistic response that began with praise and also offered constructive criticism that referenced back to paper requirements and areas for continual improvement. Her comments ranged from praise to questioning to suggestions, and they were balanced so as not to overwhelm students but to continue the conversation. If she needed to subtract points for a missing requirement, she took a moment to explain why so that students would understand how the final score was tallied.

You may have noted that throughout the inquiry unit we included less focus on structure and format, but rather asked students to build upon skills they had already studied. Unfortunately, we did not have sufficient time to engage students in any further study of grammar and mechanics. However, because this unit took place near the end of the year, Dawn was able to refer students back to skills they had worked on earlier in the year.

The issues surrounding the need for assessment are multilayered. While we must issue grades, it is essential to move students beyond the aim of simply scoring points to help them demonstrate their actual learning. By evaluating students in the context of the way they approached the MAPS (mode, media, audience, purpose, and situation) or rhetorical situation of their work, Dawn was also able to involve students in more self-assessment (in which students were fairly accurate and recognized when they were not doing 100 percent on their assessments), and to involve students in monitoring what they were learning. As part of her approach to assessment, Dawn frequently asked students to think about the following questions:

- *Are you able to identify the moves that you are making as a writer and explain how you use them in your composition?*

- *How are you showing that you understand the text?*

- *Are you thinking critically and applying your ideas in other learning moments to transfer your learning?*

This approach can be tricky, because it involves the critical thinking surrounding learning, which is more complicated than relying on a checklist. Still, when it comes to assessment and evaluation, it is essential for teachers to consider difficult questions, such as

- How do we make assessment transparent so all stakeholders—students, parents and guardians, administrators, community so we all members, and even the potential audience of congresspeople—so we all understand the manner in which we are assessing student work and learning?

- How do we help students prepare for future assessment experiences?

At the end of the inquiry unit, Dawn noted that these papers represented the best writing work that these students had produced all year. While the projects certainly allowed them to build upon skills and practices they had engaged in throughout ninth grade, the fact that we had specifically designed the unit to encourage student choice clearly increased their personal interest and buy-in, which were both reflected in the high quality of their final work.

PURPOSEFUL TECHNOLOGY INTEGRATION

We no longer need to focus students on a single tool and help them learn it to the best of their ability. Rather, we can encourage them to work with multiple

> While we must issue grades, it is essential to move students beyond the aim of simply scoring points to help them demonstrate their actual learning.

tools and experiment. When we considered effective ways to help students integrate technology into this inquiry unit, we aimed to make it purposeful. Specifically, we wanted to help students see how they could use different types of technology to make different elements of expression become a reality.

With that in mind, while most students chose to create their work digitally and share it online, we also allowed students to use more traditional print work, though much of this work also included visual literacy considerations, such as Zoya's collage. In this way, we wanted to emphasize that while digital tools can be used in important ways, they are secondary to the act of thinking and learning. Throughout the inquiry unit, students effectively used technology to help them organize ideas and keep track of research. As one student working on a research paper in a different class later noted,

I was in the middle of working on [my] research paper and was having trouble keeping up with all my sources when I remembered using a website [for organization and citation] in your class . . . it's helping me out quite a bit for this paper. So . . . thanks! :)

Even if a school offers only limited access to technology, there are many ways to work around those limitations, such as frontloading planning work on paper and then using computers, focusing on collaboration with students so they can share technologies, utilizing student phones (if available), and taking similar digital concepts and working with them on paper to eventually move to a computer or at least discuss transferring skills to digital spaces. Ultimately, we need to think creatively with students to help them take advantage of the many opportunities for growth that are available in our digital world. As Hicks and Turner (2013) conclude in an *English Journal* article, "Digital literacy is no longer a luxury, and we simply cannot wait to build the capacity in our students and colleagues, as well as ourselves" (p. 64).

CONCLUSIONS

We believe that the co-constructed teaching style (teachers and students constructing content) described in this book—an approach in which students get to explore their own questions with careful support from the teacher—is advantageous to learners because it provides authentic learning opportunities.

Specifically, when teachers move students beyond "playing the game of school"—that is, beyond having students guess a predetermined answer in the teacher's head—they give students the chance to engage in even more rich learning experiences. The possibilities of these inventive experiences become endless, particularly as students share with teachers the responsibility for their own learning and guide much of their own inquiry and reflection. Co-constructing questions and topics means teachers don't have one predetermined approach or idea. This means modeling of ideas and process are authentic in the interaction between teacher and student.

Innovation and creativity are essential for student learning (Robinson, 2011). While it can be easy for teachers to become bogged down with requirements and mandates, it is essential to recognize that within those confines we can establish rich and meaningful learning. And while it is not always easy to co-create with students, embracing uncertainty does provide time for students to think and reflect. As we wrestle with big ideas, so do students. And as this unit has shown, ultimately we meet learning requirements and goals in thoughtful and rich ways.

While students will continue to ask questions like "How long does this writing assignment need to be?" we believe that teachers can and should move students beyond that question—and the confines of scores such as with strict rubrics (though we contend there are times and places for a rubric)—to help them make their writing authentic. This is why Dawn takes a rhetorical approach to writing instruction, teaching her students to thoughtfully consider their audience and purpose, as well as the mode, media, and situation of their writing. By asking students to focus on this rhetorical approach, and to justify their choices through reflection and explanation, teachers can help students hone their critical thinking about why they make specific choices as writers and how they are thinking about major moves in compositions. Moreover, for schools and teachers focused on standardized tests, we contend that teaching students to think and critically reflect as they make rhetorical decisions will naturally help students make these thinking moves in their writing not only for writing assignments and writing in the world, but also for writing on a standardized test.

So, what does all of this mean for research writing in secondary English classrooms? Rewiring research means that as teachers design lessons on research writing, it is essential to focus on the thinking and learning opportunities for students. At the same time, we need to let go of some of the decision making, trust students, allow them to stumble and make mistakes as part of the learning process, and support them throughout the process.

We are at an exciting time in education where we can move research to another level—beyond just regurgitating what is online. Research involves much more than copying from a "digital" encyclopedia. Initially,

> While it is not always easy to co-create with students, embracing uncertainty does provide time for students to think and reflect. As we wrestle with big ideas, so do students.

students may want to take that approach because it is easy, but we need to push them to higher-level thinking. Specifically, we need to help students

- Put texts in conversation with one another

- Recognize the various tools and resources that surround them

- See digital devices as more than pure entertainment

- Embrace and pursue their natural feelings of curiosity and wonder

When teachers ask students to focus on big questions, we give them opportunities to dig a little deeper and find bigger connections across texts. This focus for reading to build textual connections and explore questions takes students beyond a simple plot-driven conversation and into conversations connected to self and the world. As these chapters have shown, we set up the start of this inquiry unit to encourage students to ask "self" and "world" questions and then relate those questions to culture as well. This approach worked well for Dawn and her students, leading us to our next takeaway.

Teaching in an inquiry-driven manner is not an add-on; it is essential if we want our students to be curious and confident as readers, writers, and thinkers.

As referenced throughout this book, we also designed this inquiry unit to give students a wide variety of writing experiences. In these lessons, students explored personal responses, reflections, responses to literature, analysis of a variety of texts, quick note taking, compositions with images, visual design, collage composition and written explanation, and media work. While a major piece of this work was indeed the inquiry-based research essay, we grounded this inquiry-based research essay in a process that focused on research writing.

By creating student-centered classrooms that offer many choices and support the students' decision making, we help learners connect ideas and make connected moves. Through lessons such as the ones described in this book, teachers can strengthen the relevancy of students' learning and ensure that the learning is interesting. As Dawn's students followed a rhetorical approach to compositions, which included explaining the moves they made as writers, they began to move away from making "easy" decisions. In this way, their critical thinking was fostered and supported. This leads to our next contention.

Providing a variety of writing experiences invites students to explore, question, reflect, and synthesize their own ideas, making smart rhetorical decisions across many types of authentic compositions.

Finally, connected learning is about making students' work relevant and related to their various interests in our world. When teachers design lessons to engage students in personal learning networks, we give them opportunities to take ownership, create connections across disciplines, and use digital writing tools for genuine communication, both in presenting their ideas and by responding to the ideas of others.

We strongly believe that rewiring research requires embracing opportunities for connected learning in the English classroom, which ensures that students are making meaning out of their personal and academic lives.

When we reflect upon the rich work of Dawn's students, we delight in their authentic and thoughtful work. Most important, as we teach students to embrace the wobble and challenges it takes to create smart work, we teach them to embrace the very process of learning. Research writing is uniquely positioned to offer students an opportunity to investigate various texts, explore ideas across disciplines, and offer reflection and publishing opportunities. In this way, students become researchers within their own personal learning community. And through this work of rethinking the research process, students are able to engage in purposeful and authentic learning, as they rewire their learning experiences.

References and
Further Reading

Al Mayassa, S. (2010). *Globalizing the local, localizing the global*. Retrieved from https://www.ted.com/talks/sheikha_al_mayassa_globalizing_the_local_localizing_the_global

Anderson, J. (2005). *Mechanically inclined*. Portland, ME: Stenhouse.

Applebee, A. N., & Langer, J. A. (2013). *Writing instruction that works: Proven methods for middle and high school classrooms*. New York, NY: Teachers College Press.

Appleman, D. (2009). *Critical encounters in high school English: Teaching literary theory to adolescents* (2nd ed.). New York, NY: Teachers College Press.

Ashbaugh, H. (2007, December 5). Teaching naked and inkshedding. *The Online Instructor*. Retrieved from http://theonlineinstructor.blogspot.com/2007/12/teaching-naked-and-ink shedding.html

Association of College and Research Libraries. (2011, October). *ACRL visual literacy competencystandards for higher education*. Retrieved from http://www.ala.org/acrl/standards/visualliteracy

Autrey, T. M., O'Berry Edington, C., Hicks, T., Kabodian, A., Lerg, N., Luft-Gardner, R., . . . Stephens, R. (2005). More than just a web site: Representing teacher research through digital portfolios. *English Journal, 95*, 65–70.

Baron, D. (2005). *Hooked on Ebonics*. Retrieved from http://www.pbs.org/speak/seatosea/american varieties/AAVE/hooked/

Beach, R., Anson, C., Breuch, L.-A. K., & Swiss, T. (2008). *Teaching writing using blogs, wikis, and other digital tools*. Norwood, MA: Christopher-Gordon.

Beach, R., & Myers, J. (2001). *Inquiry-based English instruction: Engaging students in life and literature* (1st print ed.). New York, NY: Teachers College Press.

Beach, R., Thein, A. H., & Webb, A. (2012). *Teaching to exceed the English language arts Common Core State Standards: A literacy practices approach for 6–12 classrooms*. New York, NY: Routledge.

Beers, G. K. (2003). *When kids can't read, what teachers can do: A guide for teachers, 6–12*. Portsmouth, NH: Heinemann.

Bomer, R. (2011). *Building adolescent literacy in today's English classrooms*. Portsmouth, NH: Heinemann.

Borough of Manhattan Community College. (2015). Primary vs. secondary sources. *BMCC Library*. Retrieved from http://lib1.bmcc.cuny.edu/help/sources.html

Borsheim, C., Merritt, K., & Reed, D. (2008). Beyond technology for technology's sake: Advancing multiliteracies in the twenty-first century. *The Clearing House: A Journal of Educational Strategies, Issues and Ideas, 82*(2), 87–90. http://doi.org/10.3200/TCHS.82.2.87-90

Braddock, R., Lloyd-Jones, R., & Schoer, L. (1963). *Research in written composition*. Champaign, IL: National Council of Teachers of English. Retrieved from http://smago.coe.uga.edu/Books/Braddock_et_al.pdf

Bradley, A. (2004, February 25). Adolescent brains show reduced reward anticipation. Retrieved from http://www.eurekalert.org/pub_releases/2004-02/nioa-abs022304.php

Burke, J. (2010). *What's the big idea? Question-driven units to motivate reading, writing, and thinking*. Portsmouth, NH: Heinemann.

Burke, K. (1973). *The philosophy of literary form: Studies in symbolic action* (3rd ed.). Berkeley: University of California Press.

Campbell, K. H., & Latimer, K. (2012). *Beyond the five-paragraph essay*. Portland, ME: Stenhouse.

Card, O. S. (2010). *Ender's game* (Rev. ed.). New York, NY: Tor Books.

Carnegie Corporation of New York's Council on Advancing Adolescent Literacy. (2009). *Time to act: An agenda for advancing adolescent literacy for college and career success*. Retrieved from http://carnegie.org/publications/search-publications/pub/195/

Childers, P., Fels, D., & Jordan, J. (2004, Fall). The secondary school writing center: A place to build confident, competent writers. *Praxis: A Writing Center Journal*. Retrieved from http://projects.uwc.utexas.edu/praxis/?q=node/91

Collins, S. (2008). *The hunger games*. New York, NY: Scholastic Press.

Connected Learning Research Network & Digital Media & Learning Research Hub. (n.d.). *Connected learning infographic*. Retrieved from http://connectedlearning.tv/infographic

Copeland, M. (2005). *Socratic circles: Fostering critical and creative thinking in middle and high school*. Portland, ME: Stenhouse.

Council of Writing Program Administrators, National Council of Teachers of English, & National Writing Project. (2011, January). *Framework for success in postsecondary writing*. Retrieved from http://wpacouncil.org/framework/

Crawford, J. (2001, March 7). A nation divided by one language. *The Guardian*. Retrieved from http://www.theguardian.com/theguardian/2001/mar/08/guardianweekly.guardianweekly11

Creative Commons. (n.d.). *About*. Retrieved from http://creativecommons.org/about

Crenson, M. (2001, January 1). *Parents just don't understand: Brain changes, not hormones, explain many adolescent behaviors*. Retrieved from http://www.hurriyetdailynews.com/default.aspx?pageid=438&n=parents-just-dont-understand-brain-changes-not-hormones-explain-many-adolescent-behaviors-2001-01-05

Daniels, H. (2002). *Literature circles: Voice and choice in book clubs and reading groups* (2nd ed.). Portland, ME: Stenhouse.

DNews. (2013, July 1). *Why we worship celebrities* [Video]. Retrieved from https://www.youtube.com/watch?v=9l76OX0b2fo&feature=youtu.be

Dornan, R. W., Rosen, L. M., & Wilson, M. (2002). *Within and beyond the writing process in the secondary English classroom*. Boston, MA: Pearson.

Farr, K. (2014, May 20). Is celebrity obsession bad for us? *KQED Education*. Retrieved from http://blogs.kqed.org/education/2014/05/20/is-celebrity-obsession-bad-for-us

Fecho, B. (2011). *Teaching for the students: Habits of heart, mind, and practice in the engaged classroom*. New York, NY: Teachers College Press.

Fecho, B. (2013). Globalization, localization, uncertainty and wobble: Implications for education. *International Journal for Dialogical Science, 7*(1), 115–128.

Fields, S. (2014a, April 1). How to create e-posters [Blog post]. *Balancing Books & Technology*. Retrieved from http://www.okemosschools.net/education/components/board/default.php?sectiondetailid=17504&threadid=1350

Fields, S. (2014b, May 29). The school library in an informational renaissance [Blog post]. *Balancing Books & Technology*. Retrieved from www.okemosschools.net/education/components/board/default.php?sectiondetailid=17504&threadid=1385

Fields, S. (2015, June 3). Student work displayed [Blog post]. *Balancing Books & Technology*. Retrieved from http://www.okemosschools.net/education/components/board/default.php?sectiondetailid=17504

Fisch, K., & McLeod, S. (2007). *Did you know; shift happens: Globalization; information age*. Retrieved from http://www.youtube.com/watch?v=ljbI-363A2Q

Fisher, D., & Frey, N. (2007). *Checking for understanding: Formative assessment techniques for your classroom*. Alexandria, VA: ASCD.

Fisher, D., & Frey, N. (2011). *The formative assessment action plan: Practical steps to more successful teaching and learning*. Alexandria, VA: Heinle ELT.

Fitzgerald, F. S. (1925). *The great Gatsby*. New York, NY: Scribner.

Fort, C. (1998). Wild talents: *A hypertext edition of Charles Hoy Fort's book*. Retrieved from http://www.resologist.net/talent06.htm

Gallagher, K. (2015). *In the best interest of students: Staying true to what works in the ELA classroom*. Portland, ME: Stenhouse.

Garcia, A. (Ed.). (2014). *Teaching in the connected learning classroom: The Digital Media & Learning Research Hub report series on connected learning*. Retrieved from http://www.nwp.org/cs/public/download/nwp_file/19025/teaching_in_the_CL_classroom.pdf?x-r=pcfile_d

Garfield, B. (2005, July 8). Get me rewrite. *On the Media*. Retrieved from http://www.onthemedia.org/story/129250-get-me-rewrite/

Gordon, M. J. (2005). *The Midwest accent*. Retrieved from http://www.pbs.org/speak/seatosea/americanvarieties/midwest/

Grad School Hub. (2015). *Just Google it: How Google has changed research for grad students*. Retrieved from http://www.gradschoolhub.com/google-it/

Graff, G., & Birkenstein, C. (2006). *"They say/I say": The moves that matter in academic writing*. New York, NY: Norton.

Graham, S., MacArthur, C. A., & Fitzgerald, J. (Eds.). (2013). *Best practices in writing instruction* (2nd ed.). New York, NY: Guilford Press.

Graham, S., & Perin, D. (2007). *Writing next: Effective strategies to improve writing of adolescents in middle and high schools*. New York: Carnegie Corporation of New York. Retrieved from http://www.all4ed.org/files/WritingNext.pdf

Green, M. (2014, April 11). How can we address the high cost of fashion? *KQED Do Now*. Retrieved from http://blogs.kqed.org/education/2014/04/11/sweatshops-fashion/

Greene, M. (1978). *Landscapes of learning*. New York, NY: Teachers College Press.

Greene, M. (1981). Aesthetic literacy in general education. *Philosophy and Education: 80th Yearbook of the National Society for the Study of Education*, 115–141.

Haddix, M. P. (2005). *Among the brave* (Reprint ed.). New York, NY: Simon & Schuster Books for Young Readers.

Haddon, M. (2004). *The curious incident of the dog in the night-time*. New York, NY: Vintage Books.

Harvey, S., & Goudvis, A. (2007). *Strategies that work: Teaching comprehension for understanding and engagement* (2nd ed.). Portland, ME: Stenhouse.

Hattie, J. (2008). *Visible learning: A synthesis of over 800 meta-analyses relating to achievement*. New York, NY: Routledge.

Hattie, J. (2011). *Visible learning for teachers: Maximizing impact on learning*. New York, NY: Routledge.

Heritage, H. M. (Ed.). (2010). *Formative assessment: Making it happen in the classroom*. Thousand Oaks, CA: Corwin.

Heritage, M. (2013). *Formative assessment in practice: A process of inquiry and action*. Cambridge, MA: Harvard Education Press.

Herrington, A., Hodgson, K., & Moran, C. (2009). *Teaching the new writing: Technology, change, and assessment in the 21st-century classroom*. New York, NY: Teachers College Press.

Hicks, T. (2009). *The digital writing workshop*. Portsmouth, NH: Heinemann.

Hicks, T. (2010). Multiliteracies across lifetimes: Engaging K–12 students and teachers through technology-based outreach. In J. Inman & D. Sheridan (Eds.) *Multiliteracy centers: Re-centering with new media*. Cresskill, NJ: Hampton Press.

Hicks, T. (2014). Crafting an argumentative essay with Evernote. In M. Gura (Ed.), *Teaching literacy in the digital age: Inspiration for all levels and literacies* (pp. 137–149). Eugene, OR: International Society for Technology in Education.

Hicks, T., Busch-Grabmeyer, E., Hyler, J., & Smoker, A. (2013). Write, respond, repeat: A model for teachers' professional writing groups in a digital age. In K. Pytash, R. E. Ferdig, & T. Rasinski (Eds.), *Preparing teachers to teach writing using technology* (pp. 149–161). Pittsburgh, PA: Entertainment Technology Center of Carnegie Mellon University. Retrieved from http://press.etc.cmu.edu/files/Teachers-Writing-Technology-Pytash_Ferdig_Rasinski_etal-web.pdf

Hicks, T., & Perrin, D. (2014). Beyond single modes and media: Writing as an ongoing multimodal text production. In E.-M. Jakobs & D. Perrin (Eds.), *Handbook of writing and text production* (Vol. 10, pp. 231–253). Berlin, Germany: Mouton de Gruyter.

Hicks, T., & Reed, D. (2007). Keepin' it real: Multiliteracies in the English classroom. *Language Arts Journal of Michigan: The Scholarly Journal of the Michigan Council of Teachers of English, 23*(1), 11–19.

Hicks, T., Russo, A., Autrey, T., Gardner, R., Kabodian, A., & Edington, C. (2007). Rethinking the purposes and processes for designing digital portfolios. *Journal of Adolescent & Adult Literacy, 50,* 450–458.

Hicks, T., & Turner, K. H. (2013). No longer a luxury: Digital literacy can't wait. *English Journal, 102*(6), 58–65.

Hillocks, G. (1986). *Research on written composition: New directions for teaching.* National Conference on Research in English.

Hillocks, G. (2011). *Teaching argument writing, grades 6–12: Supporting claims with relevant evidence and clear reasoning.* Portsmouth, NH: Boynton/Cook.

Hobbs, R. (2009, February 23). Copyright education: User rights, Section 107 [Music video]. Retrieved from https://www.youtube.com/watch?v=8tWhKeb-fUQ&feature=youtu.be

Hobbs, R. (2010). *Copyright clarity: How fair use supports digital learning.* Thousand Oaks, CA: Corwin.

Hobbs, R. (n.d.). Document the fair use reasoning process [Handout]. Retrieved from http://mediaeducationlab.com/document-fair-use-reasoning-process

Holmes, L., & Reed, D. (2014). Peer review in a digital space. In R. E. Ferdig, K. Pytash, & T. V. Rasinski (Eds.), *Using technology to enhance writing: Innovative approaches to literacy instruction* (pp. 193–197). Bloomington, IN: Solution Tree Press.

Homan, E. C., & Reed, D. (2014). Learning from digital students and teachers: Re-imagining writing instruction and assessment for the 21st century. In R. McClure & J. Purdy (Eds.), *The next digital scholar: A fresh approach to the Common Core State Standards in research and writing* (pp. 35–67). Medford, NJ: Information Today, Inc.

Hugo, V. (1892). *The hunchback of Notre-Dame.* New York, NY: Lupton.

Hyler, J., & Hicks, T. (2014). *Create, compose, connect! Reading, writing, and learning with digital tools.* New York, NY: Routledge.

Inman, J. A. (2006). Technologies and the secondary school writing center. *The Clearing House: A Journal of Educational Strategies, Issues and Ideas, 80*(2), 74–76. http://doi.org/10.3200/TCHS.80.2.74-76

Ito, M., Gutiérrez, K. D., Livingstone, S., Penuel, B., Rhodes, J., Salen, K., . . . Watkins, S. C. (2013). *Connected learning: An agenda for research and design.* Retrieved from http://clrn.dmlhub.net/publications/connected-learning-an-agenda-for-research-and-design

Jenkins, H., & Kelley, W. (2013). *Reading in a participatory culture: Remixing Moby-Dick in the English classroom.* New York, NY: Teachers College Press.

Jensen, K. (2012, June 26). Top 10 apocalypse survival tips I learned from YA. *School Library Journal.* Retrieved from http://www.teenlibrariantoolbox.com/2012/06/top-10-apocalypse-survival-tips-i-learned-from-ya/

Jetton, T. L., & Shanahan, C. (Eds.). (2012). *Adolescent literacy in the academic disciplines: General principles and practical strategies.* New York, NY: Guilford Press.

Johnston, P. H. (2004). *Choice words: How our language affects children's learning.* Portland, ME: Stenhouse.

Kajder, S. (2010). *Adolescents and digital literacies: Learning alongside our students.* Urbana, IL: National Council of Teachers of English. Retrieved from http://www1.ncte.org/store/books/language/130985.htm

Killing us softly 4: Trailer [Featuring Jean Kilbourne]. (2015). Retrieved from https://vimeo.com/16741828

Killough, A. (2014, February 3). *Coca-Cola Super Bowl ad ignites online debate.* Retrieved from http://politicalticker.blogs.cnn.com/2014/02/03/coca-cola-super-bowl-ad-ignites-online-debate/

Kim, M. S. (2012). Cultural-historical activity theory perspectives on constructing ICT-mediated metaphors of teaching and learning. *European Journal of Teacher Education, 35*(4), 1–14.

KQED. (n.d.). *About KQED.* Retrieved from http://www.kqed.org/about/

Lee, H. (1960). *To kill a mockingbird* [Book club]. New York, NY: Lippincott.

The machine is us/ing us [Final version]. (2007). Retrieved from https://www.youtube.com/watch?v=NLlGopyXT_g&feature=youtube_gdata_player

MacNeil, R. (2005). *Do you speak American?* [Viewer's guide]. PBS. Retrieved from https://www.pbs.org/speak/about/guide/

MacNeil, R., & Cran, W. (2004). *Do you speak American?* New York: Doubleday.

Macrorie, K. (1988). *The I-search paper.* Portsmouth, NH: Boynton/Cook, Heinemann. Retrieved from https://books.google.com/books/about/The_I_search_paper.html?id=jj1ZAAAAMAAJ

Media Education Lab & Program on Information Justice and Intellectual Property. (2009). *Code of best practices in fair use for media literacy education.* Center for Social Media, School of Communication, American University. Retrieved from http://mediaeducationlab.com/sites/mediaeducationlab.com/files/CodeofBest PracticesinFairUse.pdf

Mintz, A. P. (2002). *Web of deception: Misinformation on the Internet.* Medford, NJ: Information Today, Inc.

Mitchell, D. (1998). Fifty alternatives to the book report. *The English Journal, 87*(1), 92. http://doi.org/10.2307/822030

Mozilla Labs. (n.d.). *Hackasaurus.* Retrieved from https://mozillalabs.com/en-US/mozilla-hackasaurus/

National Council of Teachers of English. (2008a). *Writing now: A policy research brief produced by the National Council of Teachers of English.* Retrieved from http://www.ncte.org/library/NCTEFiles/Resources/PolicyResearch/WrtgResearchBrief.pdf

National Council of Teachers of English. (2008b, November). *NCTE framework for 21st century curriculum and assessment.* Retrieved from http://www.ncte.org/governance/21stcentury framework?source=gs

National Council of Teachers of English Assessment Task Force. (2013). *Formative assessment that truly informs instruction.* Urbana, IL: National Council of Teachers of English.

National Council of Teachers of English, & International Reading Association. (1996). *NCTE/IRA standards for the English language arts.* Retrieved from http://www.ncte.org/standards

National Writing Project. (n.d.). *About NWP: National Writing Project.* Retrieved from http://www.nwp.org/cs/public/print/doc/about.csp

National Writing Project, DeVoss, D., Eidman-Aadahl, E., & Hicks, T. (2010). *Because digital writing matters: Improving student writing in online and multimedia environments.* San Francisco, CA: Jossey-Bass.

National Writing Project Multimodal Assessment Project Group. (2013). Developing domains for multimodal writing assessment: The language of evaluation, the language of instruction. In H. A. McKee & D. N. DeVoss (Eds.), *Digital writing assessment and evaluation.* Logan: Computers and Composition Digital Press/Utah State University Press. Retrieved from http://ccdigitalpress.org/dwae/07_nwp.html

North, S. M. (1984). The idea of a writing center. *College English, 46*(5), 433. http://doi.org/10.2307/377047

Official Coca-Cola "big game" commercial 2014: America is beautiful. (2014). Retrieved from https://www.youtube.com/watch?v=M85Y_rN1a5A

Okemos High School Library Media Center. (2015). *Book blog: 2014.* Retrieved from http://www.okemosschools.net/education/components/board/default.php?sectiondetailid=14714&

Olinghouse, N., Zheng, J., & Reed, D. (2010). Preparing students for large-scale writing assessments: Research-based recommendations. In G. Troia, R. Shankland, & A. Heintz (Eds.), *Putting writing research into practice applications for teacher professional development* (pp. 17–44). New York, NY: Guilford Press.

Orwell, G. (1950). *1984.* New York, NY: Signet Classic.

Pariser, E. (2011). *The filter bubble: What the Internet is hiding from you.* New York, NY: Penguin Press.

Piper, T. (2006). *Evolution.* Retrieved from https://www.youtube.com/watch?v=iYhCn0jf46U&feature=youtube_gdata_player

Pirie, B. (1997). *Reshaping high school English*. Urbana, IL: National Council of Teachers of English.

Popham, W. J. (2008). *Transformative assessment*. Alexandria, VA: ASCD.

Popham, W. J. (2011). *Transformative assessment in action: An inside look at applying the process*. Alexandria, VA: ASCD.

Reed, D., & Hicks, T. (2009). From the front of the classroom to the ears of the world: Podcasting as an extension of speech class. In A. Herrington, K. Hodgson, & C. Moran (Eds.), *Teaching the new writing: Technology, change, and assessment in the 21st century classroom* (pp. 124–139). New York, NY: Teachers College Press/National Writing Project.

Richardson, W. (2010). *Blogs, wikis, podcasts, and other powerful web tools for classrooms* (3rd ed.). Thousand Oaks, CA: Corwin.

Richardson, W., & Mancabelli, R. (2011). *Personal learning networks: Using the power of connections to transform education*. Bloomington, IN: Solution Tree.

Robinson, K. (2011). *Out of our minds: Learning to be creative*. Hoboken, NJ: Wiley.

Rowse, D. (n.d.). *Rule of thirds*. Retrieved from http://digital-photography-school.com/rule-of-thirds/

Rule, C. (2006, October 8). *The original scary "Mary Poppins" recut trailer* [Video]. Retrieved from https://www.youtube.com/watch?v=2T5_0AGdFic

Russell, C. (2012, October). *Looks aren't everything. Believe me, I'm a model*. Retrieved from http://www.ted.com/talks/cameron_russell_looks_aren_t_everything_believe_me_i_m_a_model

Shakespeare, W. (n.d.). *Romeo and Juliet*. Retrieved from https://books.google.com/books/about/Romeo_and_Juliet.html?id=moYNAAAAYAAJ

Shanahan, T., & Shanahan, C. (2008). Teaching disciplinary literacy to adolescents: Rethinking content-area literacy. *Harvard Educational Review, 78*(1), 40–59.

Shannon, P. (2013). *Closer readings of the Common Core: Asking big questions about the English/language arts standards*. Portsmouth, NH: Heinemann.

Smagorinsky, P. (2007). *Teaching English by design: How to create and carry out instructional units*. Portsmouth, NH: Heinemann.

Smith, M. W., Appleman, D., & Wilhelm, J. D. (2014). *Uncommon Core: Where the authors of the standards go wrong about instruction—and how you can get it right*. Thousand Oaks, CA: Corwin.

Smith, M., Wilhelm, J. D., & Fredricksen, J. E. (2012). *Oh, yeah?! Putting argument to work both in school and out*. Portsmouth, NH: Heinemann.

Soe, K. (2006, May 24). The great cultural divide: Multiethnic teens struggle with self-identity, others' perceptions. *Wilson County News*. Retrieved from http://www.wilsoncountynews.com/article.php?id=11853&n=teen-scene-great-cultural-divide-multiethnic-teens-struggle-self-identity-others-perceptions

Stanger, M. (2012, December 28). *Branding and the psychology of color: Business insider*. Retrieved from http://www.businessinsider.com/branding-and-the-psychology-of-color-2012-12?op=1

St. John, M., & Stokes, L. (2012, March 29). *Abstract: The power of the NWP as it makes an evolutionary leap forward*. Retrieved from http://www.inverness-research.org/abstracts/ab2012-03_Slds_NWP-SpringMtg-final_050112.html

Stock, P. L. (1995). *The dialogic curriculum: Teaching and learning in a multicultural society*. Portsmouth, NH: Heinemann.

Stock, P. L. (1997). Reforming education in the land-grant university: Contributions from a writing center. *Writing Center Journal, 18*.

Swenson, J., & Mitchell, D. (2006). *Enabling communities and collaborative responses to teaching demonstrations*. Retrieved from http://www.nwp.org/cs/public/download/nwp_file/8965/Enabling_Communities_and_Collaborative_Responses_to_Teaching_Demonstrations.pdf?x-r=pcfile_d

Tan, A. (1999). Mother tongue. In S. Gillespie & R. Singleton (Eds.), *Across cultures* (pp. 26–31). Boston: Allyn and Bacon.

Time. (n.d.). Top 10 doctored photos: Photo essays. Retrieved from http://content.time.com/time/photogallery/0,29307,1924226,00.html

Toffler, A. (1980). *The third wave*. New York, NY: William Morrow.

Tovani, C. (2004). *Do I really have to teach reading? Content comprehension, grades 6–12*. Portland, ME: Stenhouse Publishers.

Turner, K. H. (2012). Digitalk as community. *English Journal, 101*(4), 37–42.

Turner, K. H. (2014). Error or strength? Competencies developed in adolescent digitalk. In R. E. Ferdig & K. Pytash (Eds.), *Exploring technology for writing and writing instruction* (pp. 114–134). Hershey, PA: IGI Global.

Turner, K. H., & Hicks, T. (2015). *Connected reading: Teaching adolescent readers in a digital world.* Urbana, IL: National Council of Teachers of English.

Weir, P. [Director], & Schulman, T. [Writer]. (1989). *Dead poets society* [Motion picture]. Burbank, CA: Touchstone Pictures.

Wesch, M. (2007, March 8). *The machine is us/ing us (final version)* [Video]. Retrieved from https://www.youtube.com/watch?v=NLl GopyXT_g

Whitney, A. E. (2011). In search of the authentic English classroom: Facing the schoolishness of school. *English Education, 44*(1), 51–62.

Why we worship celebrities. (2013). Retrieved from https://www.youtube.com/watch?v=9176O X0b2fo&feature=youtube_gdata_player

Wiggins, G. P., & McTighe, J. (2005). *Understanding by design* (Expanded 2nd ed.). Alexandria, VA: Association for Supervision and Curriculum Development. Retrieved from http://www.loc .gov/catdir/toc/ecip0422/2004021131.html

Wilhelm, J. D. (2007). *"You gotta BE the book": Teaching engaged and reflective reading with adolescents* (2nd ed.). New York, NY: Teachers College Press.

Williams, R. (2008). *The non-designer's design book: Design and typographic principles for the visual novice* (3rd ed.). Berkeley, CA: Peachpit Press.

Willis, C. (1993). *Doomsday book.* New York, NY: Spectra.

Wong, E. (n.d.). *The struggle to be an all American girl.* Retrieved from http://www.sabri .org/All-American-Girl.htm

Yale University. (2008). What are primary sources? *Primary Sources at Yale.* Retrieved from http://www.yale.edu/collections_collaborative/prima rysources/primarysources.html

Youth Voices. (n.d.). *What's Youth Voices all about?* Retrieved from http://youthvoices.net/about

Zemelman, S., Daniels, H., & Hyde, A. (2012). *Best practice: Bringing standards to life in America's classrooms* (4th ed.). Portsmouth, NH: Heinemann.

Zemliansky, P. (2008, April 30). *Chapter 10: Ethnographic research.* Retrieved from http://methods ofdiscovery.net/?q=node/19

Index

Accountability, in collaboration, 133
ACRL (Association of College and Research Libraries), 59
Adbusters, 50
Adolescents. *See* Teens
Advertisements, 81
   "America the Beautiful," 105, 107 (handout)
   Cheerios commercial, 191 (figure)
   Coca-Cola commercial, 105, 106
   Dove commercial, 82 (handout)
Al Mayassa, S., 26, 29 (handout)
"America the Beautiful" (commercial), 105, 107 (handout)
Anderson, J., 147
Annotation, 40, 41 (tech tip), 44
Anson, C., 2
Answers, right, 67, 68
Applebee, A. N., xxiv, xxvi
Appleman, D., 92
Argument, visual, 167
Argument skills, 99, 168
Artifacts of culture. *See* Cultural artifacts
Asperger's syndrome, 92
Assessment, 10–12
   approaches to, 201–203
   of blog entries, 86
   of culture collage, 69–70
   of essay assignment, 122–123, 132 (handout)
   of literature circles, 80 (handout), 101, 104
   of media project, 163 (handout)
   resources for, 11–12
   self-assessment, 98–104, 102–103 (handout), 155, 155 (box), 156 (handout), 158, 177, 177–178 (box), 179, 203

Association of College and Research Libraries (ACRL), 59
Athletes, 83
Audience, 7
   in academic spaces, 138
   for essay, 121–122, 130 (handout), 158–159, 158 (box)
   need for, xxvi
   and online profile, 32
   publishing for, 179
   reflection on, 156 (handout), 158–159
   See also MAPS
Autrey, T. M., xxii

Baron, D., 109
Beach, R., 2, 92
Beauty, 81, 92, 192–193
Because Digital Writing Matters (NWP), xxvi
Behavior
   classroom management in virtual spaces, 43 (teaching tip)
   for discussion, 97 (handout), 98
Beyond the Five Paragraph Essay (Campbell & Latimer), xxiv–xxv
Bias, 83
Bibliographic management tools, 141–142
Birkenstein, C., 173, 175 (handout)
Blogging, 16, 17, 89 (tech tip). *See also* Blog posts; Youth Voices
Blog posts
   assessment of, 86
   comments on, 89
   creating, 86, 87–88 (handout)
   decisions about, 31–32
   questioning and speculating, 114 (handout), 115, 115–116 (box)

responding to, 86, 114 (handout),
    153–154 (box)
on Youth Voices, 94, 94–95 (box),
    151, 151 (box), 153–154 (box)
Blogs
preparing students to use, 117
See also Blogging; Blog posts;
    Youth Voices
Bomer, R., 56
Book selection, for literature circles, 73–74
Borough of Manhattan Community
    College, 140
Borsheim, C., xxii
Breuch, L.-A., 2
Burke, J., xxiii–xxiv
Burke, K., 16, 89
Busch-Grabmeyer, E., xxiii

Campbell, K. H., xxiv
Card, Orson Scott, 126
CCSS (Common Core State Standards), xxv,
    58, 200, 201
Celebrity, 167–168, 171
Characteristics of culture, 24
Cheerios commercial, 191 (figure)
Childers, P., 150
Citations, managing, 141–142, 173
Citelighter, 141–142, 173
Citizenship, digital, 24, 31, 43
    (teaching tip), 86
Classroom
as community focused on critical
    thinking and questioning, 2
embracing inquiry in, 54, 56
Classroom management in virtual
    spaces, 43 (teaching tip)
Close reading, 92–95, 110–113, 124
CLRN (Connected Learning Research
    Network), xxvii, xxix
Coca-Cola commercial, 105, 106
*Code of Best Practices in Fair Use for Media
    Literacy Education* (Media Education
    Lab & Program on Information Justice
    and Intellectual Property), 182
Cognitive dissonance, provoking, 27
Collaboration, 128, 133, 137, 148
Collage. *See* Culture collage
Collins, Suzanne, 171
Colors, 60

Commercials. *See* Advertisements
Common Core State Standards (CCSS),
    xxv, 58, 200, 201
Common Sense Media, 33
Communication, through
    picture-based content, 60.
    See also Visual literacy
Communities, online, 86. *See also*
    Youth Voices
Community membership, 143
Conceptual units, 1
Connected Learning Research Network
    (CLRN), xxvii, xxix
Connected Reading (Turner & Hicks), 174
Content areas, connections
    among, 20
Conversations
adding to, 179
benefits of, 17
engaging in, 2, 15–16
in learning experience, 19
in online spaces, 35
Copeland, M., 113
Copyleft, 184 (handout)
Copyright, 41 (tech tip), 181–186,
    183–184 (handout)
Copyright Clarity (Hobbs),
    182, 183 (handout), 185
Copyright Friendly Wiki,
    184 (handout), 186
Course management technologies, 13
Crawford, J., 109
Creative Commons,
    183–184 (handout), 185–186
Creativity, 205
Credibility, 83, 136 (handout),
    137–139, 142, 148, 171
Critical media literacy skills, 16
Critical reading skills, 40, 171
Critical viewing skills, 84
Cultural artifacts, 44–48, 50, 81–83,
    133, 137
Cultural lens
reading through, 4–5
thinking through, 25–30, 29 (handout)
Culture collage, 52, 54, 55 (handout)
assessment of, 69–70
response guide for, 63, 68–69,
    71 (handout)

and risk taking, 67–68
sharing, 62–71, 64–65 (box),
    71 (handout)
Culture log, 73, 78 (handout),
    79 (handout), 80 (handout),
    92, 93 (table), 151
Curiosity, fostering culture of, 2–3
*The Curious Incident of the Dog in the
    Night-Time* (Haddon), 92–93, 100,
    151 (box), 153–154 (box), 193
Curriculum
    considerations in inquiry unit, 7–13
    enhancing, 13–21
    integrating media work into, 172–173

Daniels, H., xxvi, 58
Dead Poets Society (film), 51
Design, 60, 61 (handout)
DeVoss, Dánielle, xxvi, 44, 45, 46,
    48 (handout), 60, 85 (handout)
Did You Know? (video), 46, 49 (handout)
Differentiation, 20–21
Digital citizenship, 24, 31,
    43 (teaching tip), 86
Digital Citizenship (website), 33
Digital ID project, 33
Digital literacy, 204
Digital Media & Learning Hub, xxix
Diigo, 142
Disciplinary literacy, 20
Discomfort, 25
Discovery, 6
Discussions, 95–98, 97 (handout)
Diversity, celebrating. *See* Culture collage
"Document the Fair-Use Reasoning
    Process" (Hobbs), 183 (handout), 185
Do Now, 13, 15–16, 15 (figure), 84, 167
Doomsday Book (Willis), 126
Dornan, R. W., 121
Dove commercial, 82 (handout)
"Do You Speak American?" (PBS), 105,
    106, 107 (handout), 109

Eidman-Aadahl, E., xxvi
Eli Review, 160
Ender's Game (Card), 126
Essay, inquiry-based, 3 (table)
    audience for, 158–159, 158 (box)
    features, 3 (table)

identifying rhetorical situation,
    180 (handout)
introducing, 126, 128
reflecting on, 177, 177–178 (box),
    179, 193, 194–195 (box)
sharing, 179, 181, 181 (box)
See also Essay assignment
Essay assignment, 129–132 (handout)
    assessment of, 122–123, 132 (handout)
    audience in, 121–122, 130 (handout)
    features of, 120–123
    length requirements, 122
    media in, 121, 130 (handout)
    mode in, 120–121, 129–130 (handout)
    purpose in, 122, 130–131 (handout)
    situation in, 122, 131 (handout)
    skills for, 124–126
    sources in, 130 (handout)
    writing in, 131 (handout)
    See also Essay, inquiry-based
Ethics, of image manipulation, 83, 84
Ethnic heritage, celebrating, 65–66.
    See also Culture collage
Ethnography, 51–52, 53 (handout)
"Evolution" (commercial), 82 (handout)

Fair use, 41 (tech tip), 46, 181,
    183 (handout), 185
Falsification, of information, 168
Farr, K., 171
Fashion, 81–83
Fecho, B., 25
Feedback, 11, 150. *See also* Assessment;
    Peer response
Fels, D., 150
Fields, Sandy, 143
"Fifty Alternatives to the Book Report"
    (Mitchell), 74
Filter bubbles, 142
Fisch, K., 46
Fisher, D., 11
Fitzgerald, J., xxvi
Five *T*s, 3–6, 54
Fonts, 60
Food wrappers, 44–50, 47–48 (handout)
Formative Assessment That Truly *Informs
    Instruction* (National Council of
    Teachers of English [NCTE] Assessment
    Task Force), 11

Fort, Charles, 25
Framework for Success in Postsecondary Writing (Council of Writing Program Administrators), 5, 11, 117, 201, 202
Fredricksen, J. E., 120
Frey, N., 11

Gallagher, K., 200
Garcia, A., xxx
"Get Me Rewrite" (NPR), 136 (handout)
Globalizing the Local, Localizing the Global (Al Mayassa), 26
Goals, 1–2, 24, 120, 200
Goal setting, 72, 99
Google, 110, 185
Google Apps for Education, 19, 24, 41 (tech tip)
Google Docs, 40, 41 (tech tip)
Google Drive, 6, 19, 41 (tech tip), 70, 133
Google Forms, 75 (tech tip), 140
Google Groups, 6
Google Scholar, 110
Gordon, M. J., 109
Grabill, J., 160
Grades, 202, 203
Graff, G., 173, 175 (handout)
Graham, S., xxiv, xxv–xxvi
Graphic organizers, 177
"The Great Cultural Divide" (Soe), 39–40, 42 (handout)
Green, M., 84
Greene, M., 51
Ground rules, 40

Habits of mind, 202
Hackasaurus.org, 168
Haddon, M., 92–93, 193
Handouts
    analyzing visual culture, 49 (handout)
    for beginning the cultural conversation, 42 (handout)
    close reading of passages, 112 (handout)
    for cultural conversations online, 37–38 (handout)
    cultural questions and media literacy, 169–170 (handout)
    culture collage assignment, 55 (handout)
    culture collage sharing, 71 (handout)
    for digital identities, 34 (handout)
    engaging in active discussions, 97 (handout)
    essay assignment, 129–132 (handout)
    essential questions, 9 (handout)
    exploring basic copyright issues, 183–184 (handout)
    exploring visual culture through food wrappers, 47–48 (handout)
    fashion and image in American culture, 82 (handout)
    inquiry-based research essay and media projects, 175–176 (handout)
    intertextual connections, 127 (handout)
    introducing ethnography, 53 (handout)
    language in American culture, 107–108 (handout)
    literature circle meeting 4, 152 (handout)
    literature circles, 76–80 (handout)
    media project assignment, 162–163 (handout)
    media work, 164 (handout)
    personal inquiry reflections, 87–88 (handout)
    questioning and speculating, 114 (handout)
    reading images, 85 (handout)
    reflecting, sharing, and celebrating the final media project, 187 (handout)
    reflection and publication of the inquiry-based research essay, 180 (handout)
    researching (online and in library media center), 144 (handout)
    research skills and tips, 134–136 (handout)
    self-assessment and reflection, 102–103 (handout)
    for thinking through a cultural lens, 29 (handout)
    visual literacy and design, 61 (handout)
    writing and researching workshop, 146 (handout)
    writing workshop and peer response, 156–157 (handout)
Hart-Davidson, B., 160
Hashtags, using for research, 106, 109
Hattie, J., 11
Heritage, ethnic. *See* Culture collage
Heritage, H. M., 11
Herrington, A., xxvi

Heuristic. *See* MAPS
Hicks, T., xxii, xxiii, xxvi, xxvii, 2,
    7, 138, 150, 174, 204
Hillocks, G., xxiv, 120
Hobbs, R., 50, 182, 183 (handout), 185
Hodgson, K., xxvi
Holmes, L., 159
Homan, E. C., xxiii
"Hooked on Ebonics" (Baron), 109
Hugo, V., 92, 115–116 (box), 126
The Hunchback of Notre-Dame (Hugo),
    92, 115–116 (box), 126
The Hunger Games (Collins), 171
Hyde, A., xxvi
Hyler, J., xxiii

"The Idea of a Writing Center"
    (North), xxii
Ideas, initial, 26–30
Identities, digital, 30–33, 32, 33 (table),
    34 (handout). *See also* Profile, online
Identity, of multiethnic teens, 39–40
Images
    distortion of reality by, 62
    evaluating for reality, 86
    of fashion, 81
    manipulation of, 83–84,
        85 (handout), 171
    reading, 83–86
    remixing, 168, 171, 172, 172 (figure),
        191 (figure)
    for representing culture, 27–30
    technology for editing, 62
    visual literacy, 59–62
    and X-Ray Goggles, 167, 168,
        169–170 (handout), 171, 172
Ink shedding, 28, 70
Inman, J. A., 150
Innovation, 205
Inquiry
    co-creation of, 30
    developing, 28, 30
    embracing in connected
        classroom, 54, 56
Inquiry questions, 113–117, 124,
    124 (table)
Instruction, individualized, 20–21
Intertextual connections,
    125–126, 127 (handout)

Invention, 200
"Is Celebrity Obsession Bad
    for Us?" (Farr), 171
The I-search Paper (Macrorie), xxiii
Ito, M., xxx

Jenkins, H., xxx
Jetton, T. L., xxvi
Jigsaw reading, 106, 107 (handout)
Johnston, P. H., 3
Jordan, J., 150
Journals, dialectic, 73, 78 (handout),
    79 (handout), 80 (handout), 92, 151

Kajder, S., 2
Kelley, W., xxx
Kilbourne, J., 84
Killing Us Softly (Kilbourne), 84
Killough, A., 105
Knowledge, prior, 106
KQED Do Now, 13, 15–16, 15 (figure),
    84, 167

Langer, J. A., xxiv, xxvi
Language, academic, 174
Language, in American culture, 105–110
Latimer, K., xxiv
Learning
    celebrating, 196
    and co-constructed teaching
        style, 204–205
    connected learning, xxvii, xxix–xxxi,
        xxix (figure), 16, 206–207
    e-mails about, 197
    and feeling uncomfortable, 25
    importance of social interaction in, 19
    monitoring, 99, 100, 203
    ownership of, 100
    reflecting on, 180 (handout)
    through social media platforms, 109
Learning needs, 20–21
Length, requirements for, 122
Lenses
    reading through, 92, 154
    thinking through, 25–30
Lesson, preview, 25–30
Lesson 1, 30–35
Lesson 2, 35–39
Lesson 3, 39–44

Lesson 4, 44–50
Lesson 5, 50–54
Lesson 6, 59–62
Lesson 7, 62–71
Lesson 8, 72–80
Lesson 9, 81–83
Lesson 10, 83–86
Lesson 11, 86–89
Lesson 12, 95–98
Lesson 13, 98–104
Lesson 14, 105–110
Lesson 15, 110–113
Lesson 16, 113–117
Lesson 17, 123–128
Lesson 18, 128–142
Lesson 19, 143–145
Lesson 21, 151–154
Lesson 22, 154–160
Lesson 23, 160–166
Lesson 24, 166–173
Lesson 25, 173–177
Lesson 26, 177–181
Lesson 27, 181–186
Lesson 28, 186–189
Library, 143–145, 144 (handout)
Literacies, 58
Literacy, adolescent, 3–4
Literacy, digital, 204
Literacy, disciplinary, 20
Literacy, media, 62, 167–168,
    169–170 (handout), 171
Literacy, visual, 59–62, 61 (handout)
Literature circles, 58, 72–80
    assessment of, 101, 104
    handout for, 76–80 (handout)
    inquiry questions, 124, 124 (table)
    meeting 1, 95–98
    meeting 2, 110–113
    meeting 3, 123–128
    meeting 4, 151–154
    notes, 98, 98 (figure)
    self-assessment of, 155, 155 (box),
        156 (handout), 158
"Looks Aren't Everything. Believe Me, I'm a
    Model!" (Russell), 82 (handout), 83

MacArthur, C. A., xxvi
MacNeil, R., 105
Macrorie, K., xxiii, xxx

Mancabelli, R., 2
Mapping tools, 177
MAPS, 7, 83, 156 (handout),
        180 (handout), 203
    in essay assignment, 120–123
    in final assessment, 11
    in media project, 161, 162 (handout),
        164 (handout), 165
McLeod, M., 160
McLeod, S., 46
McTighe, J., xxiii
Meaning, creation of, 46
Mechanically Inclined (Anderson), 147
Media, 7
    connection with rhetoric, 7
    creation of, 171
    in essay assignment, 121, 130 (handout)
    See also MAPS
Media Education Lab, 50, 182
Media literacy, 62, 167–168,
        169–170 (handout), 171
Media literacy skills, 168
Media project, 3 (table), 160–166,
        162–163 (handout)
    assessment of, 163 (handout)
    citing sources in, 173–174
    and copyright issues, 181–186
    features of, 3 (table)
    MAPS in, 161, 162 (handout),
        164 (handout), 165
    peer response to ideas in,
        174, 175–176 (handout)
    publishing, 187 (handout), 188–197
    reflecting on, 186, 187 (handout),
        188, 188–189 (box), 190,
        190–191 (box), 194 (box)
    sharing, 187 (handout), 188–197
Meme Generator, 172
Memes, 172
Merritt, K., xxii
Michigan State University, xxii
"The Midwest Accent" (Gordon), 109
Mini-conferences, 104
Mistakes, online, 43 (teaching tip)
Mitchell, D., xx, 7, 74
Mode, 7, 120–121, 129–130 (handout).
        See also MAPS
Moran, C., xxvi
"Mother Tongue" (Tan), 109

Mozilla Webmaker X-Ray Goggles, 167, 169, 169–170 (handout), 171, 172
Musicians, 83
Myers, R., 92
My Pop Studio, 50

National Council of Teachers of English, xxv, 58, 59
National Public Radio (NPR), 15, 136 (handout)
National Writing Project, xxii, 13, 16, 39, 201. *See also* Youth Voices
"A Nation Divided by One Language" (Crawford), 109
The Non-Designer's Design Book (Williams), 60
North, S. M., xxii, 150
Notes, 98, 98 (figure), 101

Objectives, 10
Olinghouse, N., xxiii
"One right idea," 67
Online spaces
    classroom management in, 43 (teaching tips)
    tone for, 35–36
Online Writing Lab (OWL), 173
Ownership, 72
    of learning, 100
    of note taking, 101
    and real reasons to write, xxvi
    of research process, 141

Pariser, E., 142
Parody, 46
Passages, close reading of, 110–113
Password management, 35 (tech tip)
Peer response, 150, 156–157 (handout)
    to blog posts, 114 (handout)
    to culture collage, 63, 68–69
    to essay draft, 157 (handout), 159–160
    goals for, 70
    ink shedding, 28
    to media project ideas, 174, 175–176 (handout)
    setup for, 70, 160
    for student profiles, 36
    See also Feedback

Peer review centers, 150
"Peer Review in a Digital Space" (Holmes & Reed), 159
Perin, D., xxiv, xxv–xxvi
Perrin, D., 138
Personal inquiry reflections, 86–89
Perspectives, 51, 53 (handout)
Photography, 51. *See also* Images
Photo-sharing services, 52
Piper, T., 81
Pirie, B., 201
Plagiarism, 41 (tech tip), 185
Popcorn, 172
Popham, W. J., 11
Powerful Voices for Kids, 50
Preview lesson, 25–30, 29 (handout)
Principles, guiding, xxiii–xxxi, xxviii (table)
Profile, online, 32, 34 (handout), 36, 37–38 (handout). *See also* Identities, digital
Prosumers, 46, 168
Public Broadcasting Service (PBS), 15
    "Do You Speak American?," 105, 106, 107 (handout), 109
Public domain, 184 (handout)
Publishing, 180 (handout)
    for authentic audiences, 179
    encouraging, 179, 181, 181 (box)
    media project, 187 (handout), 188–197
Publishing, online, 31–32
Purdue University, 173
Purpose, xxvi, 7, 122, 130–131 (handout). *See also* MAPS

QR codes, 31 (figure). *See also* Videos
Questions
    essential questions, 8, 9 (handout), 42 (handout)
    inquiry questions, 113–117, 124, 124 (table)
    for literature circles, 77–78 (handout)
    self questions, 32, 33 (table), 37 (handout), 72
    as teaching strategy, xxiii–xxiv
    world questions, 32, 33 (table), 37 (handout), 72
Quotes, integrating, 173, 175 (handout). *See also* Citations

Reading
    close reading, 92–95, 110–113, 124
    collaborative reading,
        37–38 (handout), 39–40
    jigsaw reading, 106, 107 (handout)
    through different lenses, 92, 154
Reading skills, critical, 40, 171
Really simple syndication (RSS), 110
Reed, D., xxii, xxiii, 2, 159
Reflection, 94, 94–95 (box),
        102–103 (handout), 156 (handout)
    and assessment, 202
    on audience, 158–159
    on essay, 177, 177–178 (box),
        179, 193, 194–195 (box)
    on learning, 180 (handout)
    on media project, 186, 187 (handout),
        188, 188–189 (box), 190,
        190–191 (box), 194 (box)
    on media work, 165, 165 (box),
        166 (box)
    on personal inquiry, 86–89
    in writing, 86–89
    on writing workshop, 198
Reflections, digital, 39–40
Remixing, 168, 171, 172, 172 (figure),
        185, 190, 191 (figure)
Requirements
    and assessment, 202
    revisiting, 158
Research
    collaborative, 128, 133,
        134 (handout), 137, 142
    exploring sources, 128–142
    foundation for, 111, 123–124
    inquiry-based approach to,
        xxiii–xxiv, 1
    integrating with digital writing, xx
    as journey, 27
    organizational approaches, 142
    requirements for, 122
    shifts in, xxviii (table), 200
    skills and tips for, 134–136 (handout)
    students' ideas of, 90
    using library for, 143–145, 144 (handout)
Research, active, 120
Research workshop, 144 (handout)
Reshaping High School English (Pirie), 201
Revision, 36

Rhetoric, connection with choice
        of media, 7
Rhetorical situation, 7. See also MAPS
Richardson, W., 2
Risk taking, 67–68
Robinson, K., 205
Rosen, L. M., 121
RSS (really simple syndication), 110
Rule, C., 46
Russell, C., 82 (handout), 83

Safety, online, 31
Scary "Mary Poppins" (video),
        46, 49 (handout)
Scholars, acting as, 20
Search alerts, 110
Search engines, 110
Self-assessment, 98–104, 102–103 (handout),
        155, 155 (box), 156 (handout), 158, 203
    mini-conferences, 104
    reflection, written, 99–101
    reflection on essay,
        177, 177–178 (box), 179
    scaled questions, 99, 102 (handout)
    student ownership of note taking, 101
Shanahan, C., xxvi
Shanahan, T., xxvi
Shirky, C., 136 (handout)
Situation, 7, 122, 131 (handout).
        See also MAPS
Smagorinsky, P., 1, 10, 92
Smith, M., 120
Smoker, A., xxiii
Social interaction, 19. See also
        Conversations
Social media
    as reliable source, 138, 139
    student comments on, 28
    using for research, 106, 109
    See also Online spaces
Social networks, 24, 32, 39. See also Youth
        Voices
Socratic Circles (Copeland), 113
Soe, Katie, 39–40, 42 (handout)
Source code, 168
Sources, 120–121, 125, 135 (handout)
    citing, 173
    credibility of, 137–139, 142, 148, 171
    in essay assignment, 130 (handout)

evaluating, 136 (handout)
exploring, 128–142
original research, 140–141
original sources, 138
primary sources, 140
printed, 139–140
related to cultural artifacts, 133, 137
secondary sources, 140
Standards, xxv, 58, 200, 201
Stanger, M., 62
Stock, P. L., 2, 150
Storyboards, 177
"The Struggle to Be an All-American Girl"
    (Wong), 109
Success, student, 196
Surveys, 140
Swenson, J., xx, 7
Swiss, T., 2

Tagging, using for research, 106, 109
Tan, A., 109
Teachers
    as experts, 143
    role of in inquiry-based
        instruction, xxiv
    support of inquiry process, 2
Teaching
    co-constructed style of, 204–205
    in inquiry-driven manner, 206
Teaching the New Writing (Herrington,
    Hodgson, & Moran), xxvi
Teaching tips
    classroom management in virtual
        spaces, 43 (teaching tip)
Technology, 54
    for annotation, 41 (tech tip), 44
    for blogs, 89 (tech tip)
    for collaborative research, 142
    course management technologies, 13
    dependence on, 18–19
    desired features, 12
    for drafts, 177
    for editing images, 62, 84
    making decisions about, 18–19
    for notes, 98
    for peer response, 160
    photo-sharing services, 52
    purposeful integration of, 203–204
    selecting, 12–13

for tracking student participation, 133
    used in unit, 19
    used to create social networks, 39
    use of, 6
    See also Tools, online
Tech tips
    blogging, 89 (tech tip)
    Google Forms, 75 (tech tip)
    password management,
        35 (tech tip)
    using Google Apps for Education for
        annotation, 41 (tech tip)
TED Talks
    creating, 26–30, 29 (handout)
    *Globalizing the Local, Localizing
        the Global*, 26
    "Looks Aren't Everything.
        Believe Me, I'm a Model!,"
        82 (handout), 83
    Pariser's, 142
    viewing, 26, 29 (handout)
Teens, 3–4, 54
Texts, 54
    analyzing, 111
    broad definition of, 125
    building connections between,
        125–126, 127 (handouts)
    changing forms of, 58
    interacting with, 40
    marking up, 112 (handout),
        113, 126
    prosumers of, 46
    remixed, 46
    selection of, 6
    sharing, 125
Texts, mentor, 90
    digital reflections on, 39–40
    as models for thinking about media
        work, 161
    for personal inquiry reflections,
        87–88 (handout)
    for profiles, 37 (handout)
    responding to, 26
    selecting, 30
Thein, A. H., 92
Themes, xxx, 4, 8, 10
"They Say/I Say" (Graff & Birkenstein),
    173, 175 (handout)
Thinking, reflective, 26–27

The Third Wave (Toffler), 46
Time magazine, 84
Time to Act (Carnegie Corporation), 4
Timing, 4–5, 54
Toffler, A., 46
Tools, online, xx
    bibliographic management
        tools, 141–142
    for inquiry, 109
    integrating, xxvii
    for remixing, 172
    See also Technology
Topics, 5–6, 54
Transformativeness, 185
Ts, five, 3–6, 54
Turner, K. H., xxvii, 36, 174, 204
Twitter, using for research,
    106, 109

Uncertainty, 25
"User Rights, Section 107" (Hobbs),
    182, 183 (handout)

Videos
    video 1.1, 31 (figure)
    video 1.2, 36 (figure)
    video 1.3, 50 (figure)
    video 1.4, 51 (figure)
    video 2.1, 62 (figure)
    video 2.2, 74 (figure)
    video 2.3, 84 (figure)
    video 3.1, 111 (figure)
    video 4.1, 126 (figure)
    video 4.2, 128 (figure)
    video 4.3, 128 (figure)
    video 4.4, 143 (figure)
    video 5.1, 166 (figure)
    video 5.2, 196 (figure)
Viewing skills, critical, 84
Visual culture, 44–50, 47–48 (handout),
    49 (handout)
Visual literacy, 59–62,
    61 (handout)
Visuals, reading, 66–67

Web 2.0 (film), 46, 49 (handout)
Webb, A., 92
Website, for inquiry unit, 13

Websites
    evaluating, 86, 142
    source code, 168
Wesch, M., 46
What's the Big Idea (Burke), xxiii–xxiv
Whitney, A., xxiii
Wiggins, G. P., xxiii
Wikipedia, 136 (handout),
    137, 138
Wikispaces, 13, 14 (figure), 24, 133
Wild Talents (Fort), 25
Wilhelm, J. D., 74, 120
Williams, Robin, 60
Willis, Connie, 126
Wilson, M., 121
Within and Beyond the Writing Process
    in the Secondary English Classroom
    (Dornan, Rosen, & Wilson), 121
"Wobble," 25
Wong, E., 109
Workshops
    inquiry-based research essay and
        media projects, 173–177
    writing and research, 145–147,
        146 (handout)
    writing workshop, 156–157
Writing
    across disciplines, xxvi, 20
    best practices in, xxv–xxvii
    celebrating, 179
    digital writing, 2, 161–166
    in essay assignment, 131 (handout)
    inquiry-based writing, 158
    as process, 121
    purposes of, 122
    reflective writing, 26–27
    shifts in, xxviii (table)
    techniques, 173
    variety of experiences
        of, xxiv–xxvii
    for web, 89 (tech tip). *See also*
        Blogging; Blog posts
    on Wikipedia, 138
Writing center, xxii, 150
Writing Next (Graham & Perin),
    xxv–xxvi
Writing Now (NCTE), xxv
Writing skills, reviewing, 147

X-Ray Goggles, 167, 168, 169–170
    (handout), 171, 172

Yale University, 140
"You Gotta BE the Book" (Wilhelm), 74
Youth Voices, 6, 13, 16–17, 17 (figure),
    24, 39, 151
    blog posts, 86, 87–88 (handout),
        94, 94–95 (box)

joining, 36, 37 (handout)
publishing media project on,
    187 (handout)
questioning and speculating guide,
    114 (handout)
tone appropriate for, 35–36

Zemelman, S., xxvi
Zheng, J., xxiii

About the Authors

Dawn Reed is an English teacher at Okemos High School in Okemos, Michigan, and co-director of Red Cedar Writing Project at Michigan State University (MSU), a site of the National Writing Project. She earned her master's degree in rhetoric and writing in critical studies in literacy and pedagogy from MSU and continues to engage in teacher inquiry and research. Her research includes the teaching of writing, digital literacy, and authentic writing opportunities, including writing for civic engagement. She is involved with conducting professional development for teachers focused on technology integration and the teaching of writing. She has published in various journals and books, including *English Journal*, *The Next Digital Scholar* (Information Today, Inc., 2014), *Using Technology to Enhance Writing* (Solution Tree Press, 2014), and *Teaching the New Writing: Technology, Change, and Assessment* (Teachers College Press, 2009). Follow her on Twitter at @dawnreed.

Dr. Troy Hicks is a professor of English at Central Michigan University (CMU) and focuses his work on the teaching of writing, literacy and technology, and teacher education and professional development. A former middle school teacher, he collaborates with K–12 colleagues and explores how they implement newer literacies in their classrooms. Hicks directs CMU's Chippewa River Writing Project, a site of the National Writing Project. Hicks is author of the Heinemann titles *Crafting Digital Writing* (2013) and *The Digital Writing Workshop* (2009) as well as a coauthor of several books, including *Because Digital Writing Matters* (Jossey-Bass, 2010); *Create, Compose, Connect!* (Routledge/Eye on Education, 2014); and *Assessing Students' Digital Writing: Protocols for Looking Closely* (Teachers College Press, 2015). In 2011, Hicks was honored with CMU's Provost's Award, and in 2014, he was honored with the Conference on English Education's Richard A. Meade Award for scholarship in English Education. Follow him on Twitter at @hickstro.

BECAUSE ALL TEACHERS ARE LEADERS

A SAGE Company

Helping educators make the greatest impact

CORWIN HAS ONE MISSION: to enhance education through intentional professional learning.

We build long-term relationships with our authors, educators, clients, and associations who partner with us to develop and continuously improve the best evidence-based practices that establish and support lifelong learning.